D0536276

SWIM, BIKE, RUN

WES HOBSON

Clark Campbell

Mike Vickers

Human Kinetics

Library of Congress Cataloging-in-Publication Data

Hobson, Wes, 1966-
    Swim, bike, run / by Wes Hobson, Clark Campbell and Mike Vickers.
      p. cm.
    Includes index.
    ISBN 0-7360-3288-6
      1. Triathlon--Training--Handbooks, manuals, etc. I. Campbell, Clark, 1966- II.
Vickers, Mike, 1956- III. Title.

    GV1060.73 .H63 2001
    796.42'57--dc21

                                                                            00-054239

ISBN: 0-7360-3288-6

Acquisitions Editor: Martin Barnard; **Developmental Editor:** Cassandra Mitchell; **Assistant Editors:** Wendy McLaughlin, Dan Brachtesende; **Copyeditor:** John Wentworth; **Proofreader:** Erin Cler; **Indexer:** Dan Connolly; **Permission Manager:** Toni Harte; **Graphic Designer:** Stuart Cartwright; **Graphic Artist:** Tara Welsch; **Photo Managers:** Clark Brooks and Gayle Garrison; **Cover Designer:** Keith Blomberg; **Photographer (cover):** Rich Cruse; **Photographer (interior):** Tom Roberts, unless otherwise noted. Photos on pages 47-53, 56, 114, 121, 124, 126, 153, 158, 160-161, by ©Paul Bousquet.; **Art Manager:** Craig Newsom; **Illustrator:** Tom Roberts; **Printer:** Bang; **Credits:** Text pp. 76-87, 144-149 adapted, with permission, from Town and Kearney, 1994, *Swim, bike, run.* (Champaign, IL: Human Kinetics), 23-45.

Human Kinetics books are available at special discounts for bulk purchase. Special editions or book excerpts can also be created to specification. For details, contact the Special Sales Manager at Human Kinetics.

Printed in the United States of America   10 9 8 7 6 5

Human Kinetics
Web site: www.HumanKinetics.com

United States: Human Kinetics, P.O. Box 5076, Champaign, IL 61825-5076
800-747-4457
e-mail: humank@hkusa.com

Canada: Human Kinetics, 475 Devonshire Road, Unit 100, Windsor, ON N8Y 2L5
800-465-7301 (in Canada only)
e-mail: orders@hkcanada.com

Europe: Human Kinetics, 107 Bradford Road, Stanningley
Leeds LS28 6AT, United Kingdom
+44 (0) 113 255 5665
e-mail: hk@hkeurope.com

Australia: Human Kinetics, 57A Price Avenue, Lower Mitcham, South Australia 5062
08 8277 1555
e-mail: liaw@hkaustralia.com

New Zealand: Human Kinetics, Division of Sports Distributors NZ Ltd.
P.O. Box 300 226 Albany, North Shore City, Auckland
0064 9 448 1207
e-mail: blairc@hknewz.com

SWIM, BIKE, RUN

CONTENTS

ACKNOWLEDGMENTS

I want to thank the sport of triathlon. It has given me pleasure, a livelihood, and an opportunity to stay fit. I even met my wife, Jennifer, at a triathlon. If not for triathlon, I would most likely be behind a desk of a major corporation pushing papers while sweating in my coat and tie. Special thanks go to my parents, who gave me the chance to follow my dream and goal of pursuing triathlon. The thought of paying for a son's college education only to see the son toss aside the classroom work to pursue a multidisciplined physical activity after graduation would appall many a parent. My parents were very supportive; in fact, they sponsored me the first year of my pro career. Without their support and patience, I would not have had such a successful career. Mom and Dad, the education paid off, as I have written a book!

Thanks to my sponsors who have kept faith in me even during my injured years. Without them and the dedication of so many race directors and volunteers, our sport would not have grown as quickly as it has in mainstream America. Finally, this book is dedicated to my son or daughter who will be born in September, 2001. I am sad that Hobb will have never seen me race a triathlon as a professional. I hope this book lets Hobb realize the importance of triathlon in my life.

Wes Hobson

First, I would like to thank all the coaches I have had the pleasure to work with through the years. There have been so many excellent minds that I have watched, listened, and learned from. I have also been very privileged to work with many athletes at various levels of ability. Thank you for allowing me to try these ideas and theories in your quest to become champions. What each athlete has lacked in God-given talent was more than made up for with a big heart. A special thanks to Kim Wilson, my assistant coach for two years at the University of Evansville. She helped by keeping the administrative tasks of coaching under control so that I could spend more time writing. Also, Kim volunteered her time to help proofread many chapters. And last, but definitely not least, I would like to thank my best friend and wife, Cassie. She provided so much support with this project that without her understanding and help, none of this would have been possible.

Clark Campbell

I thank my wife, Caylen, for introducing me to triathlon in the first place. She competed long before I did. To all five of my children for tolerating my absences while I trained. I always justified it by thinking that they were proud and respectful of the example I was setting; I hope I'm right. To Clark

Campbell for making me a better triathlete, and to my neighbor and early training partner, Warren—back in the days when triathlon was new, exciting, and magical.

Thanks to others who helped with the book: Neil Salkind for getting Clark and me started; Dan Hughes of Sunflower Bike Shop for reviews, advice, and use of his shop; Jim Whittaker of **velotek.com**, who is my new coach and book advisor. To all my triathlon friends who kept me going: Kent, Kent, Marcel, and everyone at the Lawrence Masters Swim Club. Go, Sharks!

And a very special thanks to our HK editor, Cassandra Mitchell. Without her ability to pull (and push) the work of three authors into one cohesive book, it may never have happened. A very challenging task handled with mastery.

Mike Vickers

INTRODUCTION

When we started this book we looked to one goal: putting you in control of your destiny as a triathlete through efficient training structure and increased knowledge of every aspect related to the sport. All three of us focus on simple, results-oriented training plans and racing strategies honed with maturity over the years. This philosophy supports our collective experiences: Wes enjoys success at the elite, international level; Clark was at the elite level and is now successful in coaching; Mike represents the older amateur whose family and business demands provide limited training time. It is our hope that these three diverse perspectives result in a balanced presentation, one that benefits a broad spectrum of athletes and allows each athlete to sharpen his or her training and racing for success. Above all, we agree on the most important point: Have fun. Never lose sight of this basic perspective. If it's not fun, something is wrong. You don't have to beat yourself up to be successful in sport or in life. Employ common sense, a solid plan, and a positive attitude. If you employ these three simple ideas, you will succeed.

Part I
COMMITMENT

SWIM
BIKE
RUN

Chapter 1

BALANCING WORKOUTS TO STAY STRONG AND HEALTHY

Most of you reading this book probably fall into the category of "serious, but not professional." Likely, you have done a fair share of racing and are looking to improve your performance, but joining the professional ranks is not an option for you, perhaps for family or career reasons. You want to have fun and be successful in triathlon without giving your entire life to it. The key is to strike a balance. But balancing all the interests and pursuits in your life is not as easy as it may sound, and this is especially true for the triathlete. By its nature, triathlon can consume you if you're unprepared for the sport's demands. Ideally, triathlon should complement your life, not rule it. Balanced, well-planned training sessions and realistic competition calendars can help you stay mentally sane and healthy. In this chapter, we give you an overview of the basic structure and principles of a balanced triathlon lifestyle.

Goal Setting

First, set some basic goals and expectations. These goals should include not only athletic goals but goals in other areas of your life as well. You cannot separate one from the other, as you must determine the most effective way to interweave triathlon training into your existing life, adding to and enhancing it rather than detracting from it. From family to work, work to sport, and so on, what do you want to accomplish? Take the time to think this through, and be thorough. When setting goals, you need to come up with realistic targets that you and others in your life can live with. How much time can you invest in training and racing? How much time per day, per week, per month, per year, and per life? Remember that we're talking *really*, not ideally.

Avoid the tendency to over-reach. If you are just starting out, we highly recommend a conservative approach. If you've been at it a while, you're more familiar with the level of training you can handle. However, it's still a good idea for you, the experienced triathlete, to take a hard look at your training and its effect on your life. Are you enjoying it? Do you make the most of your training time, or are you putting in too many garbage miles?

Time Allocation

This is a simple concept but often overlooked. How much time do you really have for training, and what, based on your schedule, are your optimum training times? Too many people focus on distance: yards in the swim and miles on the bike and run. Avoid this trap! Make time primary, distance secondary. You don't really know how many miles you can put in; you do know how much time you have.

Here's how to do it. There are 168 hours in a week. That may seem like a lot, and many people at a glance think, "yes, I can train about 10 to 15 percent of total time available." Well, we can tell you that's almost assuredly wrong! Most people, unless they are on a written plan, don't have any idea how many hours they are training. Very few triathletes, unless they are pros or Ironman competitors, train 16 to 24 hours per week. Let's look at it this way:

Total hours available	168
Job	44
Preparing for job	4
Sleep	56
Eat	11
Travel	6
Shopping	6
Time with family	10
Social functions	3
Home maintenance, other hobbies, etc.	4
Relaxation and "lost time"	11
Subtotal	155
Training	13

Very few people structure their time to the hour, but we suggest that if you are training for triathlon, analyze your time similar to the above. And once you get started, one tool you *must* employ as part of your training is an exercise log. How else will you have any idea what your training really is, how you are progressing, and if you are overtraining, undertraining, and so on? A log is a must for any serious athlete.

Table 1.1 is a guideline for training time allocations at various race distance goals.

Table 1.1

Race distance	Swim per week	Bike per week	Run per week	Total
Sprint	3 workouts 3 hours total	3 workouts 4 hours total	3 workouts 3 hours total	10 hours
Olympic	3 workouts 4 hours total	3 to 4 workouts 5 hours total	3 to 4 workouts 4 hours total	13 hours
Half to full Ironman	3 to 4 workouts 5 hours total	3 to 4 workouts 8 hours total	3 to 4 workouts 6 hours total	19 hours

Table 1.1 is an outline of the average time required to maintain or improve at these race distances. Hours allocated among each sport roughly mirror time spent while racing. Certainly, if you have more time available greater gains may be had with additional training, but amounts in excess of the above likely constitute overtraining that will eventually work against you.

Once you establish how much time you have and balance that with how much time you need to train for your specific goals, the next question becomes when to train. This is very individual based on your regular life scheduling demands and training preferences. Many triathletes prefer to train with others. If you do, then you likely have a regular schedule and a starting point for time allocation. Make sure if you do train in a group that you ask yourself the following: Does the group training fit within my plan and goals? Can the group, or others, adapt to my goals? If the answer is no, then you should consider training on your own.

Once you have set goals and training time, creating a "macroplan" or long-term schedule is your next exercise. We discuss macro plans in the Training section of this book. The important point for now is to devise a written schedule for training that is not overly aggressive. Start out easy and add to training levels in small increments. Make sure the schedule is realistic, one you can achieve with relative ease and build upon. Overreaching is a certain recipe for frustration and disruption in all areas of your life.

The Triathlete Lifestyle

With the triathlon, it takes a special mind-set to reach your peak. We don't advocate dropping everything else in your life and committing all your resources to your quest for improved times. Instead, allow triathlon preparation to add dimension to your life. You can be successful, especially in shorter events, without a major time commitment to the sport. But realize that many variables affect training and racing performance. The triathlete lifestyle places a premium on fitness and time management, positively affecting the mind, body, and spirit.

The best way to improve performance in any endurance sport is to maintain physical fitness all year long. This does not mean training hard all the time; instead, enjoy being fit, and make exercise a regular part of your daily or weekly routine. Training is different from working out. When you train for an event, you put into place a detailed plan of success that will lead to peak performance. Working out, on the other hand, is akin to maintenance; it is not necessarily goal specific but more of an activity. As you likely know,

© iphotonews.com/Brooks

Improvement comes from a year-round commitment.

training takes a lot of physical, mental, and emotional energy. When you plan for a peak, you'll want to reserve a block of time within your calendar for that preparation.

Between training times, commit to maintaining a base of physical fitness by working out. Keeping fit can—and probably should—involve activities other than swimming, biking, and running. Many triathletes cross train with aerobics, in-line skating, weightlifting, cross-country skiing, rock climbing—any activity that's aerobic or strength related. Of course, you might prefer to stick with what you know and love: swimming, biking, and running. That's great, but consider adding some variety, such as swimming with a Masters team, mountain biking with friends, spinning to music, or maybe trail running in the woods. However you choose to do it, your goal is to get into great physical shape, your "base," as the coaches call it. Once you're there, you can start planning how to peak within the training program you have set for yourself.

Most nonprofessional triathletes have outside interests and pursuits that come before their sport. Adopt a mind-set of using the sport of triathlon to enhance these more vital areas of your life. Sure, you'll have some very early mornings, quick lunch-hour workouts, and late evenings. On occasion, you might have to miss a training session. But forget the guilt: it's okay to skip a session or two. If you keep the sport and your aspirations in proper perspective, you'll also keep having fun.

Another tip, borrowed from the YMCA: Treat your mind, body, and spirit with utmost respect. Training for triathlon is rigorous—you simply can't do it if the little things (not to mention the big things) are not kept in check.

Five Keys to Balanced Training

We offer the following five keys to present a general overview of the components and principles of a good training program. In later chapters we'll offer specific methods and programs to fine-tune your individual regimen, based on these principles. All principles are equally important; a training program that incorporates these keys will nearly always be successful.

Train the Three Activities Equally

Triathlon implies balance: doing three distinctively different sports in one continuous event. Achieving equilibrium in swimming, cycling, and running can be done but initially requires becoming better in all three. Many triathletes make the mistake of focusing on what they are good at. Weak swimmers think, *I'll just make up for it in the bike and run.* Weak runners say, *No problem—I'll hammer the swim and bike, and survive the run.* Others do the opposite, spending more training time on their weaknesses than on their strengths. Many good swimmers focus on running and swimming to the point that their swimming suffers.

While it may be true that one discipline will never be quite as sharp as another, you're better off if you improve your weaknesses while also improving your strengths. As you become more proficient in all three activities, your weaknesses hurt you less, and your strengths help you more. As eight-time Hawaii Ironman Champion Paula Newby-Fraser said in a workshop at the LMH Triathlon, "To be successful in triathlon think of it as one sport, not three different sports placed together." Draft-legal racing aside, the best triathletes are those who achieve balance, are "solid" in all three sports. Draft-legal racing may allow a weaker biker to excel, but most people reading this book will never compete in a draft-legal race. We've all seen athletes come to triathlon from a single discipline, thinking they can win in one sport and hang on in the others. This is not the way to success in triathlon, and our training programs show you how to balance disciplines accordingly.

Train Consistently

Our society is always looking for the fastest, easiest ways of doing things. In our sport, no pills, potions, sport drinks, or energy bars will make you better. Our "secret" is consistent preparation. For us, this means reasonable training over a long period of time (it can literally be years—remember, we're talking about a "lifestyle") and looking for long-term solutions, not quick fixes.

Hundreds of athletes have had their multisport visions crushed because they could not focus on the long term. It's so common for motivated athletes to trash themselves physically, mentally, and emotionally trying to achieve rapid improvement. Take the methodical approach, setting and meeting reasonable goals and planning a program for future success. You'll be more content this way—and injured less. For example, if you want to compete in a race on June 1, the optimum time to begin planning would be *October* of the prior year. Light but consistent base training takes place in November and December, with a more intensive build starting in January, again emphasizing consistent training over shear volume and intensity. After this base phase add some intensity over the next few months, and by the time June 1 rolls around you'll be in optimum physical shape. Many triathletes won't start training until May 1 for a June race, "cramming" for the race as if cramming for a test. You are assured to have a monumental struggle with considerable pain and an overall negative experience. Here is a general rule of race preparation: for every hour you expect the race to last, train at least two to three months in advance. So a one-hour sprint triathlon can be done on two to three months training. Of course this is insufficient time to reach a peak of competitiveness. A 12-hour Ironman race can take one to two *years* of training—but shorter races and events can (and should) be mixed in during that year or two.

Emphasizing quality workouts in training will make race day much more enjoyable.

Emphasize Quality Over Quantity

As you have probably learned by now more is not always better. In triathlon you must pace yourself while racing and training to race. Overdo it, and you'll pay the price. If you're still looking for the mix of quality training that works best for you, consider what we call "the power of two"—that is, two focused, quality workouts per week, per sport. This is plenty to help you maintain fitness and improve your skills. Details for planning these training sessions and defining "quality workouts" come later, in part V; for now, remember that every training session should be focused on a goal. Quality practices are specific workouts clearly geared toward attaining your goals.

Many athletes place too much emphasis on quantity over quality. Training can become an obsessive–compulsive behavior for many. Unable to exercise control and balance in training, the opposite begins to happen: training begins to control them, getting in the way of living a normal, sensible life. This book shows you *smart* methods of training with a structured plan, as opposed to training *hard* and *long*, wasting time putting in garbage miles with no goal or focus. We understand that anyone reading this book wants to improve performance. We'll show you how to improve performance with an emphasis on efficiency: optimal use of time to achieve specific goals, allowing you to carry on normally with all your other life's pursuits, or better yet, enhance them with all the positives of being in prime physical shape.

Optimize Training With Effectiveness and Efficiency

You may have many reasons for putting in time and effort to develop your skills in swimming, biking, and running. Maybe you want to challenge yourself in a new way, feel good after a workout, control your weight, build self-discipline, or meet people with similar interests. But if you're a serious athlete, the underlying goal of preparation is probably competition. Racing competitively is the reason you put in the hours and miles, and your training program should reflect that.

If you dissect a training program, focusing on optimal performance, you'll arrive at two questions: how efficiently can you move, and how effective are you when you move? The two questions are different, but the answers are interdependent.

Effectiveness is the ability to get the most out of yourself physically, mentally, and emotionally. How close you are to reaching your ceiling of ability is the measure of effectiveness. Highly effective people fulfill their potential, getting the most out of what they have. Reaching this peak is never achieved overnight. Our training programs get you there incrementally, in doses you can handle, with rest and recovery being an important part of the structure.

For our purposes here, *efficiency* refers to how fast you can go with the least amount of effort (not efficient time management). Watch elite athletes in any sport and see how easy they make it look. Their moves are flowing and graceful, their facial expressions relaxed and loose. How do you reach this level? In parts II, III, and IV, we discuss the elements of proper technique in all three sports. We see many athletes swim or run with the same bad habits, or bike without using their machine to its maximum potential. It takes conscientious, focused effort to change habits and improve technique. That's why we recommend things like doing some sort of swim drill at *every* practice during warm up. Practice technique every day. Remember, efficiency means going faster with less effort—that is not possible with poor technique. With rare exceptions, it takes hard work to reach the point where it looks as if you're hardly working.

Stay Healthy

To maintain the consistency you need to improve, you must stay healthy. Unless you're superhuman, you'll fall prey to colds and flu now and then, but there are ways to reduce the risks of getting sick. Above all, take care of

A Word From Wes

Overtraining and Overracing

Chronic fatigue is a state of health that modern medicine has had difficulty diagnosing. You look healthy, but when you dive into the pool you feel as if an elephant is going along for the ride. Symptoms are insomnia, sweating during sleep, loss of appetite, performance reduction, muscle aches for no reason, difficulty making decisions, and irritability. Vitamins don't help, nor does trying to train through the fatigue state.

How do I know so much about chronic fatigue? One season, I had an eight-week period where I trained 28 to 32 hours a week, which included 20,000 to 25,000 yards of swimming, 280 to 350 miles of biking, and 50 to 55 miles of running; most of this training was at a high intensity. I felt good and I needed to because I was competing in seven triathlons over a nine-week period.

After my fifth race in five weekends, I was feeling tired, but I had two weeks before the next race. At that race, after an average swim, I hopped on the bike and told myself that this is where I make my move. I hammered the first 10K, but I noticed that I wasn't dropping any of the competition. My body was not functioning at its optimal level. I got off the bike and ran . . . backwards. I finished 10th, my worst finish in a U.S. race since my first year as a pro in 1989.

For the sixth race, I only trained four and a half hours during the week and I still felt tired. On race day, I exited the water with the lead pack and I got on my bike. This time I couldn't even stay with anyone on the bike. I tried pedaling aggressively, but I wasn't even breathing hard. Twelve miles into the bike, I dropped out for the first time in my career. I was scheduled to race the following weekend in Europe, but I canceled.

I got a blood test, which turned up normal with the exception of high iron content. I also saw two Chinese medicine specialists and one internist, had a massage once a week and acupuncture three times. I tried herbal teas, vitamin supplements, and pure magnesium for better absorption into the cells. My state of fatigue didn't change for six weeks. It was taking me at least an hour to fall asleep every night even though I was exhausted. My muscles ached and I was no fun to be around.

Too much racing and too much training at a high intensity may result in a total collapse not only of the muscular system but of the immune system as well. Athletes get caught up in racing well and push beyond what the body can accept.

Chronic fatigue is more likely to affect those triathletes who also work 40-plus hours a week. They must try to fit in their training around an already hectic schedule of work and family, with minimal sleep. If you notice any of the chronic fatigue symptoms, reevaluate your schedule. Rest, and in the long run, you'll show improvement.

yourself. Drink lots of water, choose your foods wisely, get plenty of rest and don't skip meals. Failing any of these leads to a breakdown in your natural defenses against illness.

As an athlete, along with following these basic rules of health, you must also train smart, allowing adequate time for recovery. Training too much above your current fitness level is a sure ticket to illness or injury. When you're training, your body is in a state of fatigue. Viruses and bacteria look for tired hosts that are not going to fight them. If your body is constantly broken down, expect to become sick. Putting together a smart, reasonable program is your first step toward staying healthy. Be sure to recover properly between workouts and training cycles. Progress in intensity and volume in small, manageable doses. Plan a week of downtime periodically during the season to keep your system strong.

There are two types of rest, active recovery and passive rest, with important distinctions. *Active recovery* is low-intensity exercise that helps pre- and postworkout. An easy swim, bike, or run a day after a tough session in those same activities improves your ability to bounce back quickly. This is also the major premise behind warming up and cooling down, as discussed in detail later. Stretching to improve or maintain flexibility is another form of active recovery. Stretching before and after a workout makes you feel much better later in the day and during the next training bout.

Passive rest also helps you recover. Getting more sleep during periods of tough training boosts your ability to recover. Another form of passive rest is a sports massage every other week or so. After a tough couple weeks of training, a massage feels great and keeps your body relaxed, which helps prevent injury.

Hydration plays a key role in maintaining health. Drinking water throughout the day should be a priority. If you are training seriously, drink at least a gallon of water a day. Your body is mostly water, and a decrease of 1 to 2 percent in your water level can cause physical problems.

And no matter how well you take care of yourself, sometimes the germs are stronger than you. When you do become sick, rest and more rest will help you recover quicker. Get over your illnesses *completely* before returning to serious training. Continue to stay hydrated and eat smart. Never train with a fever. Once you are fully recovered, return to your program with two to three days of light endurance training. Don't try to come back until you're fully recovered—if you come back too soon or too fast, you'll just delay your recovery.

Now that you understand the basic principles of a balanced training program, let's begin to put one together that works for you. But before that, another basic but important topic must be covered. Now that you're training optimally you must "fuel" optimally as well. Balanced health cannot be achieved without a balanced diet and thorough understanding of what makes us "go." Our next chapter covers this important topic so that mind, body, and spirit are completely ready to hammer.

Chapter 2

NUTRITION AND FUEL FOR THE TRIATHLETE

Nutrition is a huge subject, worthy of a book of its own, and there are many such books out there. For our purposes, we'll address nutrition topics of interest to the triathlete, including general principles of digestion and absorption of food into energy, the basic food groups, general guidelines for diet balance, supplements, endurance foods, and some dos and don'ts for the triathlete.

Digestion and Utilization: How the Process Works

How does what we eat and drink become energy for living and muscular movement? Understanding some basics about the process will guide you in your shopping and eating habits.

All food has potential energy, just waiting for us to take advantage of it, and all food has a common origin: the sun. All food is composed of three macronutrients: carbohydrates, fats, and proteins. The majority of our energy comes from carbohydrates and fat; much less of it comes from protein. Digestion is the process through which basic nutrients are broken down, transferred to our cellular structure, and used as energy. Digestion begins when you put food in your mouth; chewing and chemicals in your saliva start the process. Once you swallow the food, the naturally produced hydrochloric acid of your stomach breaks it down further, preparing the now sludge-like material for delivery into your small intestine. The small intestine continues to break the food down, delivering it into your bloodstream in the form of glucose (from carbohydrates), fatty acids (from fats), and amino acids (from protein). Your blood then delivers these elements to your cells for even more breaking down, and it is within your cells that the "power phase" finally occurs. Hydrogen is released, which converts to ATP, which is what your muscles use as energy.

The process is complex, and how well it works depends on the quality and balance of what you put into your body. The complex interrelations among the chemical reactions occurring every moment within your body are truly critical, yet many people disrupt or even damage the process regularly because they are unaware, apathetic, rushed, confused—the list of possible reasons goes on and on. The body functions best when it's treated well. The better you treat it, the better it serves you. Diet plays a major role.

The Macronutrients and Water

All food is made up these four basic elements, and they should be ingested with strong consideration to balance and quality. Underdoing one of them or overdoing another leads to a less efficient system, which is a problem for anyone but perhaps most for athletes, who rely on attuned bodies for performance.

Carbohydrates

Carbohydrates have become synonymous with energy, but that's not completely accurate. Carbohydrates are an energy source, but so are fats and proteins. The difference lies in how your body processes and uses the different energy sources. Carbohydrates, once broken down and delivered to the bloodstream, become one basic substance: glucose. Glucose is delivered to the muscles and also added to hydrogen in the cells to produce energy. Along the way, glucose triggers your body's production of insulin, which is a necessary catalyst for your body to use glucose as energy. When this mix is delivered to your body for use, only about 50 percent goes to actual energy production. About 10 percent is stored as glycogen for future use. The remaining 40 percent goes to fat stores. This is why we should not overeat carbohydrates. Remember that fats and proteins can be converted to glucose, so the potential for energy even without carbohydrates already exists in your fat stores. The main difference is that glycogen is your short-term, high-energy source, whereas fats are your longer-term energy source.

Another important factor regarding carbohydrates is the glycemic index, or a particular food's ability to raise blood sugar and insulin. In slang terms, the distinction is "slow-burn" or "fast-burn" carbohydrates; slow-burning carbs mean a lower glycemic index, or higher-quality carbohydrates. In general, the high-glycemic carbohydrates raise blood sugar quickly, cause glycogen to be used for energy, and inhibit fat burning. Look at table 2.1 for a list of several foods and their glycemic indexes. Notice a trend? Processed foods have higher indexes, natural foods lower indexes. Generally, more processing means more added sugar. Sugar comes in many forms—sucrose, fructose, maltose, corn syrup, maltodextrin—and each has a very high glycemic index. To enhance athletic performance, avoid processed foods and go for natural, low-glycemic, slow-burn fuels.

Table 2.1

Glycemic Indexes of Common Foods

High

Glucose	100	Gatorade	91	Potato, baked	85
Cornflakes	84	Jelly beans	80	Cheerios	74
Bread, white	70	Mars bar	68	Couscous	65
Raisins	64	Oatmeal	61	Ice cream	61

Moderate

Muffin, bran	60	Orange juice	57	Potato, boiled	56
Rice, brown	55	Corn	55	Banana, overripe	52
Bulgur	48	Baked beans	48	Lentil soup	44
Orange	43	Pumpernickel bread	41	Apple juice, unsweetened	41

Low

Apple	36	PowerBar	30-35	Chocolate milk	34
Chick-peas	33	P R Bar	33	Lima beans	32
Milk, skim	32	Apricots, dried	31	Lentils	29
Barley	25	Grapefruit	25	Fructose	23

Reprinted, by permission, from Nancy Clark, 1990, *Nancy Clark's Sports Nutrition Guidebook*, 2d ed. (Champaign, IL: Human Kinetics), 110,111.

Data from food companies and K. Foster-Powell and J. Brand Miller, 1995, "International tables of glycemic index," *Am J Clin Nutr* 62: 871S-893S.

Fats

The crusade against fats maligns an essential nutrient. Yes, fats can be bad, but they can also be good, or even essential in some cases. Basically, there are three kinds of fats: omega-6, omega-3 (unsaturated), and saturated. Sources of omega-6 fat include most vegetables; safflower, peanut, and corn oils; and black currant seed oil. Sources of omega-3 fat include fish, beans, flaxseed oil, and fish oil. Sources of saturated fat (from natural sources) are milk, cheese, eggs, and other dairy products and meat. Our bodies need all three kinds of fats to survive, but most people should try to reduce their saturated and trans fat intake while eating more omega-6 and omega-3 fats.

The many benefits of fats to bodily function and overall health include enhancing hormone production, essential for good health; insulation; healthy skin and hair (with help from cholesterol); pregnancy and lactation benefits; protection against X-rays (which are around us all the time); assistance in digestion; support and protection for body parts; absorption and utilization of vitamins A, D, E, and K; and, last but not least, enhanced flavor of foods.

Unfortunately, in today's processed-food world, there's an overabundance of saturated fats. But saturated fats are not necessarily evil, as we are led to believe, and they should not be erased from your diet completely. A problem arises because processed foods rely heavily on saturated fat—or

© iphotonews.com/Brooks

"Moderate" on the Glycemic Index, the potassium-rich banana is a great pre- or postrace snack.

worse yet "trans fat," which is the worst form of saturated fat—for enhancing taste, among other reasons. Look for the word "hydrogenated" in the ingredients list. If you see the word, avoid that food. Also avoid overheated oils, such as those used in french fries, as these are modified to trans fat through the overheating process. Trans fat is the worst form of saturated fat and can actually promote inflammation within our bodies, whereas omega fats work to control inflammation.

Any discussion about fats is not complete without touching on cholesterol. Like fats, cholesterol's reputation is suffering unjustly. We need HDL cholesterol. The other type, LDL, is the "bad" type that contributes to heart disease and other vascular problems (whereas HDL actually reduces the risk of heart disease). Most saturated fats raise the level of LDL cholesterol, with the worst culprits being palm and coconut oil. Trans fats, found in hydrogenated or overheated oils, not only increase LDL but also decrease HDL. High-carbohydrate diets have also been linked to lowered HDL levels. So once again, balance is the key. Think about achieving a balance of this essential nutrient, which generally means becoming aware of your saturated and trans fat intake, reducing it, and making an effort to ingest more omega-6 and omega-3 fats.

Proteins

Proteins are made up mainly of amino acids, and higher-quality proteins contain more amino acids in a balanced state. Of the 20 or so amino acids used in our bodies, 10 are manufactured within the body, and 10 must be derived from diet. Proteins are limited as a source of energy, but they are the building blocks of the body, all the way down to the cellular level, so their importance cannot be overstressed.

How much protein is necessary for a balanced diet? The measurement standard for protein consumption is in "grams per kilogram of body weight." To make sense of this, in the United States we need to convert kilograms to pounds (although most Americans have begun to comprehend food in terms of grams). Table 2.2 translates pounds to kilograms, then recommends intake levels based on the World Health Organization's standard of .75 grams per kilogram of body weight for Western diets. Keep in mind, though, that this standard is for "regular" people, not athletes, and that other countries disagree with the standards and modify them, usually raising the amount. Australia, for instance, uses a 1.0 gram to kilogram standard. For athletes, many nutritionists suggest a 1.2 or 1.4 to 1 ratio. Bodybuilders often approach a ratio of 2 grams to kilogram of body weight. But you don't want to overconsume proteins, as any protein not used for energy or to build cells goes to fat stores. Evidence suggests that any amount over 2 grams per kilogram is excessive and anything not used will go to fat stores.

Water

Water is our most common deficiency. Most athletes know this, yet many don't drink anywhere near enough water. In fact, many athletes are in a constant state of dehydration. Even a small decrease in the body's water content due to dehydration can greatly impair performance. You may not need other nutrients during a 60- to 90-minute race or workout, but you will always need water (events lasting longer than 90 minutes require other nutrients as well). Here are some other facts about the importance of drinking enough water:

- Feeling thirsty? Then you're already dehydrated. Never wait until thirst tells you it's time to drink—by then it's too late. Thirst means you're already beginning a state of dehydration, and once dehydrated, it can take as long as 48 hours to rehydrate effectively.

Table 2.2

Protein Intake Chart

Pounds	Kilograms	Protein intake
90	40.9	30.7
100	45.5	34.1
110	50.0	37.5
120	54.5	40.9
130	59.1	44.3
140	63.6	47.7
150	68.2	51.1
160	72.7	54.5
170	77.3	58.0
180	81.8	61.4
190	86.4	64.8
200	90.9	68.2
210	95.5	71.6
220	100.0	75.0

- When you're dehydrated, blood plasma and blood flow diminish, which reduces the supply of oxygen and nutrients to the muscles. This causes your heart rate to increase and forces you to slow down.

- During dehydration, blood circulation is reduced to your skin, which can reduce your body's ability to dissipate heat, which causes your core temperature to rise—and this can cause real trouble.

- Water consumption is so critical that many athletes use their countdown timer to remind them to drink.

- You should drink 4 to 6 ounces of water every 15 to 30 minutes during athletic activity. Drink every 60 to 90 minutes while at rest.

Sixty percent of our water intake is from consumed water. Another 30 percent comes from food, and 10 percent is manufactured in your body by metabolizing the three other macronutrients. Where does all this water go? At rest, 60 percent is lost through the kidneys (urination), 30 percent through respiration, and 5 percent each through sweating and intestinal function. When exercising, suddenly 90 percent of water loss is through sweating—up to one to two liters per hour of activity.

If you're losing one liter of water per hour, you need to be drinking about the same amount to keep your blood volume steady. A rule of thumb is that for every 1 percent of dehydrative weight loss, you can expect a 2 percent decrease in your athletic output, or pace. In a long triathlon, water losses of 6 to 10 percent can be common. That's why every year at the Hawaii Ironman, there will be some people collapsing or crawling across the finish line, seemingly near death (some are closer than we'd like to think). They are completely dehydrated, and out of fuel as well, since very little is being delivered to their muscles. If you do the math, an Ironman event can take up to three additional hours, if completed at all, due to dehydration.

- Athletes with great aerobic function (those in "good shape") naturally regulate hydration and body temperature more efficiently, and they generally have lower sweat rates. Still, they need to drink plenty of water, all day, every day. Consumption should occur gradually through-

© iphotonews.com/Brooks

Hydration should be conveniently accessible while on the bike.

out the day, as drinking large amounts of water at once can inhibit thirst and invoke a diuretic response. On particularly hot days, drink extra water before working out or racing. Drink cool water (59 to 72 degrees Fahrenheit) rather than warm water, but avoid drinking ice water, which can cause stomach contractions.

- To gauge your hydration, monitor your urine and urination habits. Clear urine means you're hydrated; yellow urine means you're dehydrated (the deeper the yellow, the more dehydrated you are). If you're not urinating seven to eight times a day, you're not drinking enough water. Limit your use of diuretics, which cause water to be lost from the body. Caffeine is a diuretic and so is alcohol. Finally, after a hard athletic event or long work out, drink at least four to five cups of water, and more than that if you sweat a lot. It's very difficult to overhydrate in this situation.

Vitamins, Minerals, Supplements, and Electrolytes

Electrolytes, sodium, chloride, potassium, and magnesium are almost as important to consume as water. Electrolytes help regulate water balance and retention through regulation of thirst and salt appetite mechanisms in your brain. We won't go into the physiological process of how electrolytes work, but you should know that overtraining causes depletion of electrolytes, which leads to dehydration and possibly diarrhea and other problems.

If electrolytes are severely depleted, sodium levels drop, causing a condition called hyponatremia. Symptoms of hyponatremia include weakness, disorientation, and, in extreme cases, neurological problems including cardiovascular instability or seizures. So, ingesting sodium during training or racing is important. If your event lasts longer than an hour, drink a beverage that contains electrolytes or sodium, or add salt in small amounts to your water (just enough to taste it) or take sodium tablets. Sodium speeds stomach-emptying of water and absorption by the small intestine into the body. It also helps prevent muscle cramps. Cramps are often an indication that your sodium levels are low.

Be wary of attaining your electrolytes or sodium through drinking sports drinks, as these drinks often contain other ingredients that may have an adverse affect on training or racing. The concept of "stomach emptying" (the rate at which water is emptied from the stomach to the small intestine for absorption) is important. Studies have shown that sugar, or its concentrated forms of glucose, sucrose, or fructose, can reduce stomach emptying by almost half, which can severely impair your ability to keep up with sweat loss. Small amounts of sodium can increase your thirst, making you drink more, thus improving hydration.

© David Sanders

Load up on electrolytes before or during long training sessions.

Regarding supplements, note that "supplement" is defined as "something intended to be added to a basic element." In other words, supplements should not be a *replacement* for vitamins and minerals that you should acquire through natural food sources. You should try to meet all your nutritional needs through regular diet. When this is not possible (as is often the case), resort to supplements. Many nutritionists recommend supplementing your diet to ensure meeting your health needs. But don't just pop any vitamins you have around. A dietary analysis should be performed by a professional, and your decisions on which supplements to use should be based on that analysis.

In general, there are three kinds of supplements to choose from: *natural* supplements made from whole foods, natural herbs, and glandular products; *isolated* supplements, also made from whole foods but refined to the point of lacking other substances in that food; and *synthetic* supplements, which are chemically synthesized and have no relation to the vitamin found in its natural form.

Which type of supplement is best for you? If you're getting plenty of nutrients in their natural form through whole foods, you'll need virtually no supplements, and you are better off. If you're not getting the nutrients you need through consuming whole foods, consider natural supplements first. Natural supplements have some relation to the whole food they are derived from and are accompanied by beneficial, natural substances; they are generally easier for the body to absorb.

However, natural supplements are usually lower in doses than synthetic supplements, so if you have a severe vitamin deficiency, a higher dose synthetic supplement might be best for you. Be aware, though, that absorption rates of synthetics are often much lower, so the net effect may be about the same, or even worse. Synthetic mineral supplements, for instance, can have very poor absorption rates compared to natural versions.

Excessive vitamin and mineral consumption can cause damage. Too much iron can eventually put you at risk of heart disease. Excess doses of vitamin C or copper on top of iron can be toxic. Excess vitamin A can result in calcium loss. Use vitamin D supplements very sparingly, if at all, as vitamin D is potentially highly toxic in excess. Most athletes spend enough time outdoors to derive all the vitamin D they need from the sun.

The bottom line: Try to get all your vitamins, minerals, and electrolytes through a well-balanced, minimally preprocessed natural diet. This is always your best and safest route.

Designing Your Diet

What is the best way to maintain an optimal athletic diet? We'll close this chapter by addressing what you should and shouldn't eat and discussing good energy foods, how to shop, and how to cook.

First of all, know that what works best for us might not work best for you. We all have different metabolisms and vastly different ways in which nutrients are processed and used, based largely on what and how much we put in our bodies. If your diet is important to you (as it should be), take a diet test with a nutritionist who specializes in sport nutrition, or do a self-test using guidelines from a qualified source.

When evaluating your diet, always consider total calories; percentages of carbohydrates, proteins, and fats; vitamin and mineral levels; amino acid levels; essential fatty acid levels; omega-3 and omega-6 fat ratio; percentages of monounsaturated fats, polyunsaturated fats, and saturated fats; and amounts of fiber.

The best foods and snacks for endurance athletes are foods high in carbohydrates, such as brown rice, beans, fresh fruit and berries; foods high in proteins, such as whole eggs, lean beef, fish, and unprocessed soy; fresh

Cooking Tips

Food preparation is the final step in optimizing your diet and can significantly influence the investment you make in food. Many nutrients can be damaged or negated through poor preparation. Some tips:

- Use extra virgin olive oil for cooking. Avoid hydrogenated fats or oils.

- Don't overheat oils (to the point of smoking), as transfats are produced.

- Invest in a steamer. You might be surprised how good vegetables, rice, fish, and other foods taste when steamed.

- Don't overcook foods; it depletes nutrients.

- Use whole foods, or real foods, as ingredients.

- Try to include raw food at every meal.

- Sea salt is better than table salt.

- Relax while you eat. Relaxation aids digestion. Stress reduces proper nutrient absorption.

vegetables (potatoes and corn in moderation), including onion and garlic; fruit smoothies, made from yogurt and fruit; some fats, such as extra virgin olive, avocado, and flaxseed oils; nuts, particularly almonds, macadamias, cashews, and walnuts; cheese; broth-based soups, all-natural energy bars; and tuna or egg salad.

Many diet plans break down when you're traveling or in a rush or in a snacking mode. To help remedy this, buy high-quality snack bars and eat them instead of junk food. Bars are cheaper if you buy them in bulk or through the mail. Don't rule out the natural route either—fresh fruit is still the best snack available.

Sensible training and a balanced diet lead to optimal health. Sometimes when you make a fervent effort to shift to a balanced diet, you can see and feel the difference within two to three weeks, but if you don't, be patient—it may take you a while to determine the best diet for your needs.

Shopping Tips

It often costs more to buy natural, unprocessed, or organic foods, or even higher-quality foods. Ask yourself if the greater cost is worth it. Our reply is a resounding yes. You can't make a better investment in yourself than a high-quality, conscientious, well-balanced diet. Some tips:

- Never shop hungry—you'll buy more junk food.

- If you bring your children, make sure they have eaten. Grocery stores are well aware of the buying influence of children, and they cater to it.

- Focus on foods around the periphery of the grocery store, where the natural, less processed produce, dairy, and meat products are.

- Natural vegetables are best, frozen a close second, canned or other processed veggies a distant third.

- Read labels! In general, simpler labels mean less processing and thus better food.

- Food grown in the United States is better for you than imported foods (tighter restrictions on pesticides and herbicides), and it's better to buy food grown in your geographic region, when possible.

- Seek out healthier versions of what you routinely buy. It takes some searching but is possible almost every time.

- Whole fruits and vegetables are healthier than prepared versions.

- Always wash fruits and vegetables, using a very mild, safe soap, if desired. There are now natural fruit and vegetable washes that claim to remove most pesticide residue.

- Buy from health food stores when possible; buy organic when possible.

- Buy natural meat products (e.g., free-range chicken) and avoid ground meat products unless very fresh.

- Shop at farmers' markets for the highest-quality, cleanest, and most natural food attainable.

- After unloading your grocery cart onto the checkout counter, take a good look at the pile. How much nonfood material are you buying? What percentage of the pile is cardboard, plastic, foam, and glass? Chances are the more nonfood mass on the line, the lower quality contained within the food and your overall diet. Strive to raise percent of real food and reduce nonfood packaging.

Chapter 3

STRUCTURING YOUR TRAINING

Most triathletes focus on traditional swim-bike-run events during their competitive season. The selection of a particular race length determines the kind of training that should be employed for a successful performance. Triathlon has four basic categories of race: sprint, Olympic distance, long, and ultra. For elite competitors, sprint events usually last about an hour. Olympic (also called "International") distance events usually consist of a 1.5K swim, 40K on the bike, and a 10K run; the fastest athletes do these races in under two hours. Long events are generally at the half-Ironman distance; elite triathletes cover these in four to five hours. Ultra events are typically Ironman distance (2.4-mile swim, 112-mile bike, 26.2-mile run). Top competitors require 8 or more hours to complete a typical Ironman. Some races can even be much longer, such as the infamous Double Ironman, also known as the Ultraman, a race that lasts twenty hours, or even more than thirty for some.

Triathletes rarely can be successful in all four categories without varying their training plans. The original "Big Four" (Mark Allen, Scott Molina, Dave Scott, and Scott Tinley) found success at any distance. However, as the sport has become more specialized, athletes must customize their training to enhance performance. Sprint and Ironman triathlons are like the marathon and mile run. It's hard to train for both at the same time, and only a handful of athletes are successful in both distances.

Many athletes now plan their training and competition schedules to peak for an end-of-the-season "big event." Gone are the days of doing 10 to 20 races a season and hoping for a breakthrough race at some point. Because of the money factor, professionals still compete in multiple races each season. But most amateurs operate from a different plan, targeting certain distances and trying to peak at the end of the season for their big event. With the cost of training and travel, focusing on a couple of events seems a more reasonable approach.

Start each racing season with a fresh set of goals. Picking a big event to peak for helps tailor your training program. When it comes to goal setting, the old saying, "failing to plan is planning to fail" rings true. If you go from workout to workout with no game plan, you'll likely lose motivation to train and compete. Identify a couple of big races to peak for at the end of your season, and set your goals accordingly.

Selecting the Right Event

Take a hard, honest look at yourself and identify your strengths and weaknesses as a triathlete. Ask yourself the following questions: Am I a racer or pacer? Is speed or endurance my strong point? How much time do I have for training? The answers to these questions will help you determine your best race distance. Here are the qualities of effective competitors in the four categories of triathlon.

Sprint

The successful sprint triathlete has a high tolerance for pain. Although these events are short in duration, they are extremely high in intensity. Don't let the name fool you—when raced correctly, sprint events are about an hour of intense pain. You're basically at the highest end of your aerobic capacity for a sustained period of time. Because of the short duration, a sprint triathlete can't afford much weakness in any of the three sports. A slow swim can take you out of contention immediately, a poor bike puts you in a tough position going into the run, and a slow run results in dropping places as you fight your way to the finish line. The short duration of each segment makes each sport about equal in overall race contribution, so there's no room for error or weakness.

However, the sprint event is also a good distance for beginners or those coming back to triathlon after a long break. There may be little chance of doing well in the competition, but you can use the sprint as a stepping-stone if you plan to race longer distances later. Sprint events are particularly helpful *as a* training *springboard* for Olympic distance races because sprints let you practice race-like conditions for a short amount of time. It's easier to move up to the longer and more demanding Olympic distance race after completing several Sprint races as practice. Plus, sprint events are relatively easy to recover from, so you won't have much down time due to postrace fatigue.

Olympic Distance

The Olympic distance race places a premium on even pacing for a period of about two hours. About half your time in an Olympic distance race is spent on the bike, so the ability to hammer a solid 40K time trial is essential. If you can also run a very fast 10K at the end, that's obviously a big plus. Olympic distance races are similar to the sprint, but the pain lasts about twice as long. To be competitive, you must operate only slightly below maximum aerobic capacity for most of the race. The distance is also useful as a tune-up for a long triathlon.

Long

Weak swimmers with good bike and run skills can have reasonable success in the long races, as swim time is typically short. Most races in this category are at about half the distance of an Ironman. Typically, you'll do a 1.2-mile swim, a 56-mile bike, and a 13.1-mile run.

© Rich Cruse

Ironman Peter Reid uses his personal strengths to be one of the best in the world at the Ironman distance.

Ultra

This event is the consummate pacer. The ability to race well "within your-self" is key to success, along with sticking to a solid race strategy that includes eating and drinking. Many good ultra racers use a heart rate monitor while cycling and running to make sure they stay within their aerobic zone. In a standard ultra race you'll do Ironman distances—2.4-mile swim, 112-mile bike, and 26.2-mile run—but some ultras go much longer. You'll need to be super efficient and have good technique to compete well in an ultra.

Training and Time Needs

The longer the race you plan to compete in, the longer the training time. Some athletes can have success with minimal time investment for sprint events. Here are ballpark numbers for hours you'll need to train per week for different events. Of course, because training response is specific and individual, some triathletes will have success with less training, while others will require more.

Sprint: 4 to 10 hours a week

Olympic: 6 to 13 hours a week

Long: 12 to 22 hours a week

Ultra: 15 to 30 hours a week

Busy triathletes with many commitments outside the sport may find their niche in races that last two hours and under. If you're competing in longer events, you'll need to set aside time to do longer training, especially on weekends. Chapter 15 outlines specific programs for each of the different categories of racing.

Types of Training

To optimize your training time, you need to learn how to train each of your body's energy systems: the aerobic and the anaerobic. Aerobic energy is produced in the presence of oxygen; anaerobic energy production requires little or no oxygen. Both systems continually provide energy, even when the body is at rest. The type of activity dictates which system is predominant. Activities performed up to anaerobic threshold (the point at which lactate or ventilation threshold is crossed) depend primarily on the aerobic system. Once this point is crossed, the anaerobic system makes a greater contribution. One of the side effects of anaerobic energy production is the formation of lactic acid (which is one of the culprits behind acute muscle "burn" associated with intense activity). The ability to withstand copious amounts of lactic acid running through the blood stream is always limited, though some athletes can tolerate it more than others. Therefore, efficient aerobic energy production is of paramount importance to the triathlete, even for sprint events.

Relevant to these energy systems, there are three basic training zones for endurance athletes. All three are important, but depending on the type of event you are peaking for, they require different amounts of training time. Shorter events such as sprint and Olympic distance races call for more intense training, while longer events place more value on stamina-oriented training.

Endurance

The first type of training is endurance (EN). Training in this range is characterized by low- to moderate-intensity efforts. Most triathletes already have plenty of EN training in their current programs. These easier workouts are great for group efforts, looking at the scenery, or simply contemplating your own thoughts. EN training is what brought most of us to the sport in the first place—giving us a time in our day when we can be alone with our thoughts and provide our body exercise. EN sessions are as important for mental and emotional fitness as they are for physical improvement.

As an endurance athlete, you'll spend a lot of your time training in this zone, as it serves a crucial role. Before you can go fast, you must first learn to go easy and build a solid base in the EN zone.

We break EN training down into two types: recovery and overdistance. EN recovery efforts are short and light workouts. Swim workouts under 3,000 yards, 30- to 90-minute bike rides, and 20- to 45-minute runs, all at very low effort, are roughly the volumes associated with EN recovery-type sessions. EN recovery workouts are done once, or up to twice per weak, per discipline. An EN recovery workout is also important for postrace recovery (or hard work-out recovery), to augment vital blood/nutrient flow to potentially damaged muscle tissue and for easing post race pain. Intense training sessions (those that simulate maximum race effort) are almost always followed by an EN recovery level workout.

EN overdistance training is longer effort at a relaxed pace. Swim workouts over 5,000 yards that feature low-key sets and easy- to moderate-paced swims, bike sessions over two hours, and runs over 60 minutes are typical of overdistance sessions. Triathletes who desire success in long or ultra races should do this form of training twice weekly. For a serious competitor, one long swim and either one long ride or run (on alternating weeks for a total of two overdistance workouts per week) fit perfectly into a program geared toward long events.

A balance between training and recovery is vital for competitive intensity.

Aerobic Power

Aerobic power (AP) features training at or around race pace. The main purpose of this type of training is to raise, over time, your anaerobic threshold (AT). Elevating your AT is very important to all endurance athletes. All of us have an upper limit of maximum aerobic capacity, known as $\dot{V}O_2max$. Increasing your $\dot{V}O_2max$ is possible but only in extremely small increments, and there is a ceiling for $\dot{V}O_2max$ improvement. This maximum aerobic capacity is more influenced by genetic factors than anything else, so athletes must focus AP work on the goal of elevating anaerobic threshold as close to maximum as possible. Some elite endurance athletes' AT has been measured as high as 98 percent of maximum—which means these elite performers can train and race at 98 percent of maximum before the effect of lactic acid begins to debilitate performance. Most well-trained athletes have an AT in the range of 75 to 90 percent of $\dot{V}O_2max$. But AT can *always* be improved, and genetics plays less of a factor than it does for $\dot{V}O_2max$.

Just as in EN training, AP work has two subgroups: AP Low (AP–) and AP High (AP+). AP– training involves efforts just below AT; this level of intensity is often described as "comfortably hard." AP– training can be done within EN overdistance workouts; this training can provide a refreshing change and add interest to a long session. AP– can also be done continuously (e.g., 20 minutes of running) or as long intervals with short rest (e.g., bike 3×9 minutes with 1-minute easy spin between reps).

AP+ type training is just at or slightly above AT. A trained endurance athlete can sustain intensities over AT for about 20 to 30 minutes. After that, glycogen depletion sets in, and lactic acid levels creep up. Interval training is a very effective tool for AP+ training. The combination of work and rest allows the body to stay at AP+ for longer periods of time, thus allowing the athlete an opportunity for improvement. AP+ intervals can be anywhere from 2 to 12 minutes in duration and feature rest intervals from 15 seconds to 5 minutes between efforts. A good rule of thumb is to actively rest half of the work time (e.g., 4-minute AP+ efforts would be followed by 2-minute recovery intervals). As your fitness level improves, gradually reduce the amount of recovery between repeats.

Speed

This type of training improves your body's ability to produce energy through the anaerobic system. Your aerobic system will always be producing some energy. But once you cross AT, anaerobic energy production starts shouldering more of the load. Speed training (SP) is important and should be done by all triathletes; SP aids significantly in improving strength, lactic acid tolerance buffering, and economy. The bottom line is if you periodically train in small doses at intensities greater than race pace, your race-day effort will feel easier to maintain.

Similar to EN and AP training, SP training is also divided into two categories: short and long. Short SP efforts are simply 10- to 20-second bursts of speed that can be carried out during any EN overdistance workout. During the first half of the 10- to 20-second effort, build your tempo to a speed close to maximum velocity, then, once you're up to speed, hold it for the remaining time. This type of speed work should feel effortless; think of it as simply releasing speed. Focus on ease of movement, and just let it flow. Once you have completed your short burst of speed, ease back down to your EN pace/ intensity. Allow at least 5 to 10 minutes between these short, fast efforts.

SP long efforts are repetitive intervals, 30 to 90 seconds in duration, at race pace intensity for a race lasting between two to five minutes. In swim training, use a pace close to what you'd use in a 200-yard race. On the bike, go at a speed that you can maintain for a 2-mile time trial. Run speed training features efforts at an 800-meter intensity. SP long efforts are *not* all-out sprints!

The key component of SP long efforts is plenty of rest between repetitions. A good rule is to allow your heart rate to drop below 120 beats per minute between efforts. It's normal if it takes two to five minutes between efforts to recover. Your goal is to keep the pace of the SP long effort fast, yet relaxed. If you don't allow full recovery between repeats, you'll have a hard time maintaining the speed you want.

Training Zones Defined

An optimal program for any triathlete is a blend of all three training zones, tailored to the specific event targeted. A triathlete gearing up for races at

© Rich Cruse

Speed training helps you to sprint to the finish of a race or fight off a competitor.

Olympic distance and shorter will do more quality work in the AP+ and SP categories. A triathlete focusing on longer races spends more time doing EN and AP– training.

For simplification, we assign numbers to each zone (1 to 5). Many variations of zones and percentages exist, but upon comparison you'll find them to be very similar most of the time. The main point is that our Zone 1 and another plan or coach's Zone 1 are likely very similar. So, if someone says, "Let's do a Zone 1 workout," both of you should have the same idea in mind.

The important difference, however, is that your Zone 1 is likely not the same heart rate as someone else's; although it will be the same *percentage* of maximum heart rate (it would be the same if your maximum heart rate is the same). We also include a perceived effort scale for those without heart rate monitors, but keep in mind most serious athletes employ a heart rate monitor eventually.

So, the initial question becomes this: what is my maximum heart rate? It's important to note that maximum heart rate won't be the same for each discipline. It is fairly common for your maximum to be lowest in the swim. Whether your "absolute maximum" comes from biking or running varies from person to person, but for most triathletes it seems to come from running. Here are suggested methods for determining your maximum in each discipline:

Swim

15-minute warm-up

4 × 200 with 15 seconds rest, descending: easy, moderate, moderate, hard

1 minute rest

3 × 100 with 15 seconds rest (check heart rate each time). Push the second interval *very hard*, and you should reach your maximum.

15-minute cool-down

Bike on a trainer

20-minute warm-up, easy spinning

6 × 1 minute, easy gear with cadence 85 to 95 rpm, alternate 1 minute medium, 1 minute easy

Come to a complete stop. Choose a gear that offers solid resistance: large chain ring and 13 to 16 cogs depending on your strength. Set a timer for 30 seconds. Start it and go, jumping fairly hard, out of the saddle if necessary, and build up to maximum speed for all you're worth. Go the full 30 seconds! This is much harder than it sounds. Check your heart rate immediately. If you don't feel you reached your maximum, repeat one more time after 3 minutes of easy spinning.

15-minute cool-down, easy spinning

Run on a track

Jog to the track or on the track for 15 minutes.

Stop, perform some light stretching and some bounding, strides, or power skipping drills (see Chapter 12).

400 meters moderate pace (5K pace); 400-meter jog, 400 meters easy with four 10- to 20-second speed bursts.

200 meter jog, then 200 meters with first 100 as build and second 100 maximum effort. Record heart rate at finish.

If you don't feel as if you achieved your maximum, go right into a 400-meter easy jog, then repeat the 200-meter build to maximum and check again.

Continue with light jog for 15 minutes.

Don't do any of these workouts until you have developed at least a minimal base in that discipline, which is defined as a minimum of two months' consistent EN training. There are other good ways to measure maximum heart rate. In both cycling and running, most of us know of a "killer" hill somewhere. It should not only be steep but it should also be long (at least 500 to 1,000 meters). Again, after a thorough warm-up, build at the base of the hill and hit maximum effort at the top. Another good time to check your maximum is at the end of a race, where most people are or should be hitting their maximum, especially if the race is a shorter distance.

Now that you have your maximum heart rate, you can use table 3.1 to establish your training zones. Again, these percentages of maximum to determine zones are fairly universally accepted, and they're also used by the United States Cycling Federation (USCF) for their certified coaches training programs.

Table 3.2 is used by USCF-certified coaches and helps to explain what each zone feels like relevant to perceived effort. The column, "% of TT" means the perceived effort relevant to a 40K time trial pace. This pace and heart rate are roughly where you should be in an average length triathlon (up to and including Olympic distance). A seasoned athlete may start a sprint race in Zone 4 and build to Zone 5; a beginner may start at high Zone 3 and end at high Zone 4. It is generally accepted that all but elite athletes should try to stay in Zone 3 (or even lower) for half to full Ironman races, keeping the pace just below anaerobic threshold. Any desired pace or heart rates are very individualized and can only be determined through experience.

A gap exists between Zone 3 and 4 because many people train too much at this intensity (80 to 84 percent of maximum). This intensity is too low to train your anaerobic threshold, and training your endurance base is done better and with less stress at lower intensities.

Table 3.3 is a reference for pacing used within each zone. It is helpful in several ways: if you are training for a straight marathon or ultra triathlon, then training in zones at that pace prepares you for proper pacing on race

Table 3.1

Training Zone Guide

Type of training	Zone	% of maximum heart rate	Perceived exertion (PE)
Endurance (EN)			
Recovery	1	<65%	1-2
Overdistance	2	65-72%	1-4
Aerobic power			
Low (AP–)	3	73-80%	5-7
High (AP+)	4	84-90%	7-9
Speed (SP)			
Short	NA	NA	5-6
Long	5	91-100%	8-10

Table 3.2

USCF Training Table

Zone	% Max	% AT*	PE	PE breathing	PE feeling	% of TT
1	<65	<65	1-2	Able to sing	Very easy	50-70
2	65-72	70-75	1-4	Able to converse	Easy	70-80
3	73-83	80-95	5-7	Talking is hard	Steady/light	80-90
4	84-90	100	7-9	Forced breathing	Steady	100
5	91-100	110+	9-10	Very forced breathing	Burn/pain	110

AT = Anaerobic threshold
TT = Time trial pace

day. Pacing is very important in racing; the inexperienced almost always start too fast and run out of gas before the finish. Others may do an entire race at too easy a pace, feel like they had more to give at the finish, and be disappointed. There is a perfect race pace for everyone; it takes a lot of practice at pacing to determine what yours is. Keep in mind, though, if you don't race, you won't understand what these paces are, unless you perform practice time trials. Almost all swimming, cycling, and running clubs have

Use a heart monitor during the race to match your pace with your inner exertion levels.

organized time trials at various distances you can (and should!) participate in to determine your pace—not to mention seeing how you stack up against the competition before the actual race!

As you can see, investing in a heart rate monitor is a good idea, and a simple, inexpensive model will do the job. Even though most serious athletes have a monitor, you can still do a lot with perceived effort, provided your zones are somewhat accurate. Borrowing a monitor for a while is always an option. Once you set zones and operate in them for a time, it becomes second nature to hit them consistently in training. Beware of falling into a trap of insufficient monitoring. It's important to recheck your training heart rate from time to time, as you may need to adjust your zones. As your level of conditioning improves, for example, the amount you need to work to achieve the same heart rate will increase. If it takes running at 7-minute-per-

Table 3.3

Pace Guide for Training Zones

Sport	Zone	Pace based on race distance
Swim	EN	5,000 meter-pace
	AP−	1,500 meters
	AP+	400 meters
	SP (long)	200 meters
	SP (short)	50-100 meters
Bike—pace based on time trial	EN	Easy/conversational/PE of 1-3
	AP−	80-100K (50-60 miles)
	AP+	20-40K (12-24 miles)
	SP (long)	3-4K (2-3 miles)
	SP (short)	1K (1/2 mile, or maximum efforts as short as 100-200 meters)
Run	EN	Easy/conversational/PE of 1-3
		Easy marathon pace
	AP−	10-mile to "competitive" marathon pace
	AP+	3-10K (2-6.2 miles)
	SP (long)	800-1,600 meters (1/2-1 mile)
	SP (short)	200-400 meters

mile pace to get to 60 percent of your max heart rate, as your conditioning improves, you may find you have to run at 6:30-minute-per-mile pace to reach 60 percent of your max. We recommend rechecking your maximum about every six months. Also, if you are overtrained, heart rate rises proportionally compared to perceived effort during training. Conversely, as your fitness improves, heart rate drops while doing the same effort as before good fitness. Resting heart rate drops with fitness as well (or rises when overtrained), and recovery heart rate—the rate at which it drops when you stop exercising—is dramatically increased. This is a big plus for training and racing. Overall, one of the ultimate goals of training is going farther and faster than you previously could at a lower heart rate. In upcoming chapters we detail how to structure successful, personalized training plans based on these principles.

Part II
SWIM

SWIM
BIKE
RUN

Chapter 4

SWIMMING EQUIPMENT

Swimming is the one sport you can do with virtually no equipment—though a swim brief or suit is recommended. As technology increasingly affects sports performance, the swimsuit you choose can now make a world of difference. Check the swim competition results at the 2000 Olympics in Sydney, and you'll see that world records fell like an avalanche—many felt primarily because of the controversial new high-tech swimsuits.

Swimsuits and Swimcaps

You want a tight-fitting, high-quality suit that won't create drag in the water. For racing, men's and women's suits are available with triathlon-specific features, such as a padded crotch for cycling or a one-piece suit that's good for swimming, cycling, and running.

The only other clothing item to discuss (and an important one) is your swimcap. Caps provide a hydrodynamic advantage, keep your head warm, help hold goggles in place, and keep your hair manageable after your swim. If a regular latex cap causes irritation, consider a lycra or silicone cap, although a lycra cap is not waterproof.

Goggles

Don't scrimp to save in the goggles department. Leaky, ill-fitting goggles are a constant source of annoyance. The simple goggle has had many recent technological breakthroughs in terms of fit and performance. Goggles come in many different styles, and none is necessarily superior to another. Choose a style that best fits your eye sockets. Most have packaging that allows you to remove the goggles, try them on, and put them back in the package if they don't fit. Keep trying them on until you get the best possible fit. They should be comfortable and seal completely without your having to tighten the straps to the point of causing a headache.

Goggles have various sealing materials, including foam rubber or flexible plastic. Some goggles have hard plastic with virtually no gasket, which takes getting used to—but those who use them swear by them, as there's no gasket material to wear out. Foam rubber is the most common material for goggles and perhaps the most comfortable, but the rubber wears out over time and can harbor bacteria that leads to eye problems if not carefully cleaned and dried. (Leaving your damp swimsuit, goggles, and cap in your swim bag is one of the worst things you can do for your equipment.) The flexible plastic-type goggle may not seal quite as well or be as comfortable as foam rubber, but it stays cleaner and generally lasts longer.

Clear or lightly tinted goggles are good for indoor training or for outdoor training in overcast or dark conditions. For outdoor training and racing in sunny conditions, consider darker tinted goggles to enhance vision. It's a

Tinted goggles help with outdoor swimming in sunny conditions.

good idea to bring a pair of each on race day. Several companies provide vision-corrected goggles, which are a blessing to some athletes. If you're careful, you can wear your contact lenses under your goggles, provided you have a great fit and no leaks. Experiment before race day.

There are ways to make any goggle fog-proof. Try rubbing a thin film of toothpaste on the inside of the goggle and rinse. Or spit a small amount of saliva into the goggle. For the less creative, there are also commercially available anti-fog goggles and anti-fog drops. Of all your options, the anti-fog drops might work the best.

Swim Training Devices

There are several training devices used routinely by swimmers and coaches to enhance training and performance. None of these is a necessity, but if you're putting in mega-training yards, these devices help break monotony and can allow for gains.

Fist Gloves

If you buy just one piece of swim training equipment, make it a pair of fist gloves. They resemble a mitten and are made of latex. They force your hand into a closed fist. Wearing the gloves for short sets of 25s and 50s improves balance in your overall stroke and keeps you from "overmuscling" the water. When you take them off, you'll swim with "smart hands" that feel the size of kickboards! Use fist gloves and fins together, and you'll really improve your stroke.

You can get the same effect of fist gloves by just closing your fists (see chapter 5), but as concentration wanes, your fingers tend to open. Fist gloves make closure complete and automatic, so you can focus on other aspects of your stroke. The gloves allow you to prolong fist-swimming for hundreds of yards instead of an occasional 25, often leading to advances in your stroke technique.

Fins

Fins build leg strength, improve kicking motion, and provide extra propulsion to allow for improvements and adjustments in other areas of your stroke. The popular shorter fins work better for building leg strength. But don't rely solely on fins—always practice some kicking in your bare feet since you won't be using fins on race day.

Hand Paddles

Used for pulling, hand paddles come in different sizes and shapes. In general, the bigger, more powerful swimmer you are, the larger paddles you can handle. But be careful: paddles add a tremendous load to your muscles by increasing surface area exposed to the water (hence the muscle build-up). If you have shoulder problems or injuries, don't use paddles, as they will aggravate such problems. Otherwise, paddles can enhance stroke technique by slowing stroke rate and lengthening your glide; they can also sometimes improve stroke movement under the water.

Pull Buoys

Made of Styrofoam or plastic, pull buoys add flotation to the lower half of the body. They are crammed up as high as possible between the legs, so initially they feel uncomfortable and may be difficult to keep in place, but eventually you'll get the hang of it. Pull buoys improve your overall body position in the water and are intended to prevent kicking, thus transferring all the load to your arm stroke. But be aware that pull buoys are termed the "styro-virus" by some coaches, as some swimmers depend on them to maintain good body position. Like all devices, the key is to not overuse them.

Kickboards

The recent trend has been away from kickboards, the theory being that kicking is generally performed while on your side during the normal course of swimming as opposed to the somewhat unnatural body position a kickboard puts you in. Kickboards also disrupt body balance in the water. However, for a prolonged kicking set where the focus is solely on kicking technique and strength development, a kickboard is still the way to go. If pain develops in your lower back, quit using the kickboard.

Other Training Devices

There are many other training devices: straps or doughnuts to go around your legs to reduce kicking and increase drag; suits with pockets, called "drag suits"; monofins; latex straps tied to the side of the pool for resistance; belts with fins to enhance body rotation; and Vasa trainers for out-of-the-water swim workouts. We recommend the occasional and structured use of fins and pull gear, but unless you're a full-time swimmer the other miscellaneous devices are unnecessary.

Wetsuits

The wetsuit is the single most important piece of equipment that has forever changed triathlon. A wetsuit provides insulation from cold water—a safety feature that can't be stressed enough—and allows many more athletes to enjoy the sport of triathlon by, in effect, extending the outdoor swim season.

It was quickly discovered that wetsuits designed for swimming greatly enhance performance by increasing buoyancy and helping swimmers attain a proper horizontal posture in the water. The net performance gain is

A Word From Wes

Wetsuits: The Long and Short of It!

Until the early 1980s, only surfers and scuba divers used wetsuits to avoid hypothermia in cold water. That changed when wetsuits became the great swim equalizer in triathlons. Wetsuits are more buoyant than human fat cells. The buoyancy allows a weaker swimmer to swim more on top of the water, which typically means that person will swim faster than he or she would without the wetsuit. This buoyancy affects poorer swimmers more than stronger swimmers and thus closes the gap between the two in efficiency. Triathlon wetsuits, or "speedsuits," come in a variety of cuts and lengths. Originally, the triathlon wetsuits were five millimeters thick throughout the wetsuit, which is the maximum thickness allowed. The wetsuit was buoyant, but it didn't allow for flexibility.

Wetsuit designs changed to sleeveless and shortened leg lengths to accommodate flexibility. Now, with advances in rubber and stretch material, I think the full-body suit is the best wetsuit for speed. It may be warmer than other wetsuit versions, but I will sacrifice comfort in warmer waters for speed. Full-body suits are flexible enough for you to maintain full range of motion with your stroke. If this is the case, then why would you want a sleeveless or a short-legged suit if there is less rubber for buoyancy?

No matter what wetsuit you use, make sure you swim with it at least once before you race. If you have no open water in your area, go to a pool. The first time you wear a wetsuit for the season, you may get a claustrophobic sensation. Visualization can help ease any such anxiety.

In a race situation, Vaseline around the ankle areas will aid in removing your wetsuit. This helps the rubber slide off easier. I also use it around the neck, groin, and near the armpits to prevent chafing. Wetsuit companies say Vaseline is bad for the rubber. Although this may be true, I haven't found anything that works better. I wipe away the Vaseline soon after the race. Vaseline is also great around the ankles because it makes it harder for a competitor to grab your ankles in the swim.

decreased resistance while swimming; in fact, most agree that a wetsuit can reduce time by about 10 percent, or even more for some. As of this writing, USA Triathlon-sanctioned (USAT) races do not allow amateurs to wear wetsuits if water temperature is over 78 degrees Fahrenheit (72 degrees for pros), unless you choose to be ineligible for prizes or ranking in the race. In spite of this rule, many athletes still opt to wear a wetsuit, which indicates the benefits a wetsuit brings to racing.

The most common wetsuit is the minimal "short john," which is sleeveless and descends to just above the knee, about the same length as cycling

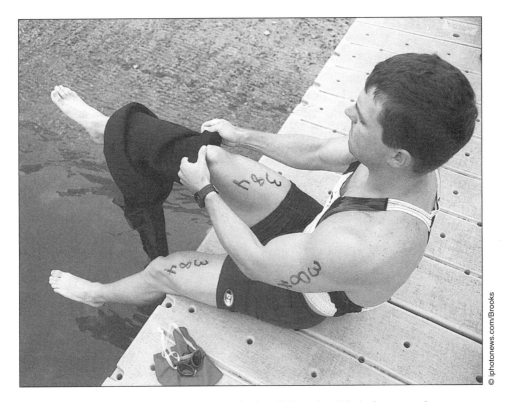

© iphotonews.com/Brooks

Wetsuits are not always easy to put on and take off. Practice this before race day.

shorts. These add buoyancy without the risk of overheating. For colder water, full-leg suits are available, and for even greater warmth, there are suits with full arms, as well. An issue worth consideration is the fabric thickness of your potential wetsuit, which can affect performance. Thicker material has greater insulating value and increased buoyancy but decreases mobility. A thickness of five millimeters is the current legal limit for racing. Many manufacturers offer wetsuits with a five-millimeter torso and hip region, coupled with three millimeters of material on the full arms and lower legs. Currently, this is the popular setup, as both buoyancy and mobility are maximized.

Wetsuits should fit snug. They can feel very constrictive and can take getting used to, especially around the neck. Try the suit on in the store to get the right fit, and be sure to train in it before racing in it. Certain areas of your body chafe, and some may feel constricted or even claustrophobic within the confines of the suit. A thin film of petroleum jelly (Vaseline) helps keep potential "hot spots" from chafing, but petroleum can degrade rubber, so use it in moderation and clean it off thoroughly afterward.

If the neck of the suit is tight or the sleeves or legs too long, carefully trim them with a sharp pair of scissors. This usually has no ill effects on the integrity of the suit. As you swim more with the wetsuit, the less restrictive it feels.

You'll want to practice quickly and smoothly removing the wetsuit. You can lose precious seconds in the transition by fumbling around. A lubricant around the lower legs of the wetsuit helps it slide off easily when you pull it down. Learn the best way to reach the zipper cord—too short a cord may be almost impossible to reach in the controlled chaos of the swim-to-bike transition.

Choosing the right equipment and learning how to wear it is the easy part. In the next chapter, we'll move to the tougher, more important part: stroke mechanics.

Chapter 5

POLISHING STROKE MECHANICS

The ultimate objective of great stroke mechanics is to swim quickly and efficiently without draining your energy reserves. You won't win a race in the swim. Sure, your race can fall apart during this first segment of the triathlon, but a successful race does not hinge on a fantastic swim (even if you're a world-class swimmer). The realistic goal for the swim is to get through it with minimal energy expenditure and place yourself in a solid position to be successful in the race. If your goal is to win the race, it makes sense to stay near the front during the swim or to maintain a position where you're confident you can catch whomever is in front of you on the bike leg. For the competitive athlete in today's triathlon world, it's tough to make up two or more minutes from a poor swim if you wasted a lot of energy, especially in an Olympic distance race or shorter.

The primary stroke for swimming a triathlon is freestyle, also known as the front crawl. The fastest of the four competitive strokes, freestyle is a graceful, artistic movement in swimmers who are technically sound. For those who are not sound, it's a water-thrashing waste of energy. Freestyle swimming is very different from running or cycling, and the aspiring triathlete must view the stroke from the swimmer's perspective in order to improve.

Freestyle stroke mechanics can get as complicated as you want. Many athletes, coaches, and sports scientists have spent full careers in the scientific study of freestyle, making discoveries at every turn. This chapter looks at the stroke in a very simple way. Often, looking at too many parts of a continuous, fluid movement results in rigid, robotic actions, which we want to avoid. To do it well, freestyle must be smooth, flowing, and graceful—the opposite of mechanical.

The basic characteristics of freestyle include balance and posture, arm motion (underwater and above water), body roll, kick, and breathing. These five components are the essence of the stroke.

Balance and Posture

Perfect horizontal posture in water is the same as perfect vertical posture on land. Standing, starting with your head, your body maintains one balanced, imaginary line to the feet. When a person is placed in water for the first time, his or her first reaction is to lift the head to breathe: a natural reflex common in all mammals. The first step in perfecting your freestyle stroke is to break this natural reflex.

Your nose should point at the bottom of the pool as you swim. The leading edge should be the crown of your head (see photo on page 47). While swimming, imagine a dot on the crown of your head, and lead the way with that dot. The only time your head comes up is to sight breathe (to see where you're going in open water). When you breathe to the side, your "dot" should still be leading the way.

Another way to improve head position is to try to minimize the curve in your neck. Drop your chin to a neutral position and feel as if you "grow" your neck. This gives you a natural proper head position in which it's nearly impossible to look forward.

Moving down the body toward proper swimming posture, you need to lean in, or down, and forward on the water, with your chest. This has the same effect of submerging a beach ball in the water: the water pushes it up. Because the chest stores the lungs, it's buoyant and floats well—in fact, a little too well compared to the lower half of the body. Leaning in and forward helps lower the front and raise the back, achieving balance and equilibrium in the water, thus reducing drag. We each have a different ability to float. Some triathletes float like corks, while others sink like stones. Most of us fall somewhere in between. The more of a "sinker" you are, the more you must learn to lean in and forward on the water to balance your body position and reduce drag.

Moving farther down the body, tip your hips up and in. This helps you flatten your back and makes it easier to roll from side to side, the key to swimming efficient freestyle. Try this on land first by lying on your back with your knees slightly bent, and simply roll your pelvis up and in. You'll feel your lower back flatten out and touch the floor. Running with your pelvis up and in is also helpful, but more on that later. If you have a cycling background, this procedure may be difficult to master, as you are taught to roll your pelvis forward and down to achieve a flat back position on the bike. A strong, flexible pelvic region is a key to triathlon success: for swim and run, rotate hips up and in; for the bike, rotate hips forward and down.

Balance is the key in swim positioning. A swimmer must be balanced in the water before arms and torso can be used for propulsion. Many novice swimmers use arms and hands for balance, reducing their abilities as propellers. Leaning in and forward significantly helps balance, as does maintaining your head in the right position by "leading with the dot."

Notice that Wes is leading the way with the crown of his head. Look down and make your neck long.

When a freestyler starts swimming, the side-to-side sequencing of the stroke must be only two smooth motions: rolling the body to the right side, then rolling the body to the left side. Any additional motion creates drag. To facilitate the proper motion, you need some rigidity through the torso. Some swimmers have "snakey" hips and lower bodies that wiggle through the water, creating resistance. Keep your torso somewhat rigid (the "straight line" previously described) as you move through the water.

Only when posture and balance are correct can you minimize drag and get the most from the propulsive forces of pulling and kicking. Wave, or turbulence, is significantly reduced through smooth action coupled with a balanced body. Because of its unique properties of viscosity, water slows you down; the faster you go, the thicker and slower the water becomes. Thus, you'll want to make "cheating the water's drag" a paramount goal in your swim training program. Think LNS: *long, narrow, straight.* Imagine yourself as a long, sleek, racing shell used in Olympic rowing events—the perfect vessel for human-powered aquatic transportation.

Arm Motion

Now we move from the antigravity concepts of swimming into the propulsive, or forward-moving, forces. Since there are limits to the power we can transfer to the water, body position is the initial key. It's always wise to consider how little resistance we can create while moving through water.

The arm stroke, or the underwater portion of the stroke, in freestyle is one of the most studied components of swimming. Much is said about lift and drag forces, angle of attack, and so on. Our philosophy is to keep this simple, so let's look at the basic components, especially regarding body rotation. If you can master the skill of using arms and torso together as one unit, you can significantly add to your body's ability to produce power.

Entry

Always enter your hand into the water in a line directly in front of your shoulder (see photo below). A common mistake among triathletes is "crossover," which occurs when the hand is placed inside the shoulder line, usually in line with the head. Crossover must be avoided, as it directs energy toward the side, instead of forward, creating side-to-side movement, a "wag," and resistance. Freestyle swimmers must always focus on directing energy forward.

Catch

Contrary to popular belief, the first thing *not* to do upon entry is immediately push water back. Instead, slide your hand smoothly forward into the water, and roll to that side of your body (see photos on page 49). As the hand slides

Wes is ready to enter the water directly in front of his shoulder. His hand and forearm are relaxed before entry.

Wes is reaching for the wall, setting up a perfect catch.

Excellent front-end extension.

forward, reach forward (as if for the wall in front of you when you are at the pool) and elevate your shoulder blade. This action is what creates the "long" component of LNS. A common error is to roll too much. Once your hand reaches its longest point, *stop your hip rotation!* The idea in the catch phase of the stroke is to put your body in the best possible position to execute the power phase of the underwater portion of the stroke. Overrotation disrupts the sequence of the stroke. Also, be sure not to overrotate your shoulders. Rotate your hips and shift shoulders forward. Digging shoulders too deep causes excessive frontal resistance, which then must be overcome. Roll forward as you go from side to side, almost as if you are ice-skating or in-line skating. Keep your body as "small" as possible in terms of presenting frontal area to the water.

Arm Pull

Once the catch is completed, it's time to anchor your hand and arm. A key concept is to think of your hands and forearms as anchors. When the underwater stroke is started, set your anchors (hand/forearm) by elevating your shoulder blade, which sets your elbows in a high position. Then, as the anchors are set, allow your body to move over them (see photo below). Don't

Allow your powerful trunk muscles to move yourself over your anchoring arm.

make the common mistake of pulling your hands past your body. Anchoring the hands requires a light touch and a reasonable feel for the water. Most triathletes are surprised how light the touch truly is upon the water. Think of holding on to "hard" water. You know you have the concept once water feels almost like a solid rather than a liquid. Keep elbows high; the higher the elbows (in relation to the surface of the water), the higher the body will be in the water. Many swimmers either take their underwater stroke too wide (outside) their body or cross over the midline, in too close. The anchors always stay within a line between the shoulder and breastbone, as that is where you can hold the hardest water. Swimmers who move the fastest through water are those who can place the reasonable pressure on the water without slipping through it. Think of yourself as "holding your ground," and anchor those hands.

Arm Recovery

The key to a great recovery lies in two areas. First, think of your elbows moving in a rough circle under and above water. This helps keep your stroke circular, much like your pedal stroke on the bike. Great freestylers have a continuous stroke, with no pauses or dead spots. Start the recovery by lifting your elbow, as if you're pulling your hand out of your pocket (see photo below). To keep your arms relaxed over the water, always have your hands lower than your elbows. Second, swing forward as if you're reaching for the

Relaxed, high-elbow recovery prevents soreness in your shoulders.

wall in front of you. Momentum is created in this way during recovery. Freely swing your arms forward, in a relaxed manner, but be careful not to swing them out to the side. Always move forward.

A great way of putting your stroke together is to repeat in your head the following sequence as you swim: lift, reach, elevate. Lift your elbows, reach/swing forward, and then elevate your shoulder blade. By the time you have gone through this sequence, it's time to lift the opposing elbow. While your anchors are under water, all you allow them to do is relax and exit where they entered. Freestyle becomes more efficient and easier if you reverse your thinking about the stroke and stop worrying about what you're doing under water. You can create a lot of momentum during the recovery phase of the stroke.

Body Roll

To maximize your ability to apply power, use the massive amount of strength of your torso and hips. As mentioned with the catch, once the arm pull is

As Wes extends to his right side, his body rolls right. His head, however, maintains a neutral position.

Anchoring and rolling creates the power you need.

ready to begin, your body has rolled to that side or your hips are facing away from your hand. Once the arm stroke is initiated, anchor with your arm while rolling your hips toward your hand at the same time. Think of a golfer swinging a club or a baseball pitcher winding up before a pitch. Anchoring and rolling at the same time create an enormous amount of power that can be applied to the water, if you're holding hard water. Remember to anchor your hands and let your body go over your anchors. Another key concept is allowing your hand to exit where it enters. Truly gifted swimmers actually exit *in front* of where they enter due to excellent streamlining between strokes and momentum created in the recovery phase of the stroke. Always think of your hands exiting where they enter with every stroke you take.

Kick

A strong kick is important for the initial explosion at the start of a race, as well as during efforts to close the gap between you and another swimmer. Freestyle uses the flutter kick, in which your feet alternate in an up and down motion. The key for a good kick is keeping it small, fast, and supple. A lot of novice swimmers kick too big. Keep your kick within the shadow of your body. The overall contribution to propulsion from the kick is only about 10 percent; a big kick creates greater drag and actually negates propulsion.

However, if your body tends to sink instead of float, the kick plays a critical role in stabilizing your position in the water. During training, find the minimal amount of kick to keep your body in a horizontal plane. Most distance-oriented swimmers use a two-beat kick (two kicks per arm cycle), and this is a reasonable kick for triathletes to adopt. Two small, quick kicks between arm strokes keep your body in great hydrodynamic position; more important, they don't rob your legs of precious energy you'll need for the bike and run.

To kick well, your ankles must be flexible, which is one reason triathletes with a nonswimming background struggle with the flutter kick. When you run and bike, your ankle is usually in a dorsi flexed position, keeping your foot fairly flat and rigid. However, during the flutter kick, your feet must be plantar flexed (toes pointed). To aid in plantar flexion, stretch your ankles by simply sitting on them. Or, while sitting down, cross one leg over the other, grab your foot, and rotate it clockwise and then counterclockwise. Kicking and swimming with fins also increase ankle flexibility.

Breathing

Your top goal in taking a breath while swimming is not to disrupt your smooth, hydrodynamic body position. Another goal is to learn how to see where you're going in open water while breathing at the same time. This is called sight breathing.

Bilateral Breathing

Normal freestyle breathing calls for the swimmer to roll the head with the body. Too often, swimmers lift their head prior to breathing, causing the hips to sink. The only time the head should move from a still, neutral position is during the breath. Think *roll my head forward with my body* and *hide my breath.* You lift your head only to sight breathe.

Many swimmers are unclear about the simple mechanics of inhalation and exhalation while swimming. While inhaling, simply let air "fall" into your lungs. Exhalation occurs under water and so needs to be somewhat forceful. A forceful exhalation helps blow out excess carbon dioxide, a cause of pain and fatigue. Exhalation should be through the mouth and nose. Novice swimmers often exhale only through the nose, which limits the amount of air expelled. Using both the mouth and nose helps the athlete lose more carbon dioxide.

The simple action of taking a breath in freestyle swimming plays a critical role in stroke symmetry. To be effective, the side-to-side action of freestyle must be symmetrical on both sides of the body. Breathing only to one side all the time in training leads to an unbalanced, lopsided stroke. Practice breathing on both sides (bilateral breathing) in training. You can practice in several ways:

1. Breathe every third stroke cycle.

2. Within each length of the pool, take two to four breaths on the right side, then switch to the left side and take two to four breaths. Make sure to take an equal number of breaths on both sides during the course of a practice.

3. Alternate entire lengths of breathing in the pool, breathing only to the right going down and to the left coming back. Again, take equal breaths right and left over the course of practice.

Bilateral breathing can be difficult in the beginning but can be quickly learned by anyone. Be patient, as breathing this way will significantly help your stroke symmetry. When training hard or racing, breathe in the pattern most comfortable to you, even if it's to only one side, and do not limit your breathing (air is good!). However, try to do most of your easy endurance swimming, including warm-up and cool-down, with a bilateral breathing pattern.

Sight Breathing

Sight breathing needs to be a seamless activity in which you combine taking a breath with looking where you are going. There are no black lines to follow in open water. The skill of sight breathing is critical to competent open-water racing to ensure you're swimming in the right direction or that the person you're drafting behind is going the right direction.

First, decide on a pattern of sight breathing. Usually every 4 to12 stroke cycles works well, depending on conditions. The worse the conditions (weather, surf, etc.), the more you need to look where you're going. By deciding on a pattern, rhythm is created, keeping your stroke more symmetrical.

Second, learn to sight and breathe in one seamless motion. To do this, lift your head and look straight in front of you (see photo on page 56). To counterbalance the head lift action, slightly increase the tempo of your kick to help keep you in a balanced horizontal position with your hips up. Once you visually establish your direction, roll to your side and take your breath.

That's it. Sounds simple, but it's a skill that should be practiced before race day. If you're confined to a pool for all your swim training, practice sight breathing every once in a while to help perfect the skill.

Incorporate a rhythm into your sight breathing technique.

Going Faster

Swimming faster comes down to this equation: V (velocity) = SL (stroke length) × SR (stroke rate). SL is how far you travel with each stroke, and SR is how fast, or the tempo of your strokes. Running and cycling are very rate oriented—you simply move your legs faster to go faster. That doesn't work with swimming. As triathletes, we probably have awesome stroke rate (SR), but to optimize our speed, we need to attend to stroke length (SL).

Counting your strokes while you're swimming is the best way to increase your SL. Vow to constantly reduce your strokes to a minimum, thus lengthening each stroke. To accomplish this, you can do three things:

1. Pull harder (hold "harder" water), but remember there's only so much force you can apply to the water before you start slipping and losing your "grip," creating turbulence and drag.

2. Streamline between strokes and stay in perfect balance. When you swim, go down the pool as "quietly" as possible, creating the least amount of waves. The more waves you create, the greater resistance you give the water.

3. Balancing both of the above is the preferred way of taking fewer strokes. The goal is to optimize efficiency and power. Work harder on the efficiency part and put the power component in later.

Stroke Drills

There are literally hundreds of drills and whole-stroke technique ideas that swimmers and coaches use to enhance form in freestyle swimming. What follows is a list of drills and technique swims to help your form. Do drills at every practice. Start each session with an easy swim to warm up, then go into a drill set in which you focus on technique. Use repeat distances of 25 and 50 yards for drill sets.

KICKING ON YOUR SIDE

Keep your lower arm (the one closest to the bottom of the pool) extended and roll your head so your face is parallel with the surface of the water, looking up. If you have problems moving forward, wear fins. You should stay horizontal and balanced in the water. Kicking on your side helps you get comfortable.

SIX KICK AND ROLL

Take six kicks on your right side, then take a freestyle arm stroke with the extended arm and recover with the opposite arm to the opposite side, looking up. Repeat this sequence down the pool. If it's a challenge to go forward, wear fins until you get the hang of it. This drill promotes the shifting of weight from side to side that's critical in correct freestyle technique. Swimming freestyle is similar to ice skating and in-line skating.

SINGLE-ARM SWIMMING

Start in your side-kicking position (lower arm extended and top arm resting against the side of your body). Once you feel balanced kicking on your side, swivel your head and look down. Get balanced in that position for a few kicks. Then take a freestyle arm stroke with the extended arm by anchoring your hand and rolling forward. Once your recovery is complete, assume the side-kicking position again. This is a great drill for balancing both sides of your stroke.

FINGERTIP DRAG

Swim freestyle and drag your fingertips across the surface of the water during recovery. Always think of keeping your body long, narrow, and straight. This helps with relaxed arm recovery and body roll.

TARZAN SWIMMING

Swim with your head completely out of the water, looking forward and keeping your head still. Increase the tempo of your kick to help with horizontal positioning. This drill helps when you sight breathe in open water.

SWIM DOWNHILL (FORM SWIM)

As you move down the pool, hide your head by lowering it slightly, and feel the sensation of going downhill by leaning in and forward on the water. If you are doing it right, you'll feel as if your hips and legs are going to run over your head.

SKATE

Think of your torso as an ice-skate blade, and skate down the pool. Take an arm stroke and skate on your side for three counts, then take another arm stroke and skate on the other side.

FIST SWIMMING

Swim an entire set with your hands closed. It feels strange, and you envision yourself as a stick figure moving down the pool. As you swim, imagine swimming "from the inside out," that is, generating power and balance from the center of the body and radiating outward to the hands and feet. This is the reverse of what many novice swimmers think is correct swimming technique—focusing solely on the movements of the arms and legs. Once you complete the set, open your hands and swim with "smart hands." Feel the power! After swimming with closed fists, your hands will be more sensitive to water flow when they are opened.

These are just a few examples of swim drills. See a local swim coach in your area to help you with technique. Also, videotaping is a great tool in analyzing your form. Have someone tape you while you're swimming, and using the checklist below, review the tape with a coach or an accomplished swimming buddy to look for ways to improve. Seeing yourself swim helps enormously in learning to swim freestyle effectively and efficiently.

Videotape Checklist

1. Head position—is it too high or too low? Are you looking down the pool or at the bottom?

2. Body position—is your body line horizontal or vertical? Do you have an excessive curve in your lower back? Are you rotating equally to both sides as you shift your weight?

3. Arm recovery—are your elbows the highest part of your arm over the water? Are your arms relaxed?

4. Arm stroke—are your arms staying between your midline and shoulder? If you are outside your shoulder, the stroke is too wide; and if you are crossing the midline, you'll lose power. Are your hands exiting where they enter?

5. Kick—is it small and supple? Does it stay within the shadow of your body?

6. Breathing—are you rolling your head with your body and going forward as you breathe? Or are you moving your head independent of your body and negating forward momentum?

Swim technique can't be overemphasized. Of the three activities that make up the triathlon, swimming is the most technique dominated. At every practice, devote time to drills and technique practice. While training intensely, look for ways to become more slippery and to use less effort.

Chapter 6

SWIMMING WORKOUTS

Swim training requires you to forget what makes you better in the run and bike. A skilled, proficient swimmer with a strong background can actually train similar to the way a runner or cyclist trains, with energy system–specific sets, triathlon swimming–specific workouts, and open-water time trials being a part of the training mix. Those new to swimming and less proficient at the sport need to think of water time as *practice* versus *training*. Just as you would take golf lessons to improve your game, swim practice makes you more proficient and fluid in the water. In this chapter we'll examine what each type of swimmer could complete in a given week.

Determining What Type of Swimmer You Are

Complete this test in a 25-yard pool. Warm up for 10 to 15 minutes of easy swimming, then complete a 100-yard time trial. Push yourself and have someone record your time while you count your strokes per length. When counting strokes, count each arm movement. For example, a full stroke with your right arm is stroke #1, a full stroke with your left arm is #2, right arm #3, left arm #4, and so on. If you take over 18 strokes (male) or 20 strokes (female) a length while swimming fast, put yourself in the "Practice Swimmer" category, in which you work on improving your efficiency. If you hold your stroke count consistently below 18/20 strokes, you could probably benefit from actual swim training.

Why count strokes? In swimming, the fastest swimmers almost always appear to be putting forth the least amount of effort. For them, everything looks so easy, graceful, and powerful. For most of us, though, moving efficiently through water is not natural, though we can learn to do it. Counting strokes gives us immediate feedback on our efficiency. The fewer strokes we need to travel a certain distance means we're channeling our power better on the water and creating less resistance with our body. For this reason, competitive swimmers spend countless hours in the water. The more you move through water, the better you get at it.

You can improve a lot by swimming easy. Just by spending more time in water, you'll become more comfortable. The Power of Two axiom states that you need only a couple of quality practices per week, but spending more time swimming easy will make you a better swimmer and help in recovering from key running and cycling workouts. If you have the luxury of swimming five to six days a week, go for it. Once you learn the art of easy, manageable swimming, you'll look more forward to your pool sessions each week.

Components of a Workout Session

Every swim session should have a basic flow and progression. Each session should begin with a warm-up between 200 and 1,000 yards. The more intense the workout or the more advanced the swimmer, the longer the warm-up. Use the first part of warm-up to forget about your nonswimming day and the last part of the warm-up to prepare for skilled swimming. After the warm-up, complete a pre-set, which can consist of drills or swimming repeats that gradually elevate your heart rate, blood flow, and muscle temperature to help get you ready for the main set.

The main set is the quality portion of practice. A training swimmer should do a set that elevates endurance, aerobic power, or speed. Practice

Easy swimming helps in recovery from running and cycling workouts.

swimmers can do similar sets but should focus on ease of movement and fluidity. Don't use the clock alone to measure your success. Also monitor stroke counts, heart rates, and perceived exertion during the main set. Remember that the best swimmers make it look effortless.

Conclude each practice session with a cool-down. Five to ten minutes of easy swimming helps you recover from solid training and brings back a natural feel of moving through water, especially if your stroke felt ragged during your set.

Sample Workouts for the Practice Swimmer

Remember that you're going to the pool to refine your technique and improve your efficiency. When you go to the pool to improve endurance, swim at relaxing speeds. Focus on swimming quietly, with no excessive splashing or waves. To build aerobic power, try swimming with low stroke counts for medium distance repeats with moderate rest intervals. To build speed, swim faster while doing short repeats with minimal strokes and lots of easy swimming between efforts. You can build fitness by thinking efficiency. Never swim sloppy or so hard that you can't maintain perfect form. Become a miser with each stroke—think of ways to travel farther with each stroke by becoming more slippery between strokes. Avoid placing maximum force on the water; imagine ease of movement.

Three sessions that contain the basic components of a swim practice session are on the following pages. The format is basic and can be modified and changed week by week. The idea is to introduce you to the types of practices that can be developed.

For those unfamiliar with workout abbreviations, use table 6.1.

Table 6.1

Warm-up	Easy swimming to prepare for the session. Keep intensity low and technique high. Feel free to mix strokes.
Drill set	Focus is on technique. This can be a combination of drills and form swimming.
Pre-set	Elevate heart rate and body temperature to prepare you for the main set.
Main set	Targets endurance, aerobic power, or speed, but with a premium on efficiency.
Cool-down	Easy swimming that brings your body back down to normal after a challenging session.

Endurance Practice Session

Warm-up: 600 yards easy swimming

Pre-set: 16×25 drill on :40 intervals

Main set: 6×200 with :20 rest between sets (swim as silently as possible)

Cool-down: 300 easy swim alternating 25 swim/25 drill

Total yards: 2,500

Aerobic Power Practice Session

Warm-up: 800 yards easy swimming

Pre-set: 12×50 on 1:05 fist swim breathing every third stroke

Main set: 10×100 with :40 rest between sets (low stroke count on each length)

Cool-down: 300 easy swim

Total yards: 2,700

Speed Practice Session

Warm-up: 1,000 yards easy swimming

Pre-set: 6×75 as 50 drill + 25 distance per stroke on 1:30 intervals

Main set: 8×100 (25 fast with the least strokes possible + 75 easy/perfect stroke)

Total yards: 2,250

Sample Workouts for the Training Swimmer

Once you achieve a proficient stroke count and feel consistently fluid in the water, you'll benefit from specific sets that target the three components of training: endurance, aerobic power, and speed. Even the most gifted swimmer can benefit from copious amounts of easy, well-done swimming. It's always a goal to find the most efficient way to move through water; this search should continue throughout your lifetime as a swimmer or triathlete.

Determining Pace

Determining training paces for different intensity levels can significantly aid in improving swimming performance. Some swimmers operate simply by feel, which can work sometimes, but at other times it can lead to over- or underperformance. Feel is important, but feel alone should not dictate the total effort. By setting paces, you stop searching for feel and let feel come to you.

Pacing yourself during the swim will put you in good shape during the transition from the swim to the bike.

To set up your training paces try the following (this can be done in yards or meters):

Warm-up: 800 (every fourth 25 nonfree)

Drill set: 12×25 on :40 intervals

Pre-set: Three sets of 3×50 on 1:00 intervals, descending

Recovery: 50 easy

Time trial: 500 to 1,000 (the better swimmer you are, the farther you should go)

Take fewer than 18 (male) or 20 (female) strokes per length (the fewer, the better). Record your heart rate and time after swim.

Cool-down: 400 easy swim

After you complete the time trial, you'll have specific numbers to work with. As an example we'll use Triathlete A, who completed her 500-yard time trial in six minutes (360 seconds). The average per 100 yards would be 1:12 (360/5.00 = 72 seconds [1:12]). Once you have that information, you can set intensities using table 6.2. (These guidelines can also be used for a meter pool as long as the time trial was also completed in meters.)

The following are the pace suggestions for Triathlete A:

Endurance (5-8 seconds slower than 500 pace) = 1:17-1:20 per 100

Aerobic power (0-3 seconds slower than 500 pace) = 1:12-1:15 per 100

Speed (3-6 seconds faster than 500 pace) = 1:06-1:09 per 100

Once you have your figures, stay at those paces to improve each training area. If you feel your fitness is improving, do another time trial and see if your time improves (while still taking a reasonable number of strokes per length during the effort). A time trial every four to eight weeks is sufficient.

Training Sessions

The same basic concepts apply to the training swimmer as to the practice swimmer. Below are a few training sessions based on a swimmer who has completed his 500-yard time trial in six minutes.

Sample Endurance Training Session

Warm-up: 3×250 (150 free + 100 nonfree)

Pre-set: 6×100 (50 free-distance per stroke, breathing every third stroke) on :50 intervals

    (50 as 25 drill + 25 distance per stroke) on :55 intervals

Main set: 5×400 on 5:30 (hold 5:08 to 5:20 per 400)

Cool-down: 200 easy swim

Total yards: 3,550

Sample Aerobic Power Training Session

Warm-up: 800 (every fourth 25 nonfree)

Pre-set: 12×50 on :55 intervals; fist swim breathing every third stroke

Main set: 8×200 on 3:10 intervals (hold 2:24 to 2:30 per 200)

Cool-down: 300 easy swim

Total yards: 3,300

Sample Speed Training Session

Warm-up: 3×300 (150 free + 100 nonfree + 50 kick)

Pre-set: 10×50 on 1:00 intervals

    Odd 50s (1, 3, 5, etc.) distance per stroke + breath every third stroke

    Even 50s (2, 4, 6, etc.), build first 25

Table 6.2

Intensity Pace Chart

500-yard time	Pace per 100-yard time trial	Endurance pace	Aerobic power pace	Speed pace
5:00	1:00	1:05-1:08	1:00-1:03	:54-:57
5:05	1:01	1:06-1:09	1:01-1:04	:55-:58
5:10	1:02	1:07-1:10	1:02-1:05	:56-:59
5:15	1:03	1:08-1:11	1:03-1:06	:57-1:00
5:20	1:04	1:09-1:12	1:04-1:07	:58-1:01
5:25	1:05	1:10-1:13	1:05-1:08	:59-1:02
5:30	1:06	1:11-1:14	1:06-1:09	1:00-1:03
5:35	1:07	1:12-1:15	1:07-1:10	1:01-1:04
5:40	1:08	1:13-1:16	1:08-1:11	1:02-1:05
5:45	1:09	1:14-1:17	1:09-1:12	1:03-1:06
5:50	1:10	1:15-1:18	1:10-1:13	1:04-1:07
5:55	1:11	1:16-1:19	1:11-1:14	1:05-1:08
6:00	1:12	1:17-1:20	1:12-1:15	1:06-1:09
6:05	1:13	1:18-1:21	1:13-1:16	1:07-1:10
6:10	1:14	1:19-1:22	1:14-1:17	1:08-1:11
6:15	1:15	1:20-1:23	1:15-1:18	1:09-1:12
6:20	1:16	1:21-1:24	1:16-1:19	1:10-1:13
6:25	1:17	1:22-1:25	1:17-1:20	1:11-1:14
6:30	1:18	1:23-1:26	1:18-1:21	1:12-1:15
6:35	1:19	1:24-1:27	1:19-1:22	1:13-1:16
6:40	1:20	1:25-1:28	1:20-1:23	1:14-1:17
6:45	1:21	1:26-1:29	1:21-1:24	1:15-1:18
6:50	1:22	1:27-1:30	1:22-1:25	1:16-1:19
6:55	1:23	1:28-1:31	1:23-1:26	1:17-1:20
7:00	1:24	1:29-1:32	1:24-1:27	1:18-1:21

Main set: 8×150 (50 fast, hold 33 to 34 seconds per 50, distance per stroke)

(100 easy with great form)

Cool-down: 200 easy swim

Total yards: 2,800

World's Best Triathlon Swim Workout

This session focuses on the key ingredients to a great triathlon swim. Most swim starts are fast and furious. The pace levels out in the middle of the swim and then quickly speeds up toward the end as athletes jockey for position. Here's a session that addresses those specifics, with paces on the triathlete who completed a 500-yard time trial in six minutes. This session would be one of the two quality sessions for the week. The other workout of the week should focus on aerobic power since speed and endurance are the focus points for this session.

Warm-up: 600 (every third 25 nonfree)

Pre-set: 12×25 drill on :40 intervals

Speed: 4×100 (75 fast, hold 50 to 52 seconds per 75) on 1:30

(25 easy on :30 leave for a fast 75 every 2:00)

Endurance: 4×300 on 4:20 (hold 3:51 to 4:00 per 300)

Speed: 6×50 on 1:15 (hold 33 to 34 seconds per 50)

Cool-down: 300 easy swim

Total yards: 3,100

As you can see, this workout is challenging, yet manageable. The idea is to learn to swim steady after already swimming fast, then trying to hold that speed while relatively fatigued. Many athletes have used this type of practice as a cornerstone of their preparation for triathlon and open-water swim competitions.

The overall goal of swim training is to prepare you to race faster. Go into each training session with the idea of "training to race" instead of "training to train." Since most triathlon racing is done in open water, pool training helps in the conditioning aspect of swim training, but it does not stop there. The next chapter on open-water swimming helps bridge the gap between the pool and the open water.

Chapter 7
OPEN-WATER SWIMMING

Most triathlons begin with an open-water swim, but preparation for these swims is usually done in a pool, as a pool is usually the most readily available aquatic environment. This is unfortunate, as open-water swimming is among the most enjoyable and natural ways of swimming. Sharing the water with fish, battling the elements, and staying clear of chlorine is the way nature intended us to swim.

Although natural and pure, open-water swimming can be intimidating and potentially disastrous for some athletes. Novices can feel disoriented with no black line to follow, but of course this can be overcome. In this chapter, we'll explore ways to help you become a competitive open-water swimmer.

Finding a Place to Train

The first and most important factor is weather—triathletes living in northern climates have a short open-water season, while those in warmer environs can practice year-round. Once you have determined your open-water season, go to a local reservoir, lake, or beach and talk with the management. Find out where you can swim legally and safely. Explain that you're a triathlete training for an event. Most park staff are extremely helpful in suggesting suitable areas to train. Obviously, you'll want a spot that limits boating. Pollution and currents are also concerns. Talk to lifeguards or park management to make sure your open-water site is clean and safe.

Once you have located a good place to swim, find a partner to escort you by boat or surfboard while you train. Describe your swim and training plan to your partner before slipping into the water, and hold to the plan as closely as possible. Also let your training partner know your desired level of effort and how long you expect to be in the water. It's always better to overprepare than to wing it; a plan puts your mind at ease and results in relaxed swimming. Another tip: Swimming parallel with the shoreline is more relaxing than going straight out into a large body of water, as you have physical markers to guide your navigation. If you're swimming in the ocean, make sure you're beyond the wave breakline or motion sickness can set in with disastrous results.

Whenever you train or race in open water, wear a brightly colored swim cap to make you visible to boaters and others using aquatic recreation vehicles. If the water is cold, try wearing two caps. You lose the majority of your body heat though your head, and wearing two caps reduces the heat loss.

Open-Water Training

Whereas pool training is interval based with its sets, reps, and send-offs, open-water training is liberating and relaxing. Once you venture into open water, swimming becomes a lot like running and cycling. Rhythm and pace come into play, which are difficult to achieve in a pool. Long, steady distance, fartlek, and time trials apply to open-water swim training as they do in running and cycling.

As previously mentioned, before training in open water, you must first learn to sight breathe. Since breathing is done while rolling your body, you must be able to look forward to stay on course without breaking stroke continuity, which means keeping your head slightly higher than you do in a pool. Before rolling to breathe, lift your head, sight quickly, then roll to breathe. Since lifting your head tends to sink your hips, slightly increase the tempo of your kick to stay horizontal.

Long, Steady Distance Training

Long, steady distance (LSD) training is probably the best way to start open-water training. Ten to 20 minutes of continuous swimming is different from doing the same in a pool. Time passes slowly while swimming in the lake or ocean, as distance is distorted in a large body of water. After some practice, you'll become a good judge of time and distance.

Your first few open-water swims should be LSD. Simply slip into the water and swim continuously for 10 to 60 minutes. Use your waterproof watch to keep track of the time, using out-and-back courses along the shoreline. Be wary of currents in the water—if you swim with the current on the way out, it naturally takes longer getting back.

LSD is a good opportunity to practice sight breathing. You'll want to establish a basic pattern for lifting your head to sight; about every 6 to 10 stroke cycles is appropriate, adjusting for rough conditions, low sun angles, and other factors that may require more frequent sighting.

As you get comfortable with open-water swimming, gradually increase the distance of each session, adding 5 to 10 minutes per swim. The intensity of the effort should be purely aerobic. Instead of thinking how fast you're

Maintain your pool techniques while training and racing in open water.

swimming, focus on breathing, keeping it slow and rhythmic. Fully exhale, and while inhaling focus on letting air "fall" into your lungs.

Fartlek Swimming

Swedish for "speed play," fartlek training has long been popular with runners and is also valuable for open-water swimmers. While racing in open water, athletes notice that pace changes frequently, similar to bicycle road racing. Drafting, pace lines, and breakaways are all components of open-water swimming. Many pool swimmers, accustomed to steady-paced swims, find the stop-and-go nature of open-water racing challenging and difficult to adapt to. Fartlek training teaches you how to handle the pace changes of triathlon swims.

After a warm-up of 5 to 10 minutes of easy swimming, swim fast for 30 to 60 seconds, and then easy again for the same duration, repeating as many times as you can without becoming fatigued. You can experiment with different formats of fartlek swimming: short, super-fast efforts with longer periods of recovery, or longer, moderate-paced efforts with very short bouts of easy swimming in between. There's no wrong way to do a fartlek workout, as long as you're varying your pace and duration. Adding patterns turns a fartlek into an interval session.

An effective way to determine lengths of efforts during fartlek sessions is to use stroke count cycles instead of time. Since it's difficult to see a watch and almost impossible to hear the beep of a timer, savvy open-water swimmers count stroke cycles. Sprint for 5 cycles (10 total strokes) and then swim easy for 20 stroke cycles (40 total strokes) to work on speed. Another type of session that focuses on aerobic power includes faster-paced efforts at 50 cycles (100 total strokes) alternated with easy swimming of 10 cycles (20 total strokes). If you use stroke cycle counting, be sure to keep your strokes long and powerful, maintaining that precious distance per stroke you have worked so hard on in the pool. After the last difficult effort, swim easy for 5 to 10 minutes as a cool-down.

A great way to incorporate fartlek sessions into your swim training is to swim with a partner of similar speed. One swimmer leads while the other one is drafting. Every 30 seconds the swimmer behind sprints ahead of the swimmer in front, and then the previous lead person drafts. This is a good drill for pacing, drafting without flip turns, closing a gap, and sprinting around a swimmer who has broken the draft chain.

Time Trials

Here's a training practice we borrowed from our cycling friends. Mark off a course 400 meters to 3,000 meters long, depending on your race goals. After a warm-up of 5 to 10 minutes, crank out a continuous time trial over your course. Record your time, try it two weeks later, and see if you improve. Invite some of your buddies along and have an informal race. As always, be sure to swim easy afterward to cool down. A time trial every two to four weeks is sufficient, especially if you're racing often.

Open-Water Racing Strategies

The more open-water racing you do, the better you become, but there are many strategies of successful open-water racing that can help you.

Mass Start

In an open-water mass start, your swimming ability will determine whether you should start fast, start on the side, or start in the back.

If you're a skilled swimmer, you'll want to start out quickly. If you don't start in the front, you'll have to swim around others as they slow. Once positioned in the front, be prepared to sprint for at least 300 meters and go anaerobic. If not, you'll be run over. Ideally you want to follow swimmers that are faster than you in the water. Typically, after the initial sprint the pace mellows into a constant pace.

If you're a moderately skilled swimmer and uncomfortable with the prospect of getting run over, you'll want to start at a far side, opposite from

A Word From Wes

Swim Segment: Where to Start?

The nerves begin weeks before the race. You are worried about the beginning of the triathlon, the swim. There can be as many as 200 people in a wave start. The Ironman distance races start as many as 1,500 people at once. The gun goes off and there is a massive churning of bubbles. So where should you start?

If you are a beginner and you don't have much confidence in your swim, then you should start behind other competitors. In doing so, you reduce the possibility of being swum over or pummeled with others' elbows, hands, and feet. You are probably unfamiliar with open-water swimming so you can follow the trail of bobbing heads to each turn buoy. However, look up every once in a while to make sure those swimmers are going in the right direction. I have known some people to swim as much as 500 meters off course in a 1,500-meter swim.

If you have great stroke technique and you don't like to get tangled up with other bodies, then you should start on the side of the wave. In doing so, you have "clean" water where you can use your swim technique to get in or near the lead. The disadvantage to this is that you may have to swim a little farther to the first turn buoy. However, if you avoid the mass of bodies, then you might go faster than the main body of swimmers.

If you are a quick starter and you have the endurance to maintain your pace, then the center and most direct route to the first buoy is the best position. You can save as much as 30 percent of your energy by drafting off a person who is equal to you in ability. If you know your competitors, then try to start next to someone faster than yourself. That way you can get on that person's feet and draft off him throughout the swim at a faster pace than what you could do yourself.

One thing to prepare for is the possibility that another person will accidentally hit you. If you are prepared for it, then you won't be so shocked if it happens. A great drill for a swim start is to get three other swimmers at swim practice. You all line up in the same lane and sprint to the other end after starting at the same time. This close contact simulates race situations.

the first turn. As the swim progresses, the pack strings out with time. As you move toward the first turn buoy, angle in toward the straight, or shortest "line."

If you're a novice open-water swimmer, you'll want to start at the back. Be prepared to pass a lot of people who were unwise in their initial pace estimate and quickly die off. As you pass, you should feel a boost of energy, which you can use to propel you through the swim.

Relax at the start of a race and try not to waste energy by thrashing around in the water.

Drafting

Drafting is completely legal in open-water racing. From bicycling, triathletes know that drafting significantly reduces resistance. Drafting also aids in swimming, though to a slightly lesser degree. Following a swimmer who is slightly faster than you or about the same speed, swim as closely behind as you can without hitting his or her toes with your hands. Etiquette is important, as it's annoying to have your feet repeatedly slapped. You can't always trust the person you're drafting behind, so be sure to sight breathe to stay on course. When not sight breathing, follow the bubbles. Through drafting, you'll use less energy while swimming and hit the bike ready to roll.

Finishing

While swimming, most of your blood is circulating in your upper body. To help with the transition from swim to bike, increase the tempo of your kick the last 100 meters of your race. Don't necessarily swim harder, but kick faster. This will get the blood flowing to your lower extremities and prepare you for cycling.

Part III
BIKE

SWIM
BIKE
RUN

Chapter 8

CYCLING EQUIPMENT AND FIT

You'll probably spend more on cycling equipment than you'll spend on the other two sports combined. Top-of-the-line swimsuits or running shoes max out at "comfortable" levels, but a bike and its related components can add up to as much as you're willing to spend. Top age-groupers and pros invest more than $5,000 in their dream machines—and if you have the cash, why not? But this type of investment is not required for success in triathlon; you can do quite well spending considerably less.

In this chapter we'll help you prioritize expenditures at a level that fits your budget. Some cycling components cut more time per dollar, so we'll explain which ones offer the most bang for your buck. With all of its technology and variables, the proposition of choosing the right cycling equipment can be intimidating. Bike-techie lingo might sound like a foreign language to the uninitiated. We'll try to get you up to pace so that when you walk into the bike shop, you'll feel comfortable and ready to talk the talk.

Frames

The basic structural element of all bicycles, frames are available in a multitude of materials and geometry, with one overriding law to abide by: it must fit your body. The most exotic, space-age frame in the world is worthless to you if the fit's no good. But we'll get to measuring and fitting your bike a little later—first we'll help you decide what frame material and geometry are right for you.

Manufacturers have given much attention to aerodynamics in creating frames and components. They've made teardrop-shaped frame tubes, routed shift and brake cables through the frame, and constructed frames of space-age materials. Scientists determined as early as 1983 that a rider must overcome 3.27 pounds of force to maintain a 20-mph speed on an aerodynamically equipped bike, compared to 3.48 pounds of force on a bike without aerodynamic modifications. The difference reflects approximately 6 percent greater efficiency when using an aerodynamically equipped bike. Six percent on a 40K time trial can mean a savings of about four minutes, which is substantial.

Frame Materials

Table 8.1 gives a comprehensive look at common frame materials: their pluses, minuses, and relative cost. You can spend countless hours on your own researching frame materials on the internet, in bike magazines, or cycling books. Other sources of information are your local bike shop or your biking buddies.

Table 8.1

Bicycle Materials

Material	Pluses	Minuses	Relative cost
Steel	Traditional material; very smooth, responsive, customizable; wide selection; good for road racing; very durable	Generally heavier, rarely special aerodynamics, rusts if scratched	Low to medium cost, high-end road racing versions can be expensive
Aluminum	Lightweight, economical, stiff and responsive, wide selection, customizable, good for road racing, aerodynamic versions, no rust	Can be overly stiff and uncomfortable on long rides, can crack or deform easier than others	Low to medium price, great recent growth in aluminum for frames
Metal matrix	Stiff and light, durable, similar to aluminum but various compounds can produce various results	Same as aluminum, except generally more durable	Medium to higher priced
Carbon or composites	Smooth and light, exotic aerodynamic design capable, no rust	Can lack stiffness, not easily customizable, some brands limited sizes, some durability problems	Medium to higher priced
Titanium	Generally accepted as the best ride available; smooth, supple, responsive, durable; no rust; customizable, aero designs	High price, limited selection	There are a few economical frames, but generally high priced

Frame Types

It's helpful to know some basic frame component terminology. See figure 8.1 for a quick rundown of terms.

Triathlon Versus Road

For most triathletes, the first question to answer is road bike or tri bike. Generally, a seat tube angle (angle of the seat tube relavent to the ground) greater than 76 degrees separates a specialized triathlon, or time trial bike, from a traditional road frame (several other factors unrelated to frame geometry also distinguish the two and are discussed further). The purpose of the "steep" seat tube angle is to move your seat and body forward, allowing for a flatter, lower aerodynamic position while cycling in your aerobars, also known as "time trialing." Another benefit of the steep seat tube is to reduce the angle of hip flexion. You open up the angle between your legs and torso, allowing for better breathing. Tri-frame geometry also allows for stable "straight-line" riding. Note also that chain stays may be shorter and the front axle may project farther forward. In the aero position, your weight is shifted forward, which can translate to a measure of instability; this special time trial frame geometry compensates for the forward position, adding stability.

If you're first and foremost a triathlete and have no aspirations to do a bicycle road race, consider purchasing a cycle with specialized tri-bike

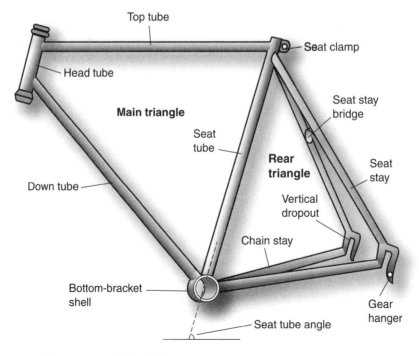

Figure 8.1   The parts of a bicycle frame.

Taken from THE RACING BIKE BOOK, published by Haynes Publishing, Sparkford, Yeobil BA227JJ. England. Tel++ 449163 442030

geometry and maybe 26-inch wheels. If you think at some point you might want to try road racing, a tri bike is a poor choice. Conversely, traditional geometry crosses over into triathlon time trialing fairly easy. The optimal solution is to own both a tri bike and a road bike, which many serious athletes end up doing.

Exotic Frames

Although many frames are available that don't conform to the "traditional frame," the geometry of these frames is the same as for the traditional frames. These cutting-edge frame designs evolve from aerodynamic testing. Different frame shapes and configurations are extensively tested in a wind tunnel and constantly monitored for wind drag.

The longer the race, the bigger role comfort plays, as discomfort causes fatigue. It's generally accepted that "beam bikes" offer the most comfort while also providing great aerodynamics. Surprisingly, even though much of the bike is simply "missing" in appearance, beam bikes do not win the

Beam bikes, with no seat tube, offer greater comfort in long races in addition to aerodynamics.

lightest-weight award. More traditional geometry in aluminum seems to be the lightest weight (but some brands are so lightweight they may be a bad choice if you're sturdily built in your human frame). If your goal is ultra distance triathlon, a beam bike is a great option. The comfort realized translates to a measurable decrease in fatigue in half or full Ironman distance races, while maintaining great aerodynamics.

Extremely exotic bikes such as the Hotta or Corima, often used by professional cyclists or triathletes, offer incredible aerodynamics and are engineering works of art. They are also very expensive. These bikes cannot be used in traditional road races, as the United States Cycling Federation and international federations do not allow them, but they are allowed and used in the time trial part of stage races, and certain versions are used in track cycling.

Most carbon frames are made from a mold instead of fabricated from lengths of tubing, so only a limited range of sizes is available. A few manufacturers, such as Calfee, have pioneered methods to "fabricate" with carbon tubing, thus allowing a full range of sizing.

Aerodynamics is a basic design concept of exotic frames, but traditional frames often use aero tubing or other features, which can reduce drag significantly, adding up to time-savings of a minute or even more in a 40K time trial. Oval tubes, fins or faring features, modified geometry, and special bladed forks are common aerodynamic modifications to standard frames.

Other Bike Parts

Now that we've dealt with the basic frame considerations involved in developing your triathlon bike, let's look at components that can improve your bike's performance and reliability. Reliability means two things: ability to withstand the many stresses that cyclists demand (durability) and the ability to perform year after year (wearability). Consider durability and wearability when purchasing the drive train, brakes, stem, and handlebars. A chain lighter in weight may break more easily. The gears on your bike may wear down quicker if they are made of a lightweight, but cheap, material. Good bike shops seldom carry low- or medium-quality replacement parts.

Also beware of buying a frame you want with a component package you don't want. The component package includes gears, cranks, shifters, handlebars, forks, and wheels and tires. We have seen great frames mixed with mediocre components. Do your homework and insist on getting what you want with your frame.

Drivetrain Components

The drivetrain is defined as gears, derailleur, and chain. The gears on the front of your bicycle are called chain rings; on a triathlon or road racing bike,

What's It Worth to You?

Cycling clearly represents the majority of the cost of becoming a triathlete. After seeing the expense involved, you may start thinking triathlon training is too expensive for you. But don't be dismayed by the costs. If necessary, you can devise cheaper ways to approach your triathlon needs. First, talk to your friends—they may have equipment you can use. Serious triathletes often have two or three of everything (hence the moniker "tri-geek") and welcome the chance to sell an item so they can go out and buy the latest technological speed advancement. If seeking used equipment, take a friend along who knows about the item, and always test before buying, especially when buying a bike.

Don't try to buy every item you run across; the dollars will add up in a hurry. Go slowly and do your research. If you spend your life's savings to participate in this new endeavor, you'll put extra pressure on yourself to perform well and perhaps sacrifice your enjoyment. Approaching the sport with moderate spending lets you participate with a healthy, guilt-free perspective.

Upgrading your cycle or getting that second bike is often more achievable through a used purchase. With the advent of the internet, access to a broad selection of used equipment is now unlimited. If you choose to buy used components, make sure you're not compromising fit, durability, or other important aspects. Our rule of thumb: if you are technically minded and like to work on your bike, used parts are a viable choice since you likely understand them. If you're short on time and are not a techie, better stick to new stuff installed by a qualified mechanic. Triathlon training takes a lot of time; wasting hours on mediocre or questionable cycling components works against getting you in shape to race.

there will be two. A 39-tooth and 53-tooth chain ring combination is normal, although others exist. The correct term for the gears on the back of your bicycle is "cogs." The smallest cog is likely to have 11 or 12 teeth; the largest cog will probably have 23 or 24 but can have as many as 32. If you haven't already, get to know your gearing and drivetrain. Many triathletes just ride along, ignoring the physics of their gearing. In the next chapter on riding technique, we'll talk about what the gearing ratios mean and how to use them. If you have been time trialing a few years and have some knowledge of the physics of various gear combinations, you may want to consider other, nontraditional gear combinations that can be especially useful on certain types of courses, such as the very flat or the very hilly course.

Gears (including the crank arms) and derailleurs and shifters are commonly referred to as the "component package," as manufacturers group these components together and sell them as a package at various levels of price and quality. How do you choose a package that's right for you? If you're just starting out, the choice is made for you: the components will be commensurate with the quality level of the bike you're considering buying—you won't find top-of-the-line components on a budget bicycle. If you want to upgrade an existing bike or are basing a large part of your overall buying decision on components, you need to do the research and also test ride the products. Our advice is not to skimp in this area, as top components are a joy. Durability and wearability qualities increase with the price tag.

Shifters

You have some choices to make when it comes to shifting your gears. You'll need to experiment to find out which type of shifter works best for you: a down tube shifter, bar-end shifter, STI shifter, or aerobar shifter.

Down tube shifters, located about four inches down from the junction of the down tube and the head tube, were the norm for many years, but they require removing your hands from the handlebars and reaching down to shift, which can disrupt aerodynamic flow and cause instability. Accurate shifting is also compromised. When shifting is difficult, you may not be inclined to shift when you should. If shifting is convenient and easy, you can shift your gears easily until you're exactly where you need to be.

Bar-end shifters are a toggle type that fit on the very end of your drop handlebars. They are much easier to access and operate than down tube shifters. Bar ends were a great upgrade when they first came out, but the next technology was really revolutionary.

STI, or integrated brake lever shifters, are the choice of the serious triathlete. These shifters are integrated with your brake levers. Pushing them one way incrementally shifts up; pushing a smaller lever the other way takes you back down. These shifters are fast, accurate, convenient, stable, and all-around wonderful. Although certainly a more expensive option, they are well worth the investment if you can afford it.

There are also integrated aerobar shifters. Any serious triathlete eventually uses aerobars for triathlon racing and training. As a result, shifting mechanisms have migrated to the aerobars in recent years, so cyclists can maintain the aero position while shifting. These shifters take on two forms: standard friction type levers or cylindrical twist shift type. The first type is basically old-style bar-end shifters moved out to the very nose of the aerobars. The second type has its origin in mountain biking, where taking your hands off the handlebars to shift can have disastrous results on rough terrain. These shifters are usually located in a convenient spot, a couple of inches back from the nose of the aerobars.

Theoretically, aerobar shifters allow you to ride an entire triathlon or time trial never leaving the aero-tuck position. Depending on conditions, this can save up to a minute or even two in a 40K time trial. However, the theory is slightly flawed; if there are hills or tight corners in your race, not to mention your training, you won't be able to stay in your aerobars much of the time without compromising speed. Shifting these units while out of the aerobars can be almost as cumbersome as using down tube shifters. The bottom line: these days, most triathletes opt for the versatility and efficiency of STI, and we recommend you do the same.

A final note: a recent development in shifting is electronic, or "automatic," shifting in which you simply push a button and your gears shift for you. Electronic shifting is top of the line and expensive (though not much more than high-end manual shift systems, like Dura-Ace or Campy Record). The electronic shifter is an impressive mechanism, and most of the bugs have been worked out so performance and durability take it beyond experimental.

Wheels

Together, the wheels and tires are the components that most affect the bike's riding characteristics, cornering ability, load-carrying tasks, acceleration, and efficiency, as reflected in minimal rolling resistance and aerodynamics.

Hubs

Thirty-six spoke wheels have long been a standard, but you won't find that many spokes on any serious triathlete's bike. At the very least, triathlon bikes have hubs with fewer than 36 spokes. A 28- to 32-spoke hub creates less wind resistance and makes the wheel lighter. Scientists Kyle and Zahradnik found this type of spoke configuration saves 106 grams of drag at 30 mph. Standard spoke wheels exist with as few as 13 spokes (the minimum International Cycling Federation legal limit). But bear in mind that fewer spokes make a wheel fragile—not wise if you race in the 190-pound plus Clydesdale category.

Other factors to consider when choosing hubs are weight and whether to get sealed bearings. Sealed bearing hubs require less maintenance, allowing longer use before replacing them. The tradeoff, however, is rolling resistance. A small compromise exists in rolling resistance between sealed and standard bearing hubs. Consider using sealed bearing hubs if you frequently train in rain or on dusty roads. Most high-end hubs these days use sealed bearings, although standard bearing hubs may still be more efficient. Hubs come in a variety of materials and weights.

Spokes

There are many kinds of spokes—double-butted (which get thinner in the middle), straight-gauge, bladed, oval, and even carbon fiber spokes. Straight-gauge spokes are the same diameter throughout. Kyle and Zahradnik found that substituting bladed spokes for straight gauge spokes saved 0.6 gram of drag for every spoke. Straight-gauge spokes are a fine choice if you weigh more than 170 pounds, are capable of applying great torque, or find yourself on rough roads. Otherwise, reduce drag and go with double-butted or bladed spokes, which come in different sizes for various weight riders.

High Performance Wheels

You'll see very few traditional spoked wheels on the bikes of serious triathletes. The growth in popularity of composite and disk wheels has been tremendous due to demand, technological advances, and performance gains. Specialized wheels greatly reduce drag via elimination of spokes and aero cross sections. Each spoke of a traditional wheel has to cut through the wind, facing resistance and causing turbulence. Fewer spokes, or *no* spokes in the case of a disk wheel, mean less resistance and turbulence. Most high-end composite wheels also offer reduced frontal area. When riding a bike with high-end wheels, you can actually sense the difference—slicing smoothly through the wind—and also hear the difference, as turbulence is reduced.

A solid disk wheel eliminates turbulence and has less frontal area than the tire. Additionally, a tailwind, or even a sidewind, is actually "caught" by

Disk wheels can provide an advantage by cutting down on turbulence. Sometimes they can give you a boost by "catching" a tailwind.

the disk, like a sail, and effectively propels you forward to a small degree. Scientists have found that a disk wheel can save more than 130 grams of drag at 30 mph, which translates into a savings of 49 second in a 40K (24.8-mile) race, not to mention the addition of the "sail" effect. Generally, disk wheels are heavier than most spoked wheels, but not appreciably. Other nondisk, spoke-type composite wheels are about the same weight or slightly less than regular spoked wheels. Weight reduction in the "rolling mass" of a bicycle is also a great advantage in terms of acceleration and sustained effort.

A drawback to the disk wheel is instability in a crosswind. If you weigh 180 pounds or more, a crosswind (unless it is severe) has little effect, but for lighter riders the effect can make handling difficult. Bringing a backup nondisk rear wheel in case conditions change right before a race is a good idea. And due to susceptibility to crosswinds, disks are rarely available for the front (don't ever use one in a triathlon).

An aerodynamic wheel costs about $400, or as much as $800 for the highest-quality wheel. But the time you'll save by having this kind of wheel can be more than three minutes if you're doing a 40K time trial in about an hour. If the purchase is within your budget, aero wheels are second only to aerobars as the greatest time-savings upgrade.

26" or 700c—What's Best for You?

A debate exists about the advantages of 26-inch versus 700c wheels (700c wheels are also called 27 inch, although they are not quite the same). The "c" has nothing to do with the metric system and is merely a size designation, and it is also not 27 inches. In any case, there are two sizes to choose from. In basic terms, 27 inch is road-racing size, and 26 inch was developed for time-trialing.

Why the difference? Most people agree that 26-inch wheels are faster for time-trialing. Advantages include lighter weight, less rolling mass, quicker acceleration, and slightly better aerodynamics due to fewer spokes and lowering the bike and rider closer to the ground. Disadvantages are in handling; the larger 700c wheels corner and handle better, thus 700c is what you see in road racing. And as certified triathlon coach and top age-grouper Kent McDonald says, for some inexplicable reason climbing is slower for some on 26-inch wheels, possibly due to leverage. In our opinion, if you're (1) a dedicated triathlete (not a roady), (2) more "slight" in physical stature or relatively short (under 5'8"), and (3) lower in "raw torque" type power (even though you may be long in endurance), then consider a rig set up for 26-inch wheels. If you're over 170 pounds (male) or 140 (female), or are tall, or have a lot of strength, then stick with 700c. If you ever intend to road race, stick with 700c—you simply don't see 26-inch wheels in a road race.

Tires and Rims

Before choosing a rim, decide which tire system to use: clinchers or tubulars. Clinchers are the more conventional design. The tire is separate from the tube and held to the rim by mating the wire-reinforced edges of the tire over the metal bead on the rim (when inflated, it "clinches" the rim). The tube consumes the space in the tire and rim and, when inflated, keeps the wire from popping off the rim. In the past, racers thought clinchers were of poor quality. The tires were big and heavy, carried low-inflation ratings (meaning more drag from increased rolling resistance), and lacked in performance.

Because the clincher system also provided some excellent qualities (e.g., lower cost and easy repair), designers began creating smaller, lighter, and higher inflation styles. In recent years, clincher tire performance has become almost equal to tubular tires. With tubulars, the tire casing completely encompasses the tube, and casing walls are sewn together on the inner side. For this reason, tubular tires are often called "sew-ups." The tubular rim, in cross section, is concave to receive the convex curvature of the tire, and it doesn't have a "bead" like a clincher rim. Proper mating of the tire to the rim is important to prevent the tire from shifting or rolling off during fast, tight turns. A special glue is used to accomplish this mating. Figure 8.2 illustrates the design differences between the two tire systems, enabling us to compare the advantages and disadvantages. Table 8.2 categorizes these comparisons.

Tires also come in different widths. Narrower tires reduce rolling resistance and wind resistance, but cornering "grip" is decreased and the ride is more harsh, leading to fatigue. Use 19-millimeter width for a relatively straight and flat time trial; step up to 21 millimeter if cornering is necessary or if the bike leg is over 40K. It's a good idea to use 23 or 25 millimeters width

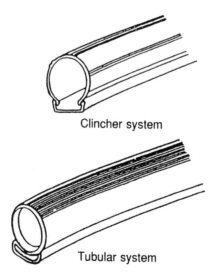

Clincher system

Tubular system

Figure 8.2 Clincher and tubular systems.

Reprinted, by permission, from Town and Kearney, 1994, *Swim, Bike, Run.* (Champaign, IL: Human Kinetics), 28.

Table 8.2

Advantages and Disadvantages of the Different Rim Systems

Tubulars	Clinchers
1. More expensive	1. Less expensive
2. Time-consuming to patch	2. Easy to patch
3. Requires gluing	3. More prone to flats from spokes and tire irons
4. Less availability	4. Readily available
5. Fast and easy to change	5. Slightly harder to change a flat
6. Overall a lighter system	6. Slightly heavier system
7. Can take higher tire pressures	7. Slightly more rolling resistance
8. Superior handling and traction	8. Satisfactory handling and traction

Reprinted, by permission, from Town and Kearney, 1994, *Swim, Bike, Run*. (Champaign IL: Human Kinetics), 28.

for off-season training for flat prevention; and when you switch from these to 19 millimeter you'll feel like you're flying! One big caveat: if your tire width is *smaller* than the rim width, you'll have turbulence when the wind hits the tire and the rim. It's better to have the tire the same size as the rim or slightly larger, so an 18-millimeter tire on a 22-millimeter rim is no good.

In addition to deciding between clinchers and tubulars, you'll need to make choices on rim width, strength, and weight. Your body weight is a factor in rim selection. Heavier triathletes with lots of raw leg power should stay away from extremely light wheels and rims, although there are plenty of wheels that are both lightweight and durable. Make sure you thoroughly research the wheels you intend to buy to ensure they are the best choice for your purposes. For instance, many companies make extremely light wheels just for road racers competing in hilly or climbing type races—the Mavic Helium is a good example. It's a great wheel for its intended purpose and not bad at all for triathlon training and racing but a poor choice for the Clydesdale competitor.

Next, you must decide how important rolling resistance is. If you're seeking the path of least rolling resistance, opt for tubular, or "sew-up," rims and tires. If you want a simpler system, consider working with a narrow clincher rim. The rim should be of an aero design (except for heavier riders) and should be no more than 19 to 21 millimeter wide. Wider rims will not accept the newer narrow-profile tires that provide lower rolling resistance.

In general, seasoned triathletes and roadies use clinchers for their training bikes or wheels, and sew-ups for racing, especially if the race is a time trial. Training on sew-ups is not really practical, as changing a flat on the road is cumbersome.

Tire Inflation

Whichever rim and tire system you choose, make sure you run the tires at proper inflation. Scientists Faria and Cavanagh found that underinflated tires increased rolling resistance about 12 percent for every 20-pound reduction in inflation pressure. An underinflated tire is inefficient and can be dangerous. Low-profile tires require optimal inflation to elevate the rim off the road's surface. Underinflated tires can allow the tire and tube to be pinched between the rim; a bump or debris in the road can easily cause a flat (called a "pinch flat," or "snakebite," because usually two holes are created) or bent rim, highly undesirable in any circumstance. Severely underinflated tires can roll completely off the rim in a hard turn, with disastrous results.

Handlebars

Aero handlebars have changed bicycle time-trialing more than any other component. Most experts agree that aerobars won the 1989 Tour de France for Greg Lemond, in the closest margin of victory ever (8 seconds in a 21-day

© iphotonews.com/Brooks

Achieve maximum aeroadvantage with aerobars.

race!). The reduction of your frontal surface area creates a knife-like effect that enables you to slice through the wind. Other benefits are the comfort derived from placing your body weight on your forearms instead of your hands, and you can relax your back and neck muscles. The lowered position also brings the powerful gluteus muscle group more into play, along with your lower back muscles.

Road-racing bicycles come with drop handlebars. Specialized triathlon bikes often come with triathlon-specific handlebars that combine aerobars with traditional hand rests and may include shifters and hydration systems in the mix. Clip-on aerobars can easily be added to standard drop handlebars, creating the same aerodynamic position as triathlon-specific aerobars.

The advantages of triathlon-specific handlebars are drag reduction and the ability to shift and hydrate without leaving the aero position, which adds up to time savings in a race. Definitely try to acquire some type of aerobar if you're going to do triathlons, as the time savings are substantial. Again, triathlon-specific bars cannot convert over to USCF road-racing compliance.

Saddles

A cheap saddle is a pain in the butt, guaranteed. If you're going to spend a lot of time on a bike, your saddle is an important investment. All new cyclists go through an initial break-in period where nerves and tissues in your crotch region must get used to and toughened up by continual riding (there's nothing quite like the agony of the first mile or so on a sore crotch). At this early point, a quality saddle is a must, but more important is making sure your saddle is correctly adjusted. Poor adjustment generally causes more initial problems than a cheap seat. After riding for a few months, talk to other riders, your bike shop, or do your own research, and consider an upgrade. If you're getting along okay without softness or gel, avoid it as it adds weight and can cause unwanted chafing by allowing too much movement while pedaling. Instead, check out the general flexibility of the seat bed and the rail system, along with the basic saddle shape. As long as you are upgrading instead of downgrading, you should be assured of enhanced comfort.

Clothing and Accessories

Often overlooked, clothing seems merely a cosmetic consideration. But choices in clothing—and helmets, shoes, gloves, and other equipment on your body—get more important with every mile you ride.

Shorts

Bicycle shorts are the single most important piece of clothing. Cheap shorts can have rough or protruding seams and thin padding. Smooth shorts with good fit and generous padding are a luxury all riders eventually appreciate, so don't scrimp on shorts. Saddle sores from cheap shorts coupled with long rides put an end to your riding quicker than any other injury.

Shorts are usually made of nylon and/or Lycra, materials that last a long time, and the best shorts are made of space-age "wicking" fabrics that draw moisture from your body, accelerating evaporative cooling. Bicycle shorts fit snugly for good reasons. Number one is aerodynamics, and number two is to enhance cooling through capillary action. Floppy, flapping clothes literally grab wind and slow you down, not to mention load up with sweat. Our most aerodynamic ride as humans would be to go naked, but that's not usually very practical. But the closer we can get to naked, the better. Most cycling shorts are dark in color, which, coupled with the lower thigh length, helps keep muscles warm and ready to hammer. Other design features keep the shorts taut, especially in the crotch region, where one little nagging fold of material can wreak havoc. Designs for men's and women's shorts are anatomically different.

Racing Briefs and Suits

For racing, swim briefs for men and swimsuits for women often feature bicycle padding. Serious triathletes jump right onto their bikes after the swim, not taking time to change to cycling shorts. Unless you're tough, buy a padded suit. They tend not to fit or stay as snug as cycling shorts, so as crazy as it sounds you may want to do a practice ride in your padded swimsuit prior to race day, to make sure you're comfortable enough.

Jerseys

For the upper body, we recommend a cycling jersey rather than a T-shirt. Cycling jerseys perform like cycling shorts in terms of aero fit. Other design features include a tight-fitting neck, zipper front, back pockets (to hold food and water bottles in the most aerodynamically advantageous spot on your body), and an elastic snug-fit bottom to go over your shorts. Most jerseys are made of a material that wicks moisture to keep you comfortable. Jerseys come in short sleeves, long sleeves, or sleeveless. A practical consideration is that sleeves protect your shoulders during a fall. United States Cycling Federation (USCF) races require participants to wear shirts with sleeves. Jerseys are not required in triathlons, but you should consider them for long races and training. Although they're expensive, they are high quality and last a long time.

Other Specialized Clothing

In straight, USCF-type time trials, competitors wear "skinsuits"—tight-fitting, one-piece short and jersey combination outfits that bring you closer to riding naked. Some are made of special, vinyl-like material that is actually "slippery" in the wind. These suits may seem extreme, but they work better in much the same way that swim briefs work better than swim trunks.

Should you wear a skinsuit in a triathlon? Strictly speaking, no, as they are not meant for swimming, but out of this technology has sprung specialized triathlon suits that are basically skin suits modified to be "swim-able." The material for these suits is great in the water (low drag) and engineered to wick moisture, keeping you cool. Again, you need to make sure this type of suit works comfortably for you before racing in it (but good luck getting your best buddy to lend you his for a trial run). Try one on in a store to check for comfort, or ask an accomplished triathlete who uses one what he or she thinks.

Gloves

Wearing cycling gloves relieves hand and wrist pressure associated with riding, which leads to pain or numbness, a real distraction on long rides or races. Gloves protect your hands when you crash, allow you to clean road glass and gravel from your tires while in motion (a technique discussed later), provide warmth on cool days, and, on hotter days, keep your sweaty hands off the handlebars and shifters. And since cold weather can make your nose run, gloves make for a handy tissue (just remember to clean them after each use). Gloves are relatively cheap, so pick up a pair or two and see if you like them. Should you wear gloves in a race? That's a matter of preference, but in short races probably not, in long races almost certainly.

Eyewear

Given the high speeds you attain while cycling and the necessity to see every car and road hazard, eyewear is an important safety consideration. Ultraviolet protection is a standard feature in all good-quality sunglasses. High-impact resistance is important but often missing in cheaper sunglasses. Possibly the most important factor is good fit coupled with light weight. Nothing is more bothersome than eyewear that slips down your nose (every time you reach up to adjust, you lose a second or two). Lens color can be important. Many athletes choose light yellow tinted lenses for cloudy days or low light conditions. Lightweight, athletic prescription sunglasses are also available.

Helmets

Helmets are mandatory in all triathlons. We train a lot with roadies, and on occasion someone shows up for a group ride without a helmet, often the younger, high-level cyclist. Going without a helmet is foolish: there's no way in the world it's worth the risk, and you set a bad example for younger athletes. Don't think that because you ride well you don't need a helmet. Many circumstances beyond your control can bring you down hard on the pavement, no matter how great you are, and at that moment your skull is no more durable than an average rider's. Get in the habit of wearing a helmet, no matter what. All three authors of this book have crashed and broken their

A Word From Wes

The Wrath of Bambi

One day during training, I had just finished a hard hill-climbing workout on my bike. Heading home, I was descending 30 to 35 mph on a steep mountain road. In the middle of the descent, I saw a fawn and its mother on the left-hand side of the road. I admired the sight and thought how incredible it was to be able to train in a city where wildlife coexists so closely with the human population. My admiration was shattered as the fawn ran across the road and continued running alongside my bike. During this two seconds of accompaniment, I thought the deer would surely turn back toward its mother.

To my surprise, the deer ran right in between my fork and frame. I flew off the bike and skidded 30-plus yards, smashing my helmet. Luckily, it was a misty day and a little cool. I had two long-sleeve jerseys on and slid on the pavement. If it weren't for a helmet I would be dead or in a coma.

A police officer trailing behind me in his car saw the whole incident and behind him was an off-duty emergency medical technician who brought me oxygen. The deer awoke from unconsciousness to go find its mother. I was transported to the emergency room in an ambulance. After I received X-rays, I was cleared to go home that evening. After receiving road rash up and down the right side of my body, I thought how lucky I was to escape worse injuries. No broken bones, just road rash and a sore neck.

The important thing to remember is that no matter how skilled you think you are at staying up on a bike, you can never account for the unexpected—whether it be a deer, a car, another cyclist, a squirrel, or any other object. A helmet provides the safest protection against changing your life for the worse. Helmets are now lighter, stronger, and more comfortable than they were many years ago.

Fast-forward six years later to the start line of the 2000 Xterra Michigan triathlon. A triathlete came up to me and asked if I had run into any deer lately. I said no. He said there are a lot of deer in Michigan and whenever they go on group rides they say, "Don't have a Hobson." I laughed. During the bike segment of that race, two deer ran in front of me. Their tails are smaller than the ones in Colorado!

helmets; without a helmet, one of us would likely not exist. There's just no advantage at all in going helmetless.

Don't count your pennies when choosing a helmet, as this is an area where quality should prevail. Choose a helmet approved by the American National Standard Institute (ANSI) or Snell. The ratings reflect the helmet's ability to withstand a crash. Most testing standards now refer to the CPSC (Consumer Protection and Safety Council) guidelines. Decent racing helmets offer great aerodynamics, ventilation, and light weight. An aerodynamic helmet will save you a few seconds in a 40K race but not much more. A more important consideration is the helmet's coolness rating. For coolness ratings, look for a bicycle magazine with helmet reviews.

Shoes and Pedals

You can use running shoes for riding, but you'll lose energy through flexing soles, and of course you can't take advantage of cleated cycling shoes. A cycling shoe has a stiff sole that transfers energy generated by your body more efficiently to the bicycle. The soft sole of a running shoe flexes when you apply pressure on the pedal. This results in less efficient energy transfer.

For a fast transition, consider clipping your shoes on the pedals first. Practice repeatedly before race day.

The direct connection of the cleated cycling shoe to the pedal takes some getting used to, but the effort is definitely worth it. With some highly advised practice, it becomes relatively simple and automatic to get your shoe in and out of the pedal. On acquiring your first cleated shoes, go to a parking lot where no one can see you (to reduce the embarrassment factor) and practice getting into and out of your cleats for half an hour or so. Such practice can be invaluable down the road. In a year or so, with ample saddle time, you'll be able to get into your cleats without even looking, which is the safest way.

Good cycling shoes are not cheap but last a long time. Consider shoes a valuable investment, not just an option. When choosing shoes, take a good look at the ease with which your foot enters and leaves the shoe. We've seen top triathletes come into transition out of the swim in the lead only to struggle with their shoes and leave in second or third place. Special triathlon bike shoes offer quick entry. Keep in mind that as you improve you'll likely wish to employ the method of leaving shoes clipped to your pedals. Pedal with your feet on top of your shoes after mounting the bike. Once you've gained sufficient momentum, reach down and secure your foot within the shoe (see photo on page 93). Reverse this for the bike-to-run transition. This is the fastest transition method. However, attempting to slide your foot into an uncooperative shoe with a difficult closure system can make this technique dangerous. In general, a shoe with one Velcro strap works best.

The first step in the evolution of pedal and shoe combinations was toe clips (also called cages) and special cycling shoes. Standard equipment on most lower range road bikes is pedals with toe clips. Don't use them: upgrade to clipless systems, and get used to them. Toe clips are generally a combination of metal and flexible straps—thus the name "cages." The toe straps (leather or plastic material used to fasten the toe clip around the shoe) must be tightened and released by hand, which can cause serious problems when you need to stop suddenly, not to mention cutting off circulation to the foot.

Drawbacks of the toe clip led to the development of the clipless pedal. The system came from snow-skiing technology, where ski bindings had already revolutionized downhill skiing. In this system, the cycling shoe uses a cleat that snaps into a slot in the pedal. The advantages are many: quick and safe entry and release; aerodynamics; 100 percent continuous, solid pedal contact; light weight; and great comfort. Rarely will you see a serious triathlete using anything else. In terms of aerodynamic impact, cycling experts Kyle and Zahradnik showed a 20-gram drag reduction with clipless pedals and translated this into a savings of at least 8 seconds in a 40K race (see their June 1987 bicycling article, "Aerodynamic Overhaul").

Hydration Systems

Weigh the importance of hydration against the low cost of water bottles and cages, and this is an easy purchase to justify. There are superlight cages

© Rich Cruse

Karen Smyers shows great aero form with convenient hydration.

available, though not a high priority on our list. However, for long training rides do what the roadies do: make sure you have two bottles. In rough terms, you should hydrate every 15 minutes on the bike, making one bottle last about an hour and a half. There is nothing worse than running out of water with a half hour or more to get home. We call that learning the hard way.

The second bottle also gives you variety: carry water in one bottle and your favorite glyco or recovery supplement in the other. Buy an insulated bottle, as drinking warm water can be unpleasant.

In recent years, hydration systems combined with aerobars have become popular. These systems accomplish up to three things: you remain constantly in the aero position and keep hammering away while still hydrating (sitting up to reach for a water bottle is an aerodynamic and cadence detriment); hydration is frequent because it's as easy as swigging a fountain drink; and many systems are very aerodynamic. Most serious triathletes use a system like this. With the "fibrous sponge" lid of some models, you can even refill them from another water bottle on the fly.

Another popular system is the camelback, or a backpack-type hydration system. This idea came from the need of mountain bikers to keep both hands on the bars while rocketing down a rough single track and still needing hydration. Triathletes figured the same feature is desirable in their sport, as the more you can stay in the aero tuck, the faster you go. However, camelback systems are banned from international road-racing competitions, as they allegedly have a positive and unfair aerodynamic effect of "smoothing out" the profile of the rider (a stretch, in our opinion).

Computers

A cyclocomputer monitors several functions, such as current, average, and maximum speed; total miles; trip miles; elapsed time; clock; cadence; and even altitude. A cyclocomputer won't make you faster but does provide valuable feedback during and after a ride.

A computer is typically an add-on item, but the wave of the future seems to be "integrated computers," where the mechanism is built into the hub, wires are strung inside the frame, and the monitor is permanent. Additionally, at least one manufacturer, Sports Instruments, also integrates a heart rate monitor into their cyclocomputers and wristwatches. Add-on units (batteries, wires, magnet alignments, calibrations) can be problematic. We know many cyclists who swear they average 25 miles an hour on their training rides (sorry, but your cyclocomputers might be miscalibrated!). Be on the lookout for these exciting new integrated technologies.

Pumps

Of the several types of pumps available, floor pumps and frame pumps are the ones you see most often. Floor pumps sit on the ground and are used to fill 120 pounds or more pressure into your tires before every ride. The "hand squeeze" tire pressure test we all use is quick but inadequate. You should check your tires with your floor pump before every foray. Another bit of advice: get a good pump. It's frustrating trying to get your tires up to pressure while having to fight a cheap pump, especially in the frantic moments before a race. A good pump should grip your valve stem solidly, have a built-in gauge, and be convertible for both Schrader and Presta valves. A good pump should last you your whole life.

A frame pump saves you when you get a flat on the road. This pump is roughly the same length as the top tube of your bike, and that's usually where you attach it, although frame pumps can parallel the seat tube or can even attach to a seat stay. They are spring loaded and fit snug within your frame parts. Make sure yours is the correct size or can be adjusted to fit your frame properly. Nothing is worse than a pump that falls off at 35 mph—a good way to make enemies on a group ride.

There are smaller, lighter-weight pumps that attach to your frame with a bracket. Pumps that attach to a bottle mount are usually "offset" so the bottle cage can still be installed. The trade-off for compactness and light weight is less pumping power than larger frame pumps, but you can generally get enough air in your tire to get home.

A final system is CO_2, a cartridge of highly compressed CO_2 gas that usually fits into a small pump apparatus that secures to your valve stem and releases CO_2 into the tube with the pull of a trigger. These systems are pretty darn slick; they fit into your jersey pocket with ease or can be taped to any convenient part of your frame, and they are far lighter than other pumps. However, most systems are designed for one shot at reinflation, so be careful. Once your CO2 is gone, it's gone (though there are some new systems on the market touting multiple inflations and lasting up to 30 days after being opened). Make sure your new tube is ready to go, or your patch job is top notch, and you have a good connection from apparatus to valve. Better yet, carry a spare cartridge. Do not ever throw your empty cartridges into the ditch. Many "green" oriented riders refuse to use CO_2 for this reason. It's like leaving oxygen tanks on Everest—not cool, hard to retrieve, and takes a few millennia to decompose: downright sacrilege.

Stationary Trainers

Cycling indoors, especially in bad weather, has become a common and preferred method of bicycle training for some. We know many triathletes who train almost exclusively indoors on their spinners, citing safety (no road hazards) and the ability to perform intense, structured, and efficient workouts (even while watching TV) as the major advantages. Although we agree in theory, a trainer will never replace the road for us. You can't develop handling skills while spinning, and these skills make for significant time savings for triathletes.

In any case, bicycling is a far too important component of triathlon for you to go days without training when you can't get outside to do it. Stationary trainers range from $150 to $350 or more.

Roller-type trainers aside, look for something that holds your bicycle solidly to prevent damage to the frame from vibration and sway. Whether the brace holds the bike at the seat post, rear axle, or front fork doesn't matter as much as a secure hold.

Options for resistance include a fan unit (which can provide cooling but is noisy), magnetic or fluid resistance, or heavy rollers. There are also several computer programs, such as the well-known "Computrainer" system that plugs into your magnetic resistance trainer, featuring programmable workouts. You can even buy programs that simulate famous races, such as the Hawaii Ironman or the Tour de France. Expect to pay considerably more for these options.

Another popular spin-off of stationary cycling is group-spinning workouts, made famous by Johnny G and others. These programs, which can be fun and intense, are covered in the training section. Be aware that some instructors lack sufficient training knowledge. Find someone you trust, or you might run the risk of being encouraged to do workouts that are inconsistent with your goals.

Fitting Your Body to the Machine

Unless you can afford to have a bicycle custom built to your anatomy, you'll need to make adjustments to your rig. As you begin to shop for your new bike, keep in mind basic fit is an absolute—nothing is more important. There are many adjustments you can make to fine-tune your body to a bike, but adjusting your frame is not one of them.

Frame Sizing

In this section we'll explain how frames are measured and how to measure your body to choose the right size frame. Frame size is measured and denoted in centimeters. Generally speaking, the measurement is taken from the center of the pedal axle straight up the seat tube (if there is one) to the exact center of the seat tube/top tube/seat stay junction (see figure 8.3). As this basic dimension increases or decreases, other frame components follow suit proportionally (although there is not a standard, per se; different manufacturers have slightly different geometric philosophies). A myriad of other measurements and associated frame geometries come into play, not to

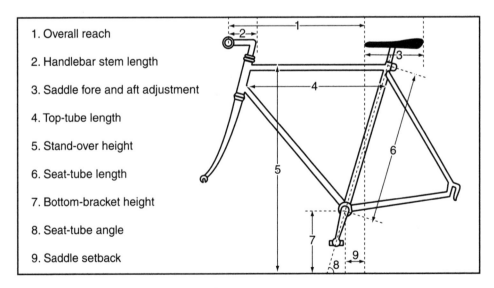

1. Overall reach
2. Handlebar stem length
3. Saddle fore and aft adjustment
4. Top-tube length
5. Stand-over height
6. Seat-tube length
7. Bottom-bracket height
8. Seat-tube angle
9. Saddle setback

Figure 8.3 The dimensions of a bicycle.

Taken from THE RACING BIKE BOOK, published by Haynes Publishing, Sparkford, Yeobil BA227JJ. England. Tel++ 449163 442030

mention the nonconforming geometries of specialized time trial frame designs. Your best bet is to become familiar with various frames and their geometry through your own research or input from a qualified technician at a bicycle shop. Ask other experienced cyclists how they approach this problem and what frame brand they like and why. An experienced cyclist or technician can approximate what size bike frame you need just by looking at your body frame. As with shoes though, sizing can be tricky: some manufacturers' 58-centimeter frames will be a little larger or smaller than others, or will fit or feel different from one another.

You can use several more or less scientific techniques to determine the proper frame size for your body (see table 8.3). The old rule of thumb was to straddle the top tube, and when the clearance between your crotch and the top tube measures about an inch, the frame size was (roughly) correct. This method, however, fails to consider differences in wheel and tire size, and ground clearance of the bottom bracket, which could lead to a substantial sizing error. Most other methods revolve around determining frame size based on your leg length. De la Rosa and Kolin suggested in their book *The Ten-Speed Bicycle* (1979) the following technique:

Measure the distance from the greater trochanter of the femur (the bony point at the side of your hip) to the floor (in bare feet). Subtract 13.75 inches (34 centimeters) from that measurement to determine the correct frame size.

Van der Plas (1986) suggested subtracting 10.5 inches from your inseam measurement to determine the appropriate frame size, converted to centimeters: (inseam – 10.5″) × 2.54 = frame size in centimeters. LeMond (1987) recommended multiplying your inseam measurement by 0.833 for proper sizing. In the final analysis, we recommend that you decide roughly what type of frame you want based on budget, material, brand, and even color,

Table 8.3

Determining Frame Size

Method	Measured by	Advantage	Disadvantage
Store clerk	Straddling the top tube	Easy	Frequently gives errors of 2 in. or more
de la Rosa and Kolin	Subtracting 13.75 in. from the length of the greater trochanter to the floor	Gives accurate results	Many people do not accurately locate the greater trochanter
Van der Plas	Subtracting 10.5 in. from your inseam	Easy	May yield low results
LeMond	Multiplying your inseam by 0.833	Easy	May yield high results

Reprinted, by permission, from Town and Kearney, 1994, *Swim, Bike, Run.* (Champaign, IL: Human Kinetics), 44.

and what size you think fits based on any of the methods above. Have your bike shop set up a stationary trainer in a corner with one of your chosen bikes. Spin away, using different hand and body positions. Allow a skilled technician to walk around and analyze your fit and position. He or she will likely give you some valuable pointers on pedaling technique and proper riding position. Allow the techie to adjust the seat and other components. Ride some more. Unless you're absolutely certain this bike and frame feel right for you, try another. As we've said, different frame manufacturers at the same size employ different geometry, and so same-size bikes feel different. You can't appreciate these differences unless you try them. Think of trying on your running shoes. Would you ever buy shoes sight unseen, without trying them on and walking around in them, and testing different sizes and types to see what felt the best? Do the same with a bike.

After you select a good fit, take a road test. Make sure the ride feels good, paying attention to handling characteristics, smoothness or ride quality, braking, and other factors not apparent in a spin test. You may want to road test a second choice to check for differences.

Finding the right frame size can take a couple of hours or more. Explain to your bike dealer in advance what you're attempting to do and work with them to pick a time when they won't be too busy. If they seem reluctant to help, go somewhere else. On the other side, if they are helpful, let them help—and if they're good, send all your friends there.

If you think selecting a frame size is time consuming, sorry, but you're just getting started. The next section explains all the other adjustments necessary to ensure good fit, resulting in maximum comfort and performance.

Saddle Height

Your saddle, or seat, has three adjustments: height; fore/aft; and tilt, or angle. Proper seat height is critically important and a subject of varying opinions. It's so important because proper seat height significantly influences your mechanical efficiency and injury potential. Hamley and Thomas (1967) pointed out that a mere 4 percent change in saddle height can affect power output by up to 5 percent. Saddle heights that are too high or low can cause knee pain or more serious injury.

To determine proper saddle height for you, we again recommend a combination of science and observation. Researchers Shennum and deVries (1976) suggested a practical technique for approximating the ideal saddle height. Stand upright wearing cycling shoes. Place your feet 12 inches apart, then measure from the floor to your crotch. Take this value and multiply it by 1.09, which represents the distance from the pedal axle to the top of the seat. It's critical to add some distance for the thickness of your pedal.

Use this measurement as a starting point. The next best step is to get on a trainer and spin. How does it feel? Keep in mind there are the two other adjustments coming up, which must be considered. Have your technician observe you from the side and the back. You shouldn't feel as if you are "reaching" at the bottom of your pedal stroke; conversely, you should not feel "cramped" with knees popping up too high at the top of the stroke, especially while in your aerobars. It's plain to see that saddle height is related to crank arm length—if you lower the seat sufficiently, but your knees pop up so high that they almost strike your chest, then your crank arms may be too long. You should feel a comfortable and powerful extension of your calf muscle, but no overextension. Your foot should travel through the bottom of the pedal stroke with neutral to slight extension, merely a few degrees beyond level. Possibly the most important viewpoint is how you look from the back. It's generally accepted that maximum power output and aerodynamics are achieved with your seat as high as possible while maintaining comfort so that your full range of muscular motion is optimized. However, your hips should never rock back and forth or up and down when being viewed from the back. They should remain level. Try intentionally raising the seat too high to see how this feels. Ride a little bit too low to see how that "cramped" feeling can reduce your perceived power output. And keep in mind that riding in your aerobars can change your body's geometry, sometimes substantially. Again, most people feel that continued riding in aerobars necessitates raising the seat a few millimeters. A higher seat position, especially coupled with aerobars, enhances aerodynamics (assuming your handlebar stem does not move up as well). Now, after doing all that, ride around with a wrench in your pack for a few weeks. Tinker with your seat height only if you feel truly uncomfortable; otherwise let it be for a while.

Other seat adjustments are important. Let's do the easier one first: tilt. Almost everyone agrees that a saddle level with the ground is proper adjustment. If you're constantly slipping forward, the saddle nose is likely angled down; if you have crotch pain or sores, the nose may be tilted up. To start with, always try level. This adjustment, along with fore and aft, can usually be accomplished by loosening one bolt under your seat that controls all adjustments (except seat height).

Next, move to fore and aft adjustments. A good saddle has rail mounts that allow you to move the saddle fore and aft several centimeters. Again, make the initial adjustment while sitting on the saddle, with your feet in the toe clips and the pedal crank arms horizontal to the ground. Position the saddle so that the center of your front knee falls no farther back than through the center of the pedal. Many multisport athletes prefer a forward position for time-trialing, and manufacturers have designed seat posts or triathlon frame geometry with steep (more vertical) seat tubes that place the saddle forward to begin with. A traditional road frame may require moving the seat as far forward as it will go to achieve comfort in the aerobar position. A string taped to the center of your knee and weighted on the other end will help you make a more exact measurement of the above methodology. Again, when all is said and done, ride and make adjustments as necessary. Keep in mind the seat adjustments also work in tandem with your handlebar adjustments, which is the next discussion.

Handlebar Adjustments

The adjustments we've discussed to this point involve fitting your lower body to the bike. Your upper-body characteristics affect your selection of correct handlebar width, stem length and height, and the pitch of the handlebars, along with aerobar positioning. Ideally, you could ask your bike dealer to determine proper stem length by using an adjustable stem. Stem adjustment can get very technical; racers use this measurement to distribute their body weight equally on each wheel, allowing for great handling and a more horizontal position. The triathlete needs a stem length that allows a

© Rich Cruse

Maintain good aeroposition—seat high, stem low, elbows in and at 90 degrees, body forward, head down, and back flat.

comfortable position. If the stem length is too short, your position is too upright (causing poor aerodynamics); if it's too long, you'll be too stretched out on the bike, likely riding on the nose of the saddle. Additionally, stem length affects bike handling; a shorter stem translates to a short lever arm, making turns somewhat "quick" and unstable. The combination of seat fore/aft position and stem length should translate to balance, wherein your crotch is centered and comfortable on the seat, your hands are comfortable on the tops of the handlebars, and you don't feel as if you are reaching, or conversely, "bunched up." Again, aerodynamics dictates that the more "stretched out" you are, the more aero you are, but not at the expense of riding forward on the nose of your seat.

Make the beginning adjustment with your hands comfortable, down in the "drops," or lower portion of the handlebars, with your wrists straight and your elbows slightly bent (important, as you should not ride with locked elbows). If your stem seems too short or long, ask for another one to try, and make sure you also try out the stem in the aero position.

Stem height is also adjustable, and for starters most agree it should be about an inch lower than the top of the saddle. Experiment. Surprisingly, in terms of comfort, stem height can affect how your crotch interacts with the saddle. As you adjust stem height, you may need to adjust seat height a little.

If you have aerobars, make the stem height adjustment in the aero position. More on proper position later, but suffice to say that the lower your front end, the better. Just don't overdo it and sacrifice comfort or power. Aerobars are also usually fore and aft adjustable, and this is important. Get your stem length right first, then mess with the aerobar length setting. The key is in your elbow placement. Above all, your upper body should rest comfortably on your elbows. The farther out your aerobars extend, the more aero you are, but again do not sacrifice comfort. The feeling of "reaching" adds upper-body muscular stress quickly resulting in fatigue, thus possibly negating aero enhancement. Remember that a feeling of balance is the key.

Stem designs allow for adjustments in the handlebar pitch or rotation around the stem. Start with your drops level with the ground. While cycling in the drops, your wrists should engage the drops directly without having to bend greatly in either direction. Bending the wrists causes discomfort through pressure on veins and nerves, resulting in numbness and other fatigue problems.

Handlebars come in different widths. Aerodynamics dictates choosing the narrowest width that feels comfortable and yet allows you to breathe fully and deeply. Again, a good bike technician can assess your body frame and make a recommendation.

Crank Arm Length

Crank arms are the mechanical "lever" that connects your foot to the drivetrain. Like any lever they differ in length, ranging from 165 to 180 millimeters. Obviously, the longer the crank arm, the higher your foot will be at top dead center (TDC, or the 12 o'clock position) and lower at bottom center (or 6 o'clock). True to mechanical rules, longer crank arms produce more leverage, or power, but also require more force, generally produced only by a longer lever arm (your leg) applying the force. Translation: the taller you are, the longer your legs, thus justifying longer crank arms. As your height and leg length increase, so does your bicycle frame size, allowing more overall room for a larger pedal circumference. Keep in mind that in cycling, you can exert your optimal muscular strength over only a limited range of motion, so a crank arm that is too long for your body size can be as detrimental to your mechanics as having your saddle too high. The general rules: a 6-foot tall person equates to 175-millimeter crank arms; for every 3- to 4-inch difference above or below this line, consider a 2.5-millimeter reduction or increase. However, the true measure is leg length, not overall height. Most frames come with crank arms proportional to the frame size. In other words a 56- or 58-centimeter frame is typically a good fit for the average 6-foot person and will likely feature 175-millimeter crank arms as standard, although some 56-centimeter road frames may have 172.5. For women with a 28- to 29-inch inseam, a crank arm length of about 160-millimeter may be appropriate. Deviating from these set proportions is advisable only if you have a disproportionate body, such as extremely long legs for your height. Again, changes in crank arm length affect seat height and other adjustments. See table 8.4 for guidelines for crank arm length.

Table 8.4

Crank Arm Length

Inseam (centimeters)	Inseam (inches)	Crank length (millimeters)
72-75	28.35-29.53	155-160
76-79	29.92-31.10	160-165
80-83	31.50-32.68	165-170
84-87	33.07-34.25	170-175
88-91	34.65-35.83	175-180
92-95	36.22-37.40	180-185

Cleat Adjustments

Just when you thought you were finished, there's one final adjustment: shoe cleats. Your cleats have slotted holes for adjustments. These adjustments can be critical.

First, there is fore and aft. Always start with a setting that balances the ball of your foot directly over the pedal axle. For most people, this will be it.

If for any reason this feels uncomfortable, adjustments can be made, but they are rare. Also make sure the direction is comfortable, as cleats can twist, or rotate. Your foot should rotate around the pedal stroke nice and straight and comfortable, with your heel being the gauge. Make sure the heel is not angled out or in, causing the heel to hit your chain stays. It is fairly standard for the heel to clear the chain by about a quarter inch to half inch. Bad pedal angle is almost certainly a recipe for knee injury.

A couple of other notes about cleats: check the mounting screws often to make sure they're not loose, which can cause serious, unexpected problems with entry and exit to the pedal. You'll inevitably end up walking some on your cleats. Over time, they wear out from this and regular cycling usage, again compromising pedal grip. Inspect them often, and if they seem worn out, they are cheap and easy to replace.

Most pedal/cleat combinations have some "float," to alleviate the potential for poor alignment problems. Some of the newer pedals offer a total floating feature and are very lightweight, allow great ground clearance in corners, and are easy to get in and out of. Many athletes swear by the advantage of this pedal system, but they agree it takes a little getting used to the free-floating feel.

Cycling shoes must fit the foot snugly yet be free enough to keep the foot from cramping. You also must consider shoe fit based on socks or bare feet. Many triathletes ride without socks because they race without them. This affects size and fit. Keep in mind too if you ride in cold weather, going barefoot simply won't work.

Preventive Maintenance

Mechanical problems can arise any time in training and competition, but there are ways to minimize the occurrences. The number one nemesis of cyclists is the flat tire. One way to avoid flats is to train on roads that are in good condition, but that's not always a choice we can make. Another factor is to invest in high-quality tires—up to $60 or $80 a tire is not uncommon. Not only is performance enhanced with these tires (improved cornering, reduced rolling resistance, durability), so is flat prevention. Another technique to avoid flats is to clean off your tires after going through loose gravel or passing over glass. As we've mentioned, this is where cycling gloves come in handy. While in motion, lightly rub the reinforced palm over the rolling surface of the front tire, with your hand in front of the fork, obviously, unless you desire broken fingers and a headlong flight over the handlebars. For the back tire, place your palm just behind the seat tube, lower it onto the rear tire, and rub it lightly. Be careful: don't push too hard and get your fingers caught. Don't be surprised to see glass fly off when you do this.

Finally, do not ride on tires with worn treads. It's unsafe, and you're just begging for a flat. If the outer layer begins to wear to the point where the inner layer is visible, change the tire immediately.

If your bike is well maintained, tire repair is your primary risk when riding. If you ride on clinchers, carry one spare tube, two tire levers, and a patch kit—and of course a pump or CO_2. All this equipment can easily fit under your seat, allowing you to forget about it until you need it. If you ride on tubulars, carry two spares. In either case, having some change tucked away comes in handy in case you must phone for help (or carry a cell phone, which is also nice to have when you want to report a dangerous driver). And if you are new to riding, practice changing a tire before you go out. Quick, problem-free tire changing is almost an art. The other option is learning the hard way, which usually entails walking many miles in cleated cycling shoes, which is no fun.

Another common riding ailment is the broken spoke. If you're mechanically minded, you can change a spoke in the field and roughly retrue your wheel, but most people just bend it around an adjacent spoke to keep it from slapping against frame parts. Make sure you do this right away, as the loose spoke can cause serious frame damage. Your wheel will be out of true at this point and almost certainly rubbing the brake pads, so you'll just have to open them up and limp home. Have your shop replace the spoke and true the wheel, and make sure they check all spokes for signs of damage or wear. The main culprit for spoke damage occurs when your derailleur is out of adjustment, causing the chain to come off the largest cog and run against the

Modifying a Road Bike to Triathlon Bike

If you want to make a road-racing frame more of a triathlon bike, consider the following modifications to enhance performance and comfort. First, check the length of the handlebar stem. In the typical road-racing bicycle, this stem is quite long, allowing the racer to stretch out his or her body while riding in the drops. Road racing in this position is more aerodynamic, and it also places the hip extensor muscles in a better position to apply pedal force. This position is fine for road racing, but being stretched out too long can make it somewhat difficult for your leg muscles to transition from bike to run. So, consider stem modification. A shorter stem allows a more upright position, which generally works better with aerobars. The following is a visual check for determining stem length when using drop handlebars: Assume a riding position on the bike, with hands in the drops. Look straight down through the top of the handlebar stem. If you see the front axle approximately two inches beyond the end of the handlebar stem, then stem length should be correct.

Next, check the saddle. A simple modification is a seat post bent to move the seat forward, called a "forward" seat post, which essentially accomplishes the same geometry as a steep seat tube. If you move your saddle forward and it still seems too far back, consider a forward seat post.

Now, let's decide how to complete your frame. In table 8.5, we detail information about wheels and tires, handlebars, pedals and shoes, and components to help you decide what you want on your bicycle. Of course, all of these items have been covered in individual detail in previous sections. Table 8.5 gives an accurate guide on the costs of "speeding up" your bike.

Table 8.5

Cost of Aero Upgrade

Item	Time saved*	Cost**	Cost per second
Aerobars	3.5	$75.00	$0.36
Aerobar end shifters	1.5	$100.00	$1.11
Aero drinking system	0.5	$50.00	$1.67
Aero helmet	1	$125.00	$2.08
18-mm tubulars @ 150 PSI	0.5	$100.00	$3.33
Deep rim front wheel	1	$400.00	$6.67
Disc wheel	1.5	$600.00	$6.67
Aero frame***	0.5	$1,000.00	$33.33
		$2,450.00	

*Time in approximate minutes

**Costs can vary; higher price may not increase time savings

***Aero frame is upgrade amount and can in effect be zero compared to expensive but non-aero frames.

spokes for a turn or two. If your chain does this, check your spokes near the cogs for abrasions. If they are deep and numerous, replace your spokes. They will break eventually from this damage.

Probably the next biggest concern in bike maintenance involves the chain. Your chain will stretch and over time will deform the teeth on both your chain rings and rear cogs. Most bike shops recommend a new chain after about 2,000 miles of riding if you want to avoid changing all your gears. A chain replacement is much cheaper than new gears. When cogs are worn, the chain can slip, usually at the most inopportune time, like when you're hammering up a hill. Simply measuring is one way to tell if your chain has stretched too much. If 12 links measure 12 inches, your chain is fine. However, if 12 links measure 12-1/8 inches or more, your chain is stretched and needs replacing.

If weather conditions are good, lubricate the chain on your bike with a chain-lubricating spray or other type. Many varieties are available and should be researched in order to make a decision on what is best for your riding conditions. Lubricating your chain is important. A well-lubricated chain is silent as it functions. Any chain noise at all signals that the chain needs attention. Check for any stiff links, and loosen them up. If you forget this measure, you may experience the frustration of a skipping chain. And there are many good chain-cleaning solvents and devices—when your chain is overly gunked, clean it well, then lubricate.

Getting caught in the rain presents maintenance problems. Your bearings have grease that can be harmed by dirt and water (even if the manufacturer claims the grease is waterproof). After getting caught in the rain once or twice, if you're mechanically minded, you may consider dismantling all moving parts not containing sealed bearings and let the frame and parts dry out before reassembling. This requires some additional shop equipment such as a crank arm extractor, but the cost is less than replacing parts ruined by dirt and rust. If you aren't inclined to perform this work yourself, take your bike to a good mechanic at least once a year for a tune-up and complete review. Make a written list of every little nagging problem that has developed throughout the year of riding, so your bike will be in great shape for the start of the new season.

Something we can't emphasize enough is the importance of doing some of your own bicycle maintenance. You should be able to perform routine maintenance to prevent road breakdowns. Tools to perform most bicycle maintenance cost about $100; there are also plenty of excellent books on the subject, including the popular choices *Zinn and the Art of Road Bike Maintenance* by Leanord Zinn (2000) and *Anybody's Bike Book by Tom Cutherthson* (1998). These resources can guide you through the maintenance of your entire bicycle.

Other maintenance measures you should perform on a less frequent basis include inspecting your rims for trueness, checking your brake pads for wear, and checking your derailleurs for proper adjustment. A well-maintained, good-quality bicycle is reliable and a sheer joy to ride.

Now that you have your dream machine, the real work begins. All this great equipment has you looking like a pro; now you must learn to ride like one as well! Our next chapter, chapter 9, covers cycling technique. Chapter 10 then presents training programs geared to optimal cycling performance. Follow all this, and you'll be at the top of your game in cycling.

Chapter 9
CYCLING TECHNIQUE

In chapter 8 we discussed the importance of fitting your bike correctly, and we want to point out again that if your bike doesn't fit you properly, if the basic element of cycling efficiency doesn't exist, then technique doesn't matter much. Gains earned through proper technique will likely be negated by improper fit because of inefficiencies, discomfort, injury, and other disorders.

Toward the end of this chapter we discuss proper time-trialing position. We'll begin here by talking about general biomechanical fit between body and bike. The key word is *comfort*. If you feel uncomfortable while cycling, something is probably wrong with the fit. Try to identify the area of discomfort and discern what adjustments might be made. For instance, when Mike began cycling, during his very first long ride (80 miles), he developed extreme discomfort in the back of the crotch region on one side, with pain extending down one leg. It turned out the seat was a little too far back, and his top tube and stem were a little too long. When we say "a little," we're talking millimeters, but when you're riding 80 miles too far forward on your saddle, the tiny numbers add up to big problems. Riding too long on the nose of the seat caused inflammation and some damage to Mike's sciatic nerve (the primary nerve running from your lower spine down your legs). Healing this condition meant suffering the humiliation of sitting on a hemorrhoid doughnut for an entire year!

Riding a bicycle defines simplicity—to wit, we use the saying, "like riding a bicycle" to refer to an activity so elementary we can do it just once and never forget it. Well, we beg to differ when it comes to triathlon training, and especially racing. Professional triathlete Marcel Vifian recently stated that great technical and performance gains can be realized by beginners in swimming and running in a relatively short time, whereas equivalent gains in cycling can take years. In running and swimming, man masters only himself, whereas in cycling we must also master a machine.

For those of you who have raced, how many times have you been struggling up a hill in the last stretch of a 40K bike leg, when suddenly a team biker in typical roadie gear (no speedo for these guys) flies by you, around

A Word From Wes

Riding With Roadies

Riding with a group of cyclists—or roadies, or wheelheads—is a great way to improve your cycling ability. I enjoy riding with them for several reasons:

1. You can get your heart rate to your anaerobic threshold and above without much perceived mental effort while you're in a group. I can easily keep my heart rate average above my AT for as long as an hour and a half of the ride by riding at the front. Training by myself, I couldn't do this. In a group, you don't realize how hard you exert yourself.

2. You can work on increasing leg speed. When in a draft of other cyclists, you exert much less effort than the leader and you can drop a gear and spin while continuing at the same pace as the leader. Drafting is easier than cycling on your own at the same speed.

3. You can improve your bike-handling skills. The peleton, or group, is constantly changing form. The peleton can be bunched up or strung out in a single-file pace line, depending on the speed. You must always be aware of your surroundings. After several rides in a group, your comfort level increases. Groups are a great way to pass time on the bike because of this constant change as well as conversations on the ride.

4. You get miles in quickly if you record your distance.

5. You get to corrupt the egotistical minds of some cyclists who think they are the kings of two wheels. After making them go totally anaerobic and blow up, you know they've got to be thinking, *[Expletive], this guy has already swum three miles and done a track workout today.*

the next corner without slowing, only to disappear quicker than he came upon you? You trudge along and think: what am I doing wrong? What's that guy's secret?

Well, the first step is to admit these guys do have some secrets. Forget about the roadie versus "tri-geek" rift and learn some of the secrets of the pros—which we impart here just for you. Something to think about: most of the awesome triathlon cyclists spend time with the roadies; many of them train and race with road cyclists.

The main advantage of riding with competitive, road cyclists is that you learn solid cycling technique. The main disadvantage is that you work out at someone else's pace or plan. Often, you are forced to go beyond your comfort zone or race pace, which, if done correctly, can adapt you to faster speeds. But you must do it correctly, or you can injure yourself. Our recommendation is that if you feel comfortable with it, go out occasionally with the road group, but stay focused on your own training schedule. If the pack begins something you don't want to do, by all means, drop off and finish on your own. Many illnesses, overtraining injuries, and other problems result from foolish competitive pride gone out of control.

Pedaling Technique

Many studies have focused on pedaling mechanics. Just as we think we know everything we need to know, we learn more. Knowledge evolves as more discoveries are made and as theories are developed, proved, disproved, and overturned. The simple act of pedaling has seen many of these evolutions, with elliptical chain rings, one-directional cranks, camming cranks, power cranks, and vastly differing technical advice (supply power 360 degrees, pull up on the backstroke, lower your heels, point your toes, and so on). We like to keep it simple. The pedal stroke hinges on a simple motion: moving in a circle, the most mathematically perfect shape in the world.

When pedaling, think, *circles:* nice, smooth, round, perfect circles. This may sound like we're telling you to supply power 360 degrees, but we're not—this concept has been disproved. Human anatomy dictates that more power is available in the pushing downward phase with the strong quadriceps muscles than in the pulling up with the hamstrings. Go ahead and imagine supplying power all the way around, but don't get hung up on the idea: don't overcompensate at any point in the circle. Keep it smooth. Imagine your thighs are piston-driven levers and your calves connecting rods. Keep the pistons moving up and down with a nice, regular rhythm thighs doing most of the work, while the lower leg travels a relaxed circle. The connecting rods transfer that power smoothly to the pedal. You'll need a smooth and quick cadence, as it is nearly impossible to perform at a low rpm.

Your calves, hamstrings, and gluteals supply a lot more power than you may feel or realize. After months or years of riding diligently, you may notice the greatest muscle mass change in your hamstrings first, then your calves, butt, and finally quads; inexperienced riders may notice quad development first. All these muscles are employed to complete a simple circular, mechanical action. Keeping it all smooth by balancing the work over these muscle groups is the key to efficient power transfer to your pedals.

Riders debate over foot angle: should it be level, toes down, heel down, or what? The answer: relax and do what comes natural. Don't make a conscientious effort to alter the angle. Keep thinking *circles, relax,* and don't lock up. Experiment however, under different conditions. When climbing a steep hill, try dropping your heels a bit; this works for many but also may work only if you change other body mechanics (more on this later). In any case, dropping your heels employs the calf muscles more, supplying additional power. Pointing your toes can be effective during high-cadence spinning workouts to reduce "hopping" in the saddle. But be careful, don't make this a habit, as pointed toes keep calf muscles contracted and can lead to cramping, especially when transitioning to the run phase.

Cadence

Cadence is defined as the revolutions per minute (rpm) with which you spin the pedals and the regularity, or rhythm, of the spinning. Most triathletes spin at too low an rpm. While cycling you should feel most of the time as if you're spinning with generally minimal effort, not overloading your legs.

So, what is a good cadence? For most people, a pace of 85 to 90 rpm is solid but not draining. (Yes, some cyclists, such as velodrome gold medallist Marty Nothsteine, operate well at a wide range of rpms, but they are not quite like the rest of us.) This cadence range is intended for more or less flat, ideal, low wind conditions, but even in conditions of wind resistance, up or down hill, or whatever, an 85 to 90 cadence is efficient for most people. Flat-out time-trialing elite athletes often maintain 100 rpm or even a little higher, but these are special cases. Dropping or adding gears to maintain a consistent, rhythmic rpm regardless of conditions is generally the best way to go. Low cadence causes excessive muscular stress, essentially trashing your legs for the upcoming run; high cadence results in high heart rate, anaerobia, and lactic acid build up—also known as pain.

How do you measure cadence? The best way is a cyclocomputer with a cadence feature (which requires a wire and magnetic sensor attached to your crank arm). Short of that, ride for a while completing one pedal revolution per second, measuring this with your watch, using it as the "metronome." This of course is 60 rpm. Get a distinct idea of what 60 rpm feels like. Now move up to 90 by counting 15 revolutions every 10 seconds, or 30 revolutions every 20 seconds. This pace is at or near your optimum cadence. If it feels a little fast, back off a tad (don't ask us to define a "tad"). Check your cadence often with the watch so you know how it feels and you can gauge where you are and make adjustments to suit your particular range of power.

Changing Gears

With 18 gears to choose from, gear changing can be confusing. Again, you'll do well to relax and keep things smooth and simple. We'll start with a simple but important definition. We all talk a lot about going "up and down" the gears; we need to be on the same page concerning what gear direction we're referring to. In this text, and in general out-on-the-road terminology, when someone says "go up" a gear they usually mean shifting to a gear that results in a heavier load. This defies sense in a way because visually "going up" on the back gears, or cogs, moves up to bigger diameter gears. Just keep in mind that up equals increasing load and down equals decreasing load. You may also hear people say, "grab a bigger gear"—again, they mean a gear that results in a heavier load, which will be a smaller, not bigger, gear on the cogs.

If you're not already, get comfortable changing gears. We've been on rides with beginners who reluctantly change gears because it's "too much trouble." If you're not comfortable changing gears, get on a section of road with some gentle hills or grade changes, and bang those gears around, all the way through, over and over until you can do it without looking or thinking. It takes time, maybe six months or a year, before you're completely comfortable—automatic, if you will—with gear changing. But it is so important! Much is made about shaving seconds off a 40K through aerodynamics, while efficient and quick gear changing is often overlooked. In shifting gears, remember that you're trying to stay around the 85- to 90-rpm range, regardless of terrain and conditions. Get used to finding the appropriate gear to hit that range as quickly and smoothly as possible.

We've described pulling along a flat section of road, striving for optimal cadence. Don't be afraid to go up or down a gear if fatigue sets in, wind changes, or you feel you can pick up a heftier gear and still be okay. Keep pedal action smooth and minimize upper-body movement by keeping relaxed. If you're tense or moving excessively from side to side, you'll waste precious energy. Imagine your legs disconnecting from your upper body, their smooth movement not affecting anything above your waist. Try focusing on your hands on the aerobars. Your grip should be relaxed, soft; some riders don't really grip at all, their hands actually dangling while cruising on the flats. Another important area to relax is your neck. Your eyes must stay on the road, but try to accomplish this by raising your eyes initially and your neck secondarily. If your neck gets stiff, roll it around a bit to keep it loose.

What gear should you be in? It depends on your power output, the wind, the grade, your weight, and many other factors. Remember your rpm goal, and gear accordingly. If you can't maintain an easy, relaxed, yet powerful spin, you likely need to move down a gear into a lighter load. You can always try going up to a bigger (heavier) gear, but if you feel as if you're "pushing," you're likely in too big a gear.

Riding Downhill

Ahhh, the pleasure of zipping down a hill, getting a break from all the exertion. Let's learn how to take the best advantage of the downhill. Hills come in different shapes and sizes, so techniques need to be adapted for various conditions. If we were not triathletes and rode without aerobars, this discussion would be different. For triathletes, the most efficient and aero way to descend is to stay in your aerobars (see photo below). For some there is a fear factor—after all, you'll be reaching speeds up to 40 miles an hour on a 19-pound machine. We've seen beginners brake out of fear while going down steep hills. We say, never do this unless a tight corner looms. Practice, practice until you're comfortable ripping down the hills in an aero tuck. Find a screamer of a hill and ride it several times, so you know the dips and bobbles and can get comfortable. How else can you pick up so much time, with so little effort? Stay relaxed yet focused as you practice transitioning smoothly from aerobars to brake handles, as you'll have to do this on occasion. At these speeds, just beginning to sit up slows you considerably because of wind resistance. Apply brake pressure smoothly.

By having his feet level, knees in, hands and elbows narrow, and head as low as possible, Wes has made himself small to cheat the wind.

Coming over the top of the hill or preparing for the descent from a flat section, look and think ahead. How long is the descent? How steep? How steep and long is the next ascent, or is it flat? It sounds complicated to plan your descents and ascents, but with time this becomes second nature. A friend who rides a tandem bicycle with his wife calls riding downhills "momentum management"—which is especially the case riding double on a tandem. The concept is a little hard to explain, so we'll try coming at it from reverse. When you slow down and have that "bogged down" feeling, your rpm drops, and it takes great strength even to go slow. You have lost your momentum. Sometimes this is inevitable, but many times the momentum attained from a fast descent can be maintained for quite a while during the following flat, or be used to power you over the next hill. This takes practice and proper gear changes at the proper time (maintain that rpm), coupled with out-of-the-saddle pedaling, if appropriate. When your speed drops below about 16 mph, there's little advantage to staying in the aero tuck, as you're going too slow for windload to have much effect. Sitting up or getting out of the saddle to gain more leverage, higher cadence, and continued momentum takes precedence over aerodynamics. If you can master momentum management, you can save seconds or even a minute or two over a long, hilly time trial.

Riding downhill is one time when deviating from the rpm rule might be in order; after all, a load reduction is being offered by gravity, meaning you can drop to a bigger (smaller on the cog) gear, use a lower rpm, and push a little harder. Roughly 10 to 30 meters before the descent starts (depending on your speed), get into the large chain ring. Changing to the big ring adds a rather serious load to the legs, so don't do it too early. If topping a hill, you may start this transition by shifting to an easier gear in the back while simultaneously, or as quickly as possible (depending on your shifting mechanism), shifting into the large chain ring. This helps reduce the transitional load from small to large ring. (The opposite, shifting to a heavier gear in the back just slightly ahead of a downshift to the small ring, prevents overspinning. Many triathletes shift to the small ring too early at the bottom of an ascent, losing their momentum.) If for some reason the shift to the big ring is too early and the load slows you down, simply bang up a gear or two more in the back. Practice this and it will make sense to you and become second nature.

Grade conditions dictate the speed with which you drop to bigger gears: a quick steep descent requires quick changes, a gradually developing descent, slower changes. Assess the descent and make as many gear changes as possible near the top of the hill before you begin to pick up a lot of speed. But don't overdo it. You can drop to lower rpms—say 60 or 70—because with gravity you'll be back up to 80 or 90 rpm quickly. As you pick up speed, continue to carefully and smoothly drop to bigger gears, until you are all out. Then, if your rpm hits 90, 100, or more, where it feels as if the power you're supplying is not adding much, you have two choices: (1) stop pedaling, level out your pedals (parallel to the road since this is the most aerodynamic), get into a nice low tuck, with your chin an inch from the handlebars, with back in flat aero position, and ride it out; or (2) continue to pedal lightly (called "soft pedaling") to make sure your legs don't cramp or load up with lactic acid. Some riders believe you should always soft pedal a descent; we say it depends on how your legs feel.

In any case as you begin to bottom out on a descent, practice being in the right gear, which may be up the rear cogs (larger) a gear or two, so that you can begin applying the right amount of steady power and cadence at the right time, again taking full advantage of your momentum, and preparing for the next flat area, or up that next hill.

Riding Uphill

The pleasure of zipping the downhill is offset by the anaerobic torture of the uphill—such is the yin and yang of cycling. All the roadies know that cycling's world premier event, the Tour de France, is won in the mountains by the great climbers, such as Marco Pantani, Jan Ullrich, Richard Virenque, and Americans Greg LeMond and Lance Armstrong (of course you must be great at all aspects of cycling to win the whole tour—Pantani and Virenque have never won the whole thing because they are climbing specialists and can't sprint or hammer the long haul). If you didn't know, Lance Armstrong was at one time one of the greatest junior triathletes in the United States. We often wonder what might have happened had he stayed in our sport (though we're glad he didn't!).

Many triathletes overlook the gains that can be had through enhanced climbing techniques. Tip number one is to change your attitude: presto! You now love hills. Believe that you are, or will be, a great climber, and you're closer to your goal already. Tip number two is to remember momentum management. As you're coming down a hill, look up the road and assess the uphill, preparing yourself mentally to smoothly ascend and power over the top.

Types of Hills

There are three basic types of hills: long hauls, steep killers, and hoppers (and of course combinations of these). Let's look at different techniques for each.

The Long Haul
A long haul is characterized by a medium to low gradient, but it goes on for a while, say 200 meters or more. Essentially, treat this kind of hill like a flat. For the most part, stay seated and in your aerobars, keep your momentum and cadence up, and slowly but steadily progress down (lighter load) the gears maintaining that rather high yet comfortable rpm. If you begin to bog down at all, go down another gear, or don't be afraid to get up out of the

© David Sanders

When staying seated on a climb, consider dropping your heels a bit, like this rider.

saddle for a few revolutions to pick up speed and cadence. Getting out of the saddle changes the muscle group you're using and can refresh you a bit to continue the climb seated. After all, for this type of climb (and most climbs for that matter), remaining seated is still the most efficient position. And, a little secret explored more in a minute: right before or simultaneous to standing, go up a gear (smaller), as standing applies much greater force to the pedals, demanding more resistance. Spinning too fast with too little resistance while standing is simply a waste; it's uncomfortable and inefficient and can cause cramping or other injury. Practice going up one, two, or even three gears (smaller) right before standing. More on out-of-the-saddle technique in a moment.

The Hopper

The hopper is the easiest kind of hill, more or less a bump of manageable proportions. However, we still see many triathletes stay in their aerobars and bog down on a hopper, when with proper technique they should fly over it as if it wasn't there. It's quite simple and goes back to the notion of momentum management. First, what is a hopper? It's a smaller hill, although it can be steep; the main feature is that your natural momentum takes you roughly halfway to the top without a gear change, or going up only one or two gears at the most. What to do? At the point where you're about to go up another gear and spin, don't! Either leave your gear alone, or actually go down to a bigger (heavier) gear, stand up and power over the top, all in one smooth motion. If done correctly with the right timing and the right gear, there's virtually no speed lost, and this hopper, for all practical purposes, never existed. Find yourself a good hopper, practice a few times, and you'll have it mastered. The key is to keep your speed and momentum up.

The Steep Killer

The steep killer is called a killer because it can wipe you out aerobically and trash your legs. So, what's the best way to manage this? First, other than the initial "run up" the hill, where you may still be at a high speed through momentum, forget about your aerobars. Once you have slowed and begun the grind of steep climbing, aerobars become a bane instead of a friend. Get out of them and grab your brake hoods firmly, wrapping at least two fingers firmly around and under. Now, depending on how steep and long the hill, you have some choices: stay seated, stand, or combine the two. After practice, you can decide what works best for you, or what works best on varying degrees of gradient. In any case, as the hill begins, keep grabbing higher gears as you load up and your rpm drops. On a steep hill this is usually pretty quick. Keep in mind the chain ring shift: if you just came down a hill, you're likely in the big ring. Leave it there for a while. Many beginners shift to the small ring a little too early. As you bottom out and begin to ascend and load up, shift up the rear cog a gear or two (or three), while pedaling smoothly. If this is a steep hill, shifts may be rapid fire. Judge your resistance, and possibly move up a couple more cogs. As you begin to slow, you'll reach a point where shifting to the small ring becomes optimal, generally when you're in the vicinity of four to six cogs up from the bottom. If the shift is at the optimal point, you should be able to shift to the small ring and continue your smooth pedal stroke more or less uninterrupted. If the ring downshift results in a sudden overrev, don't be afraid to drop down a gear or two in the back, quickly, before you lose momentum. At this point, you are sitting up. Sit back on the saddle, but keep your upper body forward and relaxed, elbows bent, and grip your bars near the stem or under the brake hoods. Don't sit up too straight; keep your back curved a bit, your head low, like a cat ready to pounce. Try dropping your heels a little, especially at the top of your pedal stroke. Keep your rpms up. If done correctly, the feeling is almost as if you're "running" on the pedals, or stepping up a set of stairs. Settle in and spin. Stay relaxed.

Figure 9.1 illustrates the shift points and riding strategy for each type of hill. No two hills are alike and many are combinations of the above but the basic strategy and principles can simply be adjusted—compacted, elongated, or combined—depending on the hill profile. In general, let momentum carry you as far as possible. Perform the first downshift as you begin to lose momentum or cadence and start to feel bogged down. One exception is the short hopper, where your mind-set should be to just fly over it like it's not even there.

Long haul

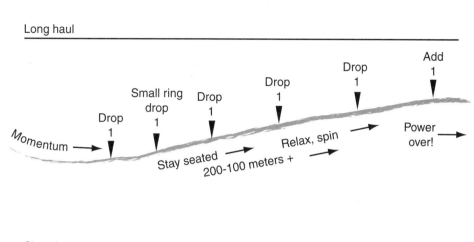

Short hopper

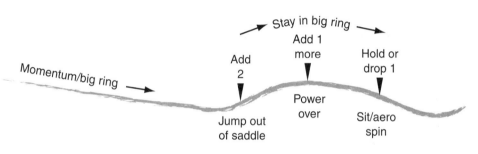

Steep killer

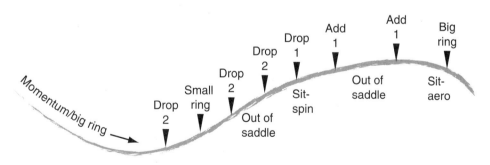

Figure 9.1 Shifting strategies for three types of hills.

Avoid blowing up during any hill climb. If you're struggling, back off, relax and spin, gather yourself, and then concurrent with the hill leveling out, begin to build even if near-maximum effort is required at that point. You're trying to acquire momentum for the next flat or hill, and momentum is easier than hammering. Practice riding hills as much as possible.

Out-of-the-Saddle Climbing

The top of the hill is coming up, but you're bogging down! Your heart rate is near max. You feel you may not make it. What now? Out-of-the-saddle climbing. It sounds simple, but this technique can take literally years to perfect—but once you do perfect it, watch out! Mountains become mere speed bumps as you dominate them with your mastery. We've already described the seated-to-standing transition. Just keep in mind that a big key here is to go to a heavier gear just before standing (unless you're already way bogged down and at a low rpm). Next, grab your brake hoods, firmly hooking your middle and ring fingers under the hoods, leaving the index finger available for shifting (if you have STI). Smoothly begin to stand as your dominant leg is coming up from the bottom on the back stroke. But wait: "standing" is a misnomer of sorts. You'll actually maintain somewhat your same "seated" body position, but you'll elevate it. Stay leaned forward a bit, bent at the waist, elbows bent, and butt just off the seat—in fact, it may still be touching the seat nose. Again, this is the classic "cat-pounce" crouch. Now, the pedaling technique: as your dominant leg (let's say it's your right leg) comes over the top of the pedal stroke, begin to pull up with your right arm on the handlebars, leaning, or pulling, your bike to the left. As you push down with the right leg, continue to pull up with the right hand, until the right foot approaches bottom (see photo on page 121). This action is similar to a rowing machine, where you push with your legs while pulling with your arms to exert maximum force on the pedal (the difference on a bike is that the push/pull alternates from right to left instead of simultaneously). In effect, you use your entire body to apply maximum force to the pedals. Now, your right leg is at the bottom, and your left is coming over the top. Pull up again with the left arm, moving the bike to the right, while pushing down with the left, and so on, back and forth, nice and smooth. If you ever have a chance to watch great road cyclists climb, you'll see them use this technique. Here are a few pointers to perfect it.

- You are, in effect, moving your bike back and forth, not your body. Keep your body vertical over the bike, letting the bike sway left and right under you.

- The technique cannot be done effectively or easily at high rpm, so adhere to the rule of dropping a gear or two. Remember that you're also applying maximum full-body power at this point, so the extra gear load should be manageable.

- If you are overrevving, the first thing you'll notice is instead of pulling up on the bars, you transition to pushing down or left and right to keep the "wag" going. This is okay, but it also usually means it's time to do one of two things: sit down, as you have lost your standing efficiency, or drop another gear or two.

- You don't need to sit down to change gears. Unless you have really poor shifting components, you can easily drop a gear while standing.

Time your downshift (or upshift) in between the power strokes, usually on an upstroke of the dominant leg. Back off the pressure just a little, shift, and then push. With practice, this becomes easy.

• Finally, the best way to practice out-of-the-saddle riding is on the flats, and then move to hills later. While cruising along, go up a gear or two (smaller) and smoothly stand up, crank a few strokes, pick up speed, then drop another gear. Smoothly transition back to seated and change gears back up. If you devote one full ride to getting up and down in the saddle, you'll be close to having it mastered. Practicing on the flats is easier than on hills at first.

Wes shows good form for out-of-the-saddle climbing. His bike leans in coordination with the downward power stroke of his right leg and upward pull of his right arm.

Going Over the Top

One of the keys to climbing is to manage hills efficiently, so you're not "blown up" as you near the top. We're all familiar with the concept of building speed in a swim workout, and this is how a hill should be approached when possible. Start out nice and relaxed, and settle in; if you start to "load up," change gears or get out of the saddle. If at all possible, try to save energy to get you over the top. Until you're in good condition and have mastered hill techniques, this may be difficult. We've all seen riders near the crest of a hill completely wasted, with no choice but to dog it over the top and simply coast the downhill. A better approach is just as the hill begins to flatten out, conserve enough energy to "build" rpm, and drop to a bigger gear. The concept is to power over the top and be in good position from a momentum-management standpoint to accelerate down the back side, leaving the novices in your wake, wondering what happened.

Riding Corners

One area where triathletes really seem to miss the boat is cornering. Unless you have raced a criterium (short course, lap-type bicycle race with tight corners), chances are you aren't getting the most out of cornering. We bring up the criterium because many triathlon cycling courses that go around a lake contain features similar to a criterium course, not to mention some nasty hills. In any case, all races have corners, and the more there are in a race, the more important it is to prepare for them.

Rule number one: trust your tires. It's amazing how well the rubber of a good tire holds the road. Typically, the more expensive the tire, the better it holds the road. Many medium-priced bikes come with poor tires, so beware. Also, remember that the narrower the tire, the more grip is reduced during corners. Many time-trial tires are narrow (19 millimeter), so for a course with many tight corners, consider a wider tire.

Next, learn to set up properly for a corner and pick a line. Figure 9.2 shows the most efficient line through a corner. In essence, you're "flattening out" the corner as much as possible. The sequence can be described this way: swing as wide as possible away from the "crux" of the corner while still a considerable distance away from it. On a right turn, swing way over to the left, and do the opposite for a left turn. (Note that most triathlons have a "yellow line" rule, meaning you cannot cross the yellow line without being disqualified. If this rule is enforced, hug the yellow line on the right turn; if not, go over it into the oncoming lane, provided it's safe to do so. For a left turn, the setup isn't critical since you're far right of the line anyway, but be careful about cutting the corner too close to the inside—this may cause a yellow line time penalty.)

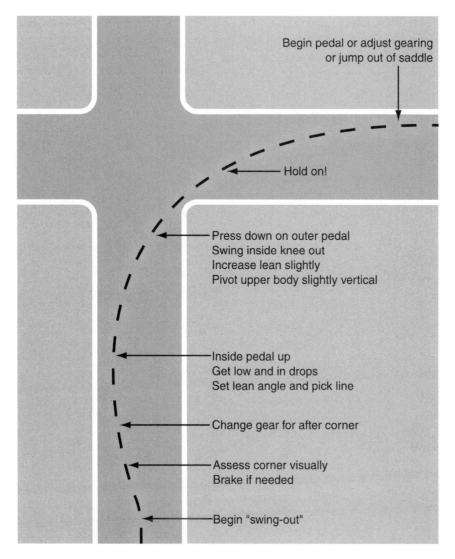

Begin pedal or adjust gearing or jump out of saddle

Hold on!

Press down on outer pedal
Swing inside knee out
Increase lean slightly
Pivot upper body slightly vertical

Inside pedal up
Get low and in drops
Set lean angle and pick line

Change gear for after corner

Assess corner visually
Brake if needed

Begin "swing-out"

Figure 9.2 Riding through a corner.

So, you're in position and ready to "pick your line." At this point, you should have an eye on the whole corner, a sort of macroview. At a point approximately 45 degrees with the corner, start your turn. Depending on speed, skill level, and the severity of the corner, some people refer to this as "diving" into the corner. Be careful, though, as doing this wrong can put you in the ditch on the other side of the corner. Also, watch for obstructions at this point, such as parked cars or road signs.

Some tips on swishing through the corner: if you've picked the right line and have your speed about right, you should sail through smoothly, without having to adjust, wiggle, or bobble. One supreme no-no: don't use your brakes in the corner. Use them before the corner, trying to set your speed just right. If you're in a corner and feel you're too fast, well, about your only choice is to hang on and trust those tires. Lean the bike farther over if disaster is impending. Even a light tap on the front or rear brake *may* bring you down. If you absolutely must brake, relax and gently feather both brakes equally, but even this can ruin an otherwise good day.

As for body position in the corner, keep your body somewhat upright, and "push" the bike down. Once you have picked your line, make sure your inner pedal is up, keep it up, and stop pedaling. Catching a pedal on the pavement is another sure way to send you flying into the ditch. With your outer leg bottomed out, literally press down on this pedal, while slightly angling your torso up, or more vertical (see photo below). This "sets" the bike

Wes' position forces momentum onto the bike. His outer leg is pushing down. His inner knee provides balance. Notice that the front wheel is straight, allowing his lean to take him through the corner.

and tires lower against the turn. You can also angle the inner knee out and down slightly to help compensate and balance.

Once you master this technique, a strange thing happens: you can actually pick up speed going around a corner, instead of slowing down. Yes, you must slow before the corner, but once you pick your line and set your bike, the vector forces involved can actually accelerate you through the corner. This can be quite exhilarating. As you hit the apex, or end of the curve on the far side, just as your bike begins to move back to vertical, smoothly begin to pedal again, using the acceleration of the corner to blast you past all those who don't know how to do it. If the corner is followed by even a slight uphill, consider jumping out of the saddle right after the corner. Whatever you do, make sure you're in the right gear after the corner (this should be set up before the corner).

Some words of caution while cornering:

- Cornering is a high-speed maneuver that must be done carefully. When practicing it, pick a good corner, safe from traffic, and ride it 5 to 10 times from both directions (the difference for some between handling a right and left turn can be remarkable). Experiment with different combinations of the above techniques. Come back to the same corner a week later, ride it some more, then try some other corners.

- You need to decide whether to get out of your aerobars on a corner. Most of the techniques described above are much better and safer if done out of the aerobars. If you're not sure, we recommend getting into your drops. If it is more of a curve than a corner, stay in the aero position; you also may not swing out at all, and you can and should pedal through a curve.

- Be careful in a crowded field. Once you pick your line and go for it, there's little room for adjustment to avoid another, slower biker. It's entirely acceptable to courteously let a cyclist in front of you know you are passing "on your right" or "on your left" by yelling, but it's not acceptable to simply yell at them to get out of the way.

- In wet conditions or if there's sand on the road, do not try to power around corners. You can still use a version of the method, but you must go slow enough to greatly reduce the lean angle on your bike. The bike must stay much more upright—or you won't.

- Really try to see the whole corner; if you can't, back off, as you don't know what might surprise you on the other side.

- When possible, ride the course in advance. Get to know your corners and your lines.

Much has been made about shaving time off a triathlon time trial through aerodynamics and weight reduction, while handling techniques get overlooked. Some triathlon courses have as many as 20 or 30 corners. Take that number and multiply it times the one or two seconds you'll gain per corner, and again you've picked up time with minimal effort and cost.

Aero Positioning

Aero positioning is all about getting flat and presenting the smallest possible frontal area to the wind. Recall the concept discussed in chapter 5 of attempting to "swim through the smallest hole possible." The same concept holds true for time trial cycling.

When you first begin riding in the aero position, it will feel uncomfortable. Relax. Keep your upper body loose, don't overgrip with your hands, don't overflatten your back and rock your pelvis too far forward. Take some time to get used to it. If after a while you still have discomfort, isolate the

Wes in aero position. He's flat and relaxed, not cramped or over-reaching.

affected area and think about what might be the cause. Try making equipment and body adjustments to alleviate the problem. Remember the full range of adjustments available:

- Seat: up, down, forward, back, and tilt, plus shape and cushioning (the aero position places more pressure on certain crotch areas, which takes getting used to, but this can be alleviated with adjustments or a new seat)
- Stem: height and length
- Aerobar: pad placement, nose placement, and extension length
- Cleat orientation to pedal

From Sprint to Stop

Sprinting is seldom used in triathlon, so we'll give it a brief mention only. Sprinting is essentially the same as climbing but usually done on flat ground. You may want to employ a sprint to rocket past a competitor for psychological advantage, or to increase cadence when bogged down, or to gain a leg up on competitors going into transition.

Stopping, or braking, skills are essential. In general, start with your back brake first, applying even and graduating pressure. As soon as you begin to feel some slowing, feather in the front brake, if needed. Adding the front brake supplies a lot of stopping power, so be careful. If you're slowing just a bit, using the back brake only should be fine. If you're in a position where you must stop quickly, body position becomes important. For instance, if you lock up your brakes, especially the front, while in a normal riding position, you could fly over the handlebars, known by mountain bikers as an "endo" or, worse yet, a "face-plant," a term that needs no further description.

If you're going downhill, all the physics of stopping are magnified. What to do? As quickly as possible, even before braking if you can, shift your body weight way back in the saddle. Mountain bikers often shift so far back that they drop off the back of the seat and behind it. If you're in this position, it's practically impossible to endo. For this kind of power stop, your front wheel must be straight. If it's turned at all, down you go, almost every time.

Drafting

Riding in a peleton? If you don't know the word, it's French for ball, cluster, clump, or bunch. And that's what it is while riding: being clumped up with a bunch of riders, drafting to save energy. In the United States, most triathlons don't allow drafting, but in Europe, it's often legal, and in international or Olympic events, it's the norm. We won't enter the great ethical debate of whether drafting should be allowed, as most readers will never race a draft-legal triathlon anyway. The greater worry arises when you've just started to train on your cycle, and you happen to go out riding with a group of road cyclists one day. How do you keep from making them angry, or keep yourself from being intimidated? Here's a few pointers:

- Stay out of your aerobars, period. You can leave them on your bike, but don't use them. They are way too unstable for a group ride.

- The peleton usually works fairly orderly, circulating riders from back to front. This circulating group, known as a paceline, is either a single or double column of riders. If you're uncomfortable, feel free to let the group know you intend to "stay off the back," meaning as lead riders drift out around the paceline to the back, you make room for them to get back into the paceline, catching a draft off the back of the pack.

- Now, you're ready to move through the paceline like the other riders. What do you do? First, relax. It's scary being that close, but tensing up only decreases your bike-handling skills. If it's a double paceline, go through a few times on the inside first, not the outside (outside means the right side or closer to the edge of the road). This way you'll feel less trapped. How close should you ride? Elite riders stay within inches, but you can gain draft advantages at two to three feet. Also, don't follow directly behind. Instead, drift to the right or left just an inch or two, and look up the road. Don't look directly at the butt or wheel right in front of you. Go easy on the brakes. Maintain a steady pace, lightly feathering the brakes only if you must.

There's a lot more information on pack riding and drafting, but if you're new to group riding, these few principles should get you through your first ride. Before long, you'll be rubbing elbows with others at 30-plus mph and thinking nothing of it.

Cycling Drills

Cycling drills can improve your cycling technique in all phases of climbing, descending, sprinting, and hammering the flats. Riding hills returns about the best gain in cycling power and fitness. Here are some things to try:

- During training, sit on most hills. This develops quad strength, which transfers best to flat riding. Sit, and then finish off the hill accelerating over the last third.

- Do your hill repeats in a bigger gear while sitting, with rpms at 50 to 60, focusing on smooth pedaling and keeping the upper body quiet.

- Steady tempo rides on hills, 30 to 60 minutes, under race pace (*tempo* means time is continuous and pace is steady).

- Hill pyramids: on 1 to 3K hill, practice racing up part way, extending the "finish line" each time. If it's a short hill, move the finish line all the way to the top and then back down.

- Hill sprints: jam up a 30- to 60-second hill as hard as you can, with a full recovery in between. Go for quality, repeating 4 to 6 times. Always quit intervals when you're blown—never practice going slow.

- Isolated leg training (ILT): clip one leg into a pedal and rest the other on a chair or on your wind trainer. Spin in an easy gear, concentrating on smooth circles. A good sequence for ILTs is left leg for 30 seconds at 65 rpm; right leg for 30 seconds at 65 rpm; easy pedaling for 1 minute; repeat the set. Then do left leg for 30 seconds at 55 rpm; right leg for 30 seconds at 55 rpm; repeat the set. Over time, increase the duration of each leg spin slowly to a maximum of 2 minutes; always keep rpm between 40 and 65 and gear load low, or easy.

- Try "cruise intervals" of 2 to 4 or 6 to 12 minutes each, hard but *below* race pace. Keep relief periods the same as work periods.

- Pyramid intervals: 1 on–1 off, 2 on–2 off, 3 on–3 off, 2 on–2 off, 1 on–1 off, keeping rest and work periods equal.

- Lactate tolerance, or intervals with incomplete recovery. Just like the pyramids but not as fancy. One to two sets of 4 to 6 reps each, 1 minute on–1 minute off, or varying intervals, should start easy and make it harder, or build. Example: 30 seconds on–1 minute off; next week, 30 seconds on–45 seconds off or 45 seconds on–1 minute off

- Occasional long "mock" time trials of 5K to 10K. We like 5K on trainer or flat wind sheltered road to monitor performance.

- High-cadence work: 5 to 10 minutes, with spin-ups for maximum leg speed.

- Strength/endurance work: 50 to 60 rpms for 3 to 6 minutes each, staying seated, with relaxed upper body, riding into wind or up slight hill, using brakes to add resistance. Repeat three to five times.

- Sprint training. Sprints always presume full recovery, at 4 to 10 minutes between, and 10 to 15 seconds duration only for each sprint. Do four to six reps. Always do less than you know you can—you need to save some energy for training adaptation.

Nothing is quite as exciting as being physically fit; having a great, light, aero bike with trick wheels; being in command of your machine with great fit and biomechanics; and slicing through a time trial with confidence, power, and very little wind noise. Zipping along in the wind rush of a peleton is a close second sensation, and much can be learned from the road-riding side of the equation. When all is in balance, you'll feel like you own the road, with your machine and you operating as one.

Chapter 10

CYCLING WORKOUTS

In this chapter we'll summarize the different types of workouts for cycling, their general purpose, and provide information on how to perform workouts for optimum results. In part V we'll discuss how to put these workouts together in a training program.

Training Zones Summary

Athletes and coaches today realize heart rate is one of the best ways to train for endurance sports. However, it isn't the only way to monitor and evaluate intensity and should be used in conjunction with other systems. Heart rate measures oxygen consumption and your body's "stress" level. Other methods, such as wattage, measure power, a more absolute measurement. Many times, the overly scientific heart rate approach to training becomes so complex that people are inclined to just forget about it and simply work out, as it's too much trouble to understand and organize all the information. Our answer is to set simple rules that make sense and are easy to comprehend. This way you're inclined to consistently follow the plan—which is the key to improvement and eventual success in reaching your goals. The difference between simply exercising randomly or sticking to a structured plan (even if your random exercise is voluminous) is remarkable; in fact if you're pressed for time, you can make greater gains with much less time, if you just follow a plan!

Table 10.1 presents different types of cycling workouts appropriate for each training zone. In this table we show approximate heart rate and percentage of maximum heart rate, and perceived effort (PE). You don't train continuously in Zones 4 and 5; rather these intensities are mixed in as manageable doses within a structured workout, and only after a solid base phase of several weeks has been completed in Zones 1 to 3.

Table 10.1

Cycling Workouts

Training Intensity	Zone: %	PE	Type of workouts	Duration
EN recovery	1: <65	1-2	Solo ride—indoor/outdoor	30-90 min
EN overdistance	2: 65-72	1-4	Solo ride—indoor/outdoor Tour, or up to century-easy	120 min +/-
AP low	3: 73-80	5-7	Solo ride—indoor/outdoor Moderate group ride	20-30 min continuous or intervals
AP high	4: 84-90	7-9	Solo ride—indoor/outdoor Indoor-outdoor intervals Practice time trial Group ride Medium distance road race Moderate/long hill repeats "Brick" workouts	2-12 min duration intervals
SP short	NA	5-6	Indoor/outdoor intervals "Bursts" of speed during any workout	10-20 seconds
SP long	5:91-100	8-10	Indoor/outdoor intervals Criterium road race Medium distance road race Hill repeats "Brick" workouts	30-90 seconds

Sample Workouts

As a supplement to the above guidelines, the following are some sample workouts for each of the training zones.

EN Recovery

Here are some examples of cycling recovery sessions.

- 30 minutes at Zone 1 (under 65 percent of maximum heart rate).
- 40 minutes total: 15 minutes at Zone 1; 10 minutes at Zone 3; 15 minutes at Zone 1.
- 40 minutes total: 15 minutes at Zone 1; 10 minutes of spin up to 120 rpm for 10 seconds every 2 minutes; 15 minutes at Zone 1.

EN Overdistance

The EN overdistance training zone includes any ride of 1.5 hours or more in Zone 2 (about 65 to 72 percent of maximum heart rate). On a hilly course, dipping into Zone 1 and breaking into Zone 3 are inevitable, but try to stay in Zone 2 as much as possible. Add in high cadence spin-ups (120 rpm for 10 to 20 seconds) every 10 or 15 minutes. After base phase is over, increase duration of these workouts incrementally to 2 or 2.5 hours, or longer if training for ultra events.

Long, slow distance rides can sometimes be boring, mind-numbing affairs. While we believe optimal gain comes from an individualized, structured training plan, working out with groups can be highly beneficial for long workouts, breaking the monotony and the possible lack of motivation that may come from training on your own. When training with others, keep your heart rate monitor on. Try to make sure your group workout meets your individual goals. If it doesn't, you can always pull off from the group and finish up with a workout that fits your plan.

You could also try going to your local bike shop and looking for flyers about tours, especially half centuries (50-mile rides) and centuries (100-mile rides). The advantages of these rides include a structured, generally safe ride; distance and route are pre-set and marked; repair services are available; camaraderie; you can learn drafting skills; and, best of all, food is usually served.

It's important to equip yourself on all rides but especially your long-slow-distance rides. Don't learn the hard way! A checklist should include a pump or CO2 cartridge and filler, a spare tube or two, a patch kit; basic tools to change a tire (levers) and make adjustments (Allen wrenches), and maybe also a spoke wrench, one water bottle per ride and two bottles if your ride is over an hour (one of the two should be an energy drink), food of some sort (gel, energy bar, or similar), a cell phone or money for a phone call, and a map.

AP Low

Here are some sample AP low workouts.

- 59 minutes total: 15 minutes warm-up at Zone 2; 5 sets of 5 minutes at Zone 3 with 1 minute rest between; 15 minutes at Zone 1.

- 60 minutes total: 15 minutes at Zone 1; 3×8 minutes at Zone 3 with 3 minutes rest between; 15 minutes at Zone 1.

- 75 minutes total: 10 minutes at Zone 2; 10 minutes at Zone 3; 5 minutes at Zone 2; 20 minutes at Zone 3; 10 minutes at Zone 2; 10 minutes at Zone 3; 10 minutes at Zone 2.

- Steady tempo rides on hills, 30 to 60 minutes, under race pace ("tempo" means time is continuous and pace is steady).

© iphotonews.com/Brooks

Finish off a long hill with an out-of-the-saddle push over the top.

AP High

Here are some sample AP high workouts.

- 50 minutes total: 15 minutes at Zone 1; 5×1 minute at Zone 4 with 30 seconds rest between; 5 minutes rest; 3×2 minutes at Zone 4 with 1 minute rest between; 15 minutes at Zone 1.

- 60 minutes total: 15 minutes at Zone 2; 1 set of 2 on–1 off/4 on–2 off/8 on–4 off/4 on–2 off/2 on–1 off (on is Zone 4, off is easy spin); 15 minutes at Zone 2.

- 60 minutes total: 20 minutes at Zone 1; 2 minutes at Zone 3; 1 minute at Zone 4; 1 minute off; 4 minutes at Zone 3, 2 minutes at Zone 4. 2

minutes off; 2 minutes at Zone 3, 4 minutes at Zone 4, 2 minutes off; 1 minute at Zone 3, 2 minutes at Zone 4, 1 minute at Zone 3; 16 minutes at Zone 1.

- Hill repeats in big gear and sitting, low rpms 50 to 60, focus on smooth pedaling and keeping the upper body "quiet." Do 4 to 6 repeats up a 1-to-3 minute hill, 5+ minutes full recovery in between.

SP Short

SP short training includes bursts of speed (about 10 to 20 seconds) at a high cadence. Depending on overall duration, do 5 to 10 of these bursts during the ride with a full 5 to 10 minutes rest between each effort.

Another method is to pick something such as a street sign, parked car, or telephone pole about 50 meters away as your finish line. Build up speed and sprint to this marker; competing with a friend makes it more fun.

SP Long

The following are some sample SP long workouts.

- 55 minutes total: 20 minutes at Zone 1; 3×30 seconds build to near-max (90-percent) effort, easy spin until heart rate drops to 120; 3×1 minute slow build to max effort, easy spin to heart rate (HR) 120; 3×30 again, rest to 120; 20 minutes at Zone 1. Make sure heart rate drops to a sustained less than 65 percent.

- 67 minutes total: 15 minutes at Zone 1; 30 seconds on, 1 minute off, 1 minute on, 2 minutes off, 1.5 minutes on, 3 minutes off, 1 minute on, 2 minutes off, 30 seconds on; 6 minutes off; repeat "ladder" one more full set; 15 minutes at Zone 1. (On is sustainable [85 to 90 percent] maximum effort; off is very easy recovery spin, but keep spinning, don't coast.)

- During the middle 60 minutes of a 120-minute EN overdistance ride, every 10 minutes choose a marker 100 to 200 meters down the road. Slowly and steadily build to the mark, finishing at near 90-percent effort. Five to six efforts, start at shorter, 100-meter length and increase incrementally to 200 meters. Don't stop to do these; pick the marker while cruising; approximate the 200-meter distance down the road.

- After a thorough warm-up, find a medium-steep hill that takes at least 1 but not more than 2 minutes to climb. Spin up the hill as comfortably as possible, powerful but not maxed-out; leave some juice to go over the top, but don't go over; cruise easy back down, at least 200 meters past the base; turn around and repeat. Do your first set at 4 reps, add one per week up to 8 or as many as 12. Make sure these efforts coincide with your race and training schedule for "peaking" purposes; don't do this workout the last week before a race. Even if an upcoming race is flat, this workout is highly beneficial for building all-purpose power.

Indoor Training

It's amazing the impact triathlon has had on its three sports. So many technologies, concepts, and changes have been spawned from our sport. For instance, cyclists have been spinning on their rollers for years, but it took triathletes, with their intensely structured, indoor group workouts to create a whole new pursuit: indoor spinning. You can now go to any gym in the country, or even to specialized spinning gyms such as the "Johnny G" chain, and spin until you drop.

There is some basic equipment you'll need for indoor training:

- Stationary trainer (see chapter 8 for options)
- Block for front wheel. Most trainers elevate your back wheel 2 to 3 inches. Doing a workout while slowly but constantly sliding off the seat is no fun. A 2-inch-by-4-inch block is fine; the fancier molded plastic units intended for this purpose are nice, as they hold your front wheel steady.
- Heart rate monitor. If you're doing a coached class or your own workout, you need a heart rate monitor for an effective session. With no hills, wind, or competitive companions, you need something to motivate you and create road-like conditions. With a monitor, you can actually improve over road conditions to some degree, as you control the action, not the road.
- Cyclocomputer. Another must; options are covered in chapter 8. We recommend getting a computer with a cadence feature. Nothing is better for "mike-ing in" cadence than indoor spinning. Many spinning workouts use a combination of heart rate, cadence, and speed to optimize time spent in the saddle.
- Towels/headband. Believe us, you're going to sweat. Since you're stationary, there's no cooling from the wind. Placing a fan in front of you is a good idea, but placing a towel underneath you is a must if you don't want to ruin your floor. A headband is also a good idea.
- Sweat guard. This device straps on your bike over the top tube to protect your bike from dripping sweat, which can be corrosive.

One of the great advantages of indoor spinning is that you can do structured, detailed, and targeted workouts that are difficult, if not impossible, to perform outdoors. The following 12-week workout is an example. Provided by elite cycling coach Jim Whittaker of Velo Tek Training, this plan is tailored for his athletes to perform over the winter on a bike trainer after a postseason rest phase, to prepare for the upcoming season. They can also be done on a stationary bike. These workouts can be done once a week, assuming other workouts are done elsewhere during the week, or can be accelerated to twice a week for a 6-week program, but don't overdo it, as the

© Mike Vickers

Indoor spinning is a good way to keep training through the winter.

workouts are more demanding than they may seem. Assuming you have completed other training as well, after completing this schedule, you'll be ready to roll into your first triathlon of the season with strength and confidence in the bike leg.

WEEK 1

0-5 Warm up at 90 to 100 rpm at 60 to 70% maximum heart rate (MHR).

5-8 90 to 100 rpm at 75% MHR.

8-10 Light gear, 95 to 105 rpm.

10-15 Spin-ups. In moderate gear, start at 100 rpm, increase 5 rpm per minute, up to 120 last minute.

15-17 Light gear, 90 to 100 rpm.

17-22 Spin-ups. In moderate gear, start at 100 rpm, increase 5 rpm per minute, up to 120 last minute.

22-25 Light gear, 90 to 100 rpm.

25-34 Isolated leg training (ILT). Pedal circles with one leg using gear that allows you to pedal at a maximum of 65 rpm. One minute each leg, recover for 1 minute light spin both legs, repeat 3 times.

34-36 Light gear, 90 to 100 rpm.

36-41 Spin-ups. In light gear pedal at 140+ rpm for 20 seconds; recover at your own pace for the rest of the minute. Repeat 5 times.

41-43 Light gear, 90 to 100 rpm.

43-51 Isolated leg training. Pedal circles with one leg using gear that allows you to pedal at a maximum of 75 rpm. 30 seconds each leg, recover for 1 minute, repeat 4 times.

51-60 Cool down in light gear, HR < 65% MHR.

WEEK 2

0-5 Warm up at 90 to 100 rpm at 60 to 70% MHR.

5-8 90 to 100 rpm at 75% MHR.

8-10 Light gear.

10-16 Spin-ups. In moderate gear, start at 100 rpm, increase 5 rpm per minute, up to 125 last minute.

16-18 Light gear, 90 to 100 rpm.

18-30 Isolated leg training. Pedal circles with one leg using gear that allows you to pedal at a maximum of 65 rpm. 45 seconds each leg, recover for 45 seconds, repeat 5 times.

30-32 Light gear.

32-42 10 minutes at 80% MHR, normal cadence.

42-45 Light gear.

45-51 Spin-ups. In light gear pedal at 140+ rpm for 20 seconds; recover at your own pace for the rest of the minute. Repeat 6 times.

51-60 Cool down in light gear, until HR < 65% MHR.

WEEK 3

0-5 Warm up at 90 to 100 rpm at 60 to 70% MHR.

5-8 90 to 100 rpm at 75% MHR.

8-10 Light gear.

10-25 Isolated leg training. Pedal circles with one leg using gear that allows you to pedal at a maximum of 80 rpm. 1 minute each leg, then recover for 1 minute, repeat 5 times.

25-27 Light gear.

27-45 Strength endurance pyramid. Pedal a heavy gear with both legs at 50 rpm. Heart rate will be 80 to 90% of MHR. 1:00/2:00/3:00/2:00/1:00, equal time for recovery at 90+ rpm in low gear. Example: 1 minute on/1 minute off, 2 minutes on/2 minutes off.

45-47 Light gear.

47-57 10 minutes at 80% MHR, normal cadence.

57-65 Cool down in light gear, until HR < 65% MHR.

WEEK 4

0-5 Warm up at 90 to 100 rpm at 60 to 70% MHR.

5-8 90 to 100 rpm at 75% MHR.

8-10 Light gear.

10-16 Spin-ups. In light gear pedal at top rpm for 15 seconds, recover at your own pace for the rest of the minute. Repeat 6 times.

16-18 Light gear.

18-38 Strength endurance, 5×2 minutes; pedal a heavy gear with both legs at 50 rpm. Heart rate will be 80 to 90% of MHR. 2 minutes on/2 minutes off; recover in light gear.

38-40 Light gear.

40-50 10 minutes at 80-85% MHR, 60 to 75 rpm. Simulated climbing, alternate in and out of saddle.

50-60 Cool down in light gear, until HR < 65% MHR.

WEEK 5

0-5 Warm up at 90 to 100 rpm at 60 to 70% MHR.

5-8 90 to 100 rpm at 75% MHR.

8-10 Light gear.

10-16 Spin-ups. In light gear pedal at top rpm for 15 seconds; recover at your own pace for the rest of the minute. Repeat 6 times.

16-26 Isolated leg training. Pedal circles with one leg using gear that allows you to pedal at a maximum of 75 rpm. 45 seconds each leg, recover for 30 seconds, repeat 5 times.

26-28 Light gear.

28-48 Strength endurance, 10×1 minute; pedal a heavy gear with both legs at 60 rpm. Heart rate will be 80 to 90% of MHR. 1 minute on/1 minute off; recover in lowest gear at 100 rpm.

48-60 Cool down in light gear, until HR < 65% MHR.

WEEK 6

0-5	Warm up at 90 to 100 rpm at 60 to 70% MHR.
5-8	90 to 100 rpm at 75% MHR.
8-10	105 rpm at 80% MHR.
10-12	110 rpm at 85% MHR.
12-14	115 rpm at 85% MHR.
14-17	Light gear.
17-27	Up-n-downs, 80 rpm out of saddle, 110 rpm in saddle, both at 80 to 85% MHR.
27-31	Light gear.
31-33	115 rpm at 87% MHR.
33-36	110 rpm at 85% MHR.
36-40	105 rpm at 80% MHR.
40-42	Light gear.
42-50	90 to 100 rpm at 80% MHR; big gear acceleration while seated.
50-60	Cool down in light gear until HR < 65% MHR.

WEEK 7

0-5	Warm up at 90 to 100 rpm at 60 to 70% MHR.
5-8	90 to 100 rpm at 75% MHR.
8-23	3×3 on/2 off, at 85 to 90% MHR, 110 rpm.
23-25	Light gear.
25-40	3×3 on/2 off, at 85 to 90% MHR, 100 rpm.
40-42	Light gear.
42-57	3×3 on/2 off, at 85 to 90% MHR, 90 rpm.
57-67	Cool down in light gear until HR < 65% MHR.

WEEK 8

Your choice of rpm during intervals; obtaining target heart rate is more important.

10-minute warm-up, 90 to 100 rpm at 60 to 70% MHR:

4 on/2 off	85% of MHR
4 on/2 off	87% of MHR
3 on/3 off	90% of MHR
2 on/2 off	92% of MHR

3 on/3 off	90% of MHR
2 on/2 off	92% of MHR
4 on/2 off	87% of MHR

6- to 10-minute cool-down in light gear until HR < 65% MHR

WEEK 9

Your choice of rpm during intervals; obtaining target heart rate is more important.

10-minute warm-up, 90 to 100 rpm at 60 to 70% MHR:

4 on/2 off	85% of MHR
4 on/2 off	87% of MHR
3 on/3 off	90% of MHR
2 on/2 off	92% of MHR
3 on/3 off	90% of MHR
2 on/2 off	92% of MHR
4 on/2 off	87% of MHR

6- to 10-minute cool-down in light gear until HR < 65% MHR

WEEK 10

Your choice of rpm during intervals; obtaining target heart rate is more important.

10-minute warm-up, 90 to 100 rpm at 60 to 70% MHR:

2:00	85% of MHR
2:00	87% of MHR
2:00	90% of MHR
2:00	92% of MHR
2:00	90% of MHR
2:00	87% of MHR
2:00	85% of MHR
5:00	70% of MHR
4:00	85% of MHR
3:00	87% of MHR
2:00	90% of MHR
2:00	70% of MHR
4:00	85% of MHR
3:00	87% of MHR
2:00	90% of MHR

6- to 10-minute cool-down in light gear until HR < 65% MHR

WEEK 11

Your choice of rpm during intervals; obtaining target heart rate is more important.

10-minute warm-up, 90 to 100 rpm at 60 to 70% MHR:

4:00	85% of MHR
2:00	70% of MHR
6:00	87% of MHR
2:00	70% of MHR
10:00	Under 90% 1st half; race pace 2nd half
6:00	70% of MHR
10:00	Race pace time trial

6- to 10-minute cool-down in light gear until HR < 65% MHR

WEEK 12

Your choice of rpm during intervals; obtaining target heart rate is more important.

10-minute warm-up, 90 to 100 rpm at 60 to 70% MHR:

4:00	85% of MHR
2:00	70% of MHR
6:00	87% of MHR
2:00	70% of MHR
10:00	Under 90% 1st half; race pace 2nd half
6:00	70% of MHR
10:00	Race pace time trial

6- to 10-minute cool-down in light gear until HR < 65% MHR

Reprinted, by permission, from Jim Whittaker M.S., 2001, *Velo tek training*. (Lawrence KS).

Advantages and Disadvantages of Indoor Spinning

Indoor spinning is a favored mode of bicycle training by many triathletes. It carries distinct advantages, along with some disadvantages. We'll list both here so you can decide if indoor spinning is right for you.

Advantages

- It's safer, with no traffic to contend with, so it presents slight risk of injury.
- It's a fantastic option when the weather is grim.
- No more, "Oh my god, I have a flat, I'm all alone, it's getting dark, I forgot my pump!"
- You can really focus on the highly beneficial concept of "spinning" at high rpm.

- You can load your legs up with a heavy gear and low rpm, as a pure strength workout.
- Isolated leg training is possible (and recommended).
- It's much easier to do a structured workout that you're in complete control of.
- A spinning workout can be actively coached, like a Masters swim workout.
- Precise heart rates, speeds, and cadences can be achieved, so it's generally a more efficient, less time-consuming workout.
- No time is spent "coasting"; typically, you are pedaling all the time. Most coaches acknowledge that this is equal to spending one and a half to two times the same amount of time on the road.
- If you want to, you can listen to blaring funky music the whole time or watch TV.

Disadvantages

- You won't learn bicycle-handling techniques.
- The bike doesn't move at all (with the slight exception of rollers, where balance is required). Thus, balance is not enhanced, and pedaling out of the saddle is rather meaningless.
- It's a hot and sweaty endeavor.
- There are no corners to practice negotiating.
- Climbing a hill cannot be replicated.
- There's no beautiful scenery or fresh air.
- There's no benefits of drafting or peleton fun.
- There's no learning to ride in wind, rain, or other crappy conditions.
- There's no aerodynamic feel.
- In general, indoor spinning is much less physically and mentally challenging than the open road.

What do we recommend? Spin in the winter, focusing on pedaling technique and building your base. As spring hits, go outside on the nice days, and stay inside and spin on the bad days. As spring gives way to summer's splendor, go outside and stay outside. As fall approaches, stay outside as much and as long as you can. When old man winter comes, take a break from it all for a couple of weeks, or consider riding your mountain bike on gravel roads, if you have one. If you have the good fortune to live in a warm climate year-round, our advice is to train outside as much as you can. It's the best way to get ready for a race, which, unless things really change, will always be outside.

Part IV
RUN

SWIM
BIKE
RUN

Chapter 11

RUNNING EQUIPMENT

After acquiring all that biking gear, your checkbook might be hammered. The good news is that running equipment is going to cost you much less (less than swimming, too, if you factor in monthly pool or Master's fees). For running, the only real expense is shoes. But your choice of which shoes to buy is an important one. Because of the highly repetitive use of certain muscles and the related impact on tendons and joints, running carries the highest risk of injury. A quality pair of shoes with correct fit and the right features for your gait go a long way toward injury prevention. Most other items we mention are useful and comfortable, but you can decide whether you really need $16 socks or not.

Finding the Right Shoe

Running need not be the injury nemesis of triathletes. You can avoid many of the typical injuries by training and racing in a quality pair of shoes. Don't even consider running in cross-training shoes—or in tennis shoes, basketball shoes, or any other shoe not made specifically for running. These shoes are designed completely different from running shoes and are no good for sustained running. For some activities you need a shoe that supports a lot of lateral motion, and if you're into these activities, you'll need to buy separate shoes. Running is a straight-ahead, heel-strike activity. While running, your heel strike produces a force many times that of your body weight, and this force is transferred up your legs and back. The degree of impact and other forces, such as pronation, are controlled by your shoes. High-quality shoes provide exceptional cushioning that absorbs impact. Cheap shoes often don't provide enough cushioning. So don't be a cheapskate when it comes to your shoes—remember that you're protecting much more than your feet.

Features of running shoes to protect your body from impact with the ground become more sophisticated each year. Before you select your running shoes, you need to know which category of runner you are relevant to foot motion. Every foot and leg go through the same basic motion while running; the foot starts by rolling out to prepare for impact. Most people land on the outside of the heel, then the foot relaxes and rolls inward; this rolling in is called pronation. The rolling motion allows the foot and body to adapt to different surfaces and absorb shock. After the pronation, which is the "neutral" part of the cycle, body weight transfers over the ball of the foot to prepare for springing off the ground. Runners fall into one of three categories: neutral pronation, overpronation (excessive inward motion), and underpronation (not enough inward motion). Motion other than neutral pronation can lead to pain or injury.

You can determine your pronation category in two ways: by analyzing your old running shoes, which can give you a good idea of your pronation style and subsequent shoe solution (see figure 11.1); or by doing the wet foot test. To do the wet foot test, lay paper on a hard floor, dip your foot in water, and take a stride on the paper. Match your footprint to those shown in figure 11.2 to determine your run mechanics and shoe category.

Here are a few other tips for picking your shoes:

- Take your time. There are hundreds of shoe brands, and they all feel different. Shoe "feel" is a very personal thing.

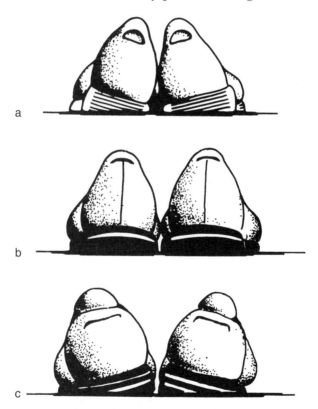

a

b

c

Figure 11.1 (a) You can see the excessive rotation of the foot in the inside wear on the shoes. (b) Normal rotation is evident when there is even wear on the shoes. (c) Lack of rotation is apparent when shoes wear on the outside.

Reprinted, by permission, from Town and Kearney, 1994, *Swim, Bike, Run.* (Champaign, IL: Human Kinetics), 44.

Overpronator
- Motion control shoe
- Straight shape
- Board or combination last

Neutral
- Stability shoe
- Semicurved shape
- Combination or sciplast

Underpronator
- Motion control shoe
- Board or combination last
- Possible extra cushioning, add arch support inserts

Figure 11.2 The wet-foot test guide.

- Once you narrow your choice to two or three, put one brand on one foot and another on the other foot to compare the differences.

- Make sure you ask about the seller's return policy. Many shoe dealers let you return shoes even after you have run in them once or twice, so keep out of the mud or run on a treadmill your first couple of runs in case you change your mind about the shoes.

- Once you find a shoe brand and style you really like, you'll probably want to stick with it. But when you need a new pair, go ahead and try on different brands to confirm that your usual shoes are still the most comfortable.

- Feet swell throughout a day or after a workout, so try new shoes on late in the day or after a run.

- The heel and midfoot areas should fit snug, but the forefoot area should have ample room.

- Most triathletes usually don't wear socks. If that's your preference make sure your shoes fit well without them.

A primary consideration in shoe selection is your weight, as greater weight means higher impact. If you're a man who weighs more than 180 pounds or a woman who weighs more than 150 pounds, consider buying heavier duty shoes with firmer cushioning and increased overall stability. The extra support is worth the extra weight of the shoe.

After a run, the cushioning foam in shoes is compressed but has "memory"—in other words, it takes awhile for the foam to re-expand to its original form. This is why most elite runners have two or more pairs of training shoes. With the mega-mileage they put in, often running twice a day, they alternate shoes to ensure maximum cushioning at all times. Even if you're training once a day, you can benefit by alternating shoes from day to day.

How often should you replace your shoes? As often as you can afford to. Most experts agree that you shouldn't try to get more than 400 to 500 miles out of a pair of shoes—and if you're heavy, you'll get significantly less. A worn-out shoe almost always leads to injury. Slapping on new shoes after racking up mileage on your old treads is like a run in the clouds.

Several factors can make running shoes more comfortable for you. Consider the following details when selecting a pair of shoes:

- A notch in the back of the heel collar can prevent irritation of the Achilles tendon.

- An external "heel counter" provides additional support and controls overpronation.

- A forefoot stability strap, made of leather or plastic, reinforces the upper part of the shoe, providing stability and support

- How well vented is the shoe? Look for a shoe with "breathability."

- Check for ample forefoot cushioning—some runners need more than others. Talk to an expert if you're not sure how much you need.

- Is the shoe easy to get on and off?

- There are different ways to lace a running shoe, with different results. Talk to your favorite shoe expert about your options.

- If you have high arches, look for shoes with extra arch pads that can be placed under the shoe inserts. If you have arch pain during or after a run, try putting the pads in. If you don't like them, you can always take them out again. Even better, consider buying high-quality shoe inserts (made by Scholls, Sorbothane, and others) that cover a variety of possible problems and enhance your shoe's performance. Make sure, though, that you get the right size shoe to allow room for the inserts.

Training shoes are made to absorb the force produced from foot strikes in your everyday training runs. When it comes to shoes, quality is critical, as poor quality or incorrect shoes can put you at risk of serious injury. Don't let the price prevent you from purchasing the best shoe for your foot. Anything that lowers injury risk is a valuable investment. Steer clear of cheap training shoes—they are made for people who run little or not at all.

Racing Flats

A whole other category of shoes is the racing flat. During your distance training runs, speed is not of much concern. Getting fit and preventing injury are your priorities. When it comes to racing, you might want to consider buying racing flats. Lighter than training shoes, flats can give you a slight

Make sure shoes are easy to slip on for fast transitions.

improvement in speed (for many runners, the difference is just a second or two per mile). Because they are lighter, racing flats do not provide as much cushioning and support as training shoes do.

Since in a triathlon you're already fatigued from the swim and the bike by the time you start running, the weight saved by wearing a racing flat may not outweigh the comfort and protection the training shoe offers. Conversely, for some athletes, the weight saving may help overcome some fatigue. In any case, before convincing yourself that you must have a pair of racing flats, consider if you want to sacrifice extra comfort and protection for a slight gain in speed. Most athletes think flats are beneficial at distances of 10K and less, and that regular shoes are better for longer races.

In chapter 13 we cover speedwork, or interval training. We don't recommend doing all your speedwork in racing flats, but this is a good opportunity to determine if flats are right for you. Try them during speedwork and see how they feel. For many, the difference in "feel" is great—what might be described almost as barefoot running. So, some of the gain by using flats may be psychological, and that alone may be worth the investment. If you feel like you're flying, maybe that will help you fly. However, any foot or knee pain that develops is not worth the real or perceived gain. If you're a heavy runner, you probably shouldn't race in flats.

Trail Shoes

And a brief word about trail shoes: If you train heavily on trails, and some do because of the great cushioning offered as compared with the streets and sidewalks, you may want to consider trail shoes. The general difference between trail and regular shoes is a more aggressive tread design and increased stiffness. But be careful! This rigidity and durability can translate into decreased cushioning. We tend to avoid trail shoes; regular running shoes still work fine on most trails anyway.

Clothing

Clothing considerations for running focus on comfort, whereas in cycling, the focus is on performance. Since, in the long run, comfort affects performance, we recommend investing in good running accessories.

Socks

You've got plenty of socks in your drawer already, so why buy more? Because athletic socks are cushioned to protect your feet, and they supplement shoe cushioning. Many are also made from high-tech fibers that wick moisture to keep feet dry, cool, and blister free. Keep in mind, though, that many competitive triathletes don't bother with socks in races because pulling dry socks on over wet feet after the swim significantly slows transition time (an exception is ultradistance racing, where socks are generally a good idea). If you opt out of socks for racing, make sure you do considerable training in this mode so that you avoid blistering. Blister prevention is a prime function of socks. As you probably know, a one-centimeter blister in the wrong spot can bring down the mightiest triathlete.

Whether you wear socks or not should influence your selection of shoe size. Ill-fitting shoes are the primary cause of blisters. Shoes should fit well and be laced firmly to prevent blisters. Saving five seconds in transition by not properly lacing can lose you much more time during the race, if you develop blisters. Wet feet can also cause blisters, so have a towel ready in transition and dry your feet quickly before putting on your shoes—dry feet go into shoes much easier, anyway.

Shorts and Tights

Good running shorts are light, comfortable, and inexpensive. They are cut in a way that allows free, unencumbered movement and made from material that keeps you dry. Most shorts have "built-in" underwear negating the need to wear anything underneath.

If you're running in the cold, then along with a good, breathable running jacket, hat, and gloves, we recommend that you wear running tights, which come in different weights for different temperatures and which are much more comfortable than wearing floppy sweats. Running in cold weather is tricky, as you must strive to be comfortable; being too cold is miserable and dangerous, and if you're too hot, you sweat, which can cause potentially unnoticed dehydration and dangerously cold conditions (since you are wet). Experiment with combinations of clothes to see what works best for you. Numerous, breathable layers are usually best, as you can shed them or don them incrementally as temperatures change.

© iphotonews.com/Brooks

This triathlete gets an advantage by wearing well-designed racing attire.

Tops

A singlet is a tank top made of lightweight material, designed to fit snugly and keep you cool. A T-shirt works fine but tends to soak up sweat and not evaporate or disperse it. Racing in a singlet keeps you cooler and makes you feel better. Any clothing flapping in the breeze during running, cycling, or (worst of all) swimming adds fatigue because of unnecessary drag.

For women, a sports bra is a must. Conventional bras lead to cuts and abrasions that can be more severe than blisters from bad shoes. In fact, some women wear two sports bras for extra support and comfort. Most are designed to be worn with nothing over the top, for maximum cooling. For racing, women should wear a swimsuit that offers adequate support or consider wearing a sports bra under the swimsuit; this way, drag is not increased but support is there for the run.

Other Accessories

If you're running in the heat, you may need a hat for cooling and UV protection. The sun beating down on your head and face can be dangerous. UV rays in the eyes are also dangerous, so wear your sunglasses, preferably ones that won't slip down your sweaty nose and that offer protection from wind and debris while biking. Protecting your eyes and face from the sun keeps your face relaxed, which triggers a degree of relaxation throughout your body.

Hydration while running is also a consideration, especially for those doing long runs while training for ultra-distance events. Making water stops or stashing water is one answer, but several companies make good quality belts for carrying water, and a "camelback" is another option, although it can be uncomfortable. When evaluating a running belt, think comfort. If running causes your water-laden belt to jiggle around annoyingly, you simply won't use it. Some water belts hold water in multiple containers for better loading. This also allows you to separate water from your favorite sports drink. Many water belts feature useful pouches for stashing solid foods as well.

Once you have found the right shoes and everything else you need for running, you can turn your attention to running technique.

Chapter 12

RUNNING TECHNIQUE AND TRAINING

Serious runners who want to run faster and longer while staying healthy and minimizing risk of injury spend considerable time practicing and perfecting their running technique. Good running technique is especially important for the triathlete. Even the strongest runners struggle to find a comfortable stride coming off the bike. Cycling emphasizes different leg muscles than running. Your legs have to go through an incredible transition from cycling to running and they will likely feel like concrete. Add this to the fact that you are already fatigued from the first two events. But since the run is the last event in a triathlon, it can make or break you. Learning to run efficiently with good technique is crucial to saving energy, preventing injury, and is the key to successful training and racing.

Running Posture

The next time you get a chance to watch Michael Johnson run the 200 or 400, pay close attention to his running posture. You'll notice that his upper body is so upright that he seems almost to be leaning backward. His hips seem thrust somewhat forward, and his leg cycle is centered, or balanced, below his body. Of course, all of this is most clearly seen when you watch a film of Johnson in slow motion. In real life, his speed is just a blur.

Watch any other great sprinter, middle-distance runner, or distance runner, and you'll see they all share the same, upright posture. They seem to float over the ground effortlessly, with grace and agility. Most novice runners lean too far forward, which results in a "putting on the brakes" effect—they must overstride to compensate for the forward body lean. Overstriding adds stress on the legs, from the pelvis down, and is a principal cause of injury. At 1,000 to 1,500 strides per mile, extra impact caused by poor posture and overstriding eventually adds up to tendon and joint problems, stress fractures, fasciitis, back problems, and other injuries.

152

You avoid overstriding by running with proper posture. The starting point for gaining proper posture is your hips. Focus on literally rotating, or tipping, your hips upward. Practice this while standing. Proper posture has been described as imagining your hips as a bucket filled with water; most people must rotate hips forward to keep water from spilling out of the front, so the final correct rotation of your hips should be relatively level. This rotation has the net effect of moving your upper body to vertical and your overall stride forward (see photo below). This forward movement alleviates overstriding, as your stride is not "reaching" to compensate for forward body lean. It's important to have your complete stride cycle centered below your upper body; imagine each leg cycle as a smooth circle, with exactly 50 percent of the circle in front of your body and 50 percent behind. You'll find

Wes shows good running posture. He is upright with his head up, hips forward, and knee high. Notice the straight line from the middle of his hip to his ear.

that along with correct posture a shorter stride facilitates this balance much easier.

Check out Michael Johnson's stride. His stride is so short and quick you may wonder how he can be so fast. The answer is that his form is close to perfect. If you perfect your form, you'll be faster, expend less energy, and reduce your risk of injury. When running with correct form, your gait is smooth and comfortable, with a decreased impact and a balanced stride, and your head is slightly back, up, and smooth. Always focus your eyes on the horizon or on a point about 50 feet in front of you, not on the ground at your feet. Head position is very important to maintaining good posture, along with pulling your shoulders back. The first signs of fatigue are drooping head and shoulders (watch novice runners toward the end of a marathon); this impairs your overall posture and efficiency.

Moving down the body, the arms should be relaxed while maintaining a ninety-degree elbow bend. Hands are held partially open or in a relaxed fist and move forward and backward in the direction you are going, not side to side.

Your stride should be relaxed and smooth. A key to balance a smooth yet powerful stride under your body is to pull your knees up slighty to start the

Checklist for Effective Running Form

Several things should be on your mind as you're trying to perfect your technique. Once you gain the right technique and practice it, the technique will become automatic, but until then you'll need to focus on getting it right. Here's a checklist to use while you're on the road or track.

- Head position: prop your chin and keep the back of your head in line with your back; keep neck curve to a minimum.

- Shoulder position: down and back; think of your shoulder blades as almost touching.

- Hip position: tip hips up and in; support the low back with the abs.

- Arm position: keep your elbows at 90 degrees and swing forward and back; minimize the arms crossing the body.

- Knee position: keep knees moving horizontally; avoid excessive up-and-down movement.

- Foot plant: let your foot fall directly below your knee, and then swing it forward; minimize the contact time your foot has with the ground.

- Stride tempo: strive for a quick turnover instead of increasing stride length; if you minimize ground contact time, your legs will be off the ground more, creating momentum.

cycle. You should feel as if your knee is "driven" through the upper, or forward, part of the stride, with the lower leg relaxed, almost "dangling." Foot plant should be light and quick, straight forward (not crossing over) but also under your body (not overstriding), with a balanced heel/toe strike. On the back side of the cycle begin with a good forward push off with the ball of the foot and toes, relax and allow the lower leg and heel to pendulum up (the "kick") and begin to elevate the knee and drive it forward, to start over again. Your overall stride cycle is better if it's shorter and quick tempo as opposed to a long, loping gait. A lot to think about? Yes, but you'll be amazed at how much small improvements in your running form can result in big gains. The only way to break bad habits and start good ones is to practice. The drills at the end of this chapter are designed to help improve form. Note too that the best time to work on your running form is during the off-season.

Common Technical Errors

It's easy to decrease your technical errors in running technique if you're willing to slow down a little and think about form. The "naturalness" of running is a double-edged sword; it can be easy to do but equally easy to fall into inefficient habits. The key to effective multisport running is to make it as efficient as possible. Some common mistakes are overstriding, crossing over, and excessive bouncing.

Overstriding

Overstriding is a common fault among triathletes. It occurs when the foot lands out in front of the knee, and it has the same effect as putting on a brake. Overstriding results in a too lengthy foot–ground contact time; the less time the feet are on the ground, the more time they have to create momentum. If your running shoes wear out quickly at the heel, you are likely an overstrider.

Faster running is more a function of stride frequency (the number of strides taken) than stride length (distance of each stride). Most of us have plenty of stride length, as long as we're flexible in the hip flexors and hamstrings. Many triathletes and novice runners feel if they take longer strides, they will go faster; but this always results in overstride. Pick up your stride frequency and focus on keeping your feet below your knees at the front.

To correct overstriding, let your foot drop below your knee as you finish the forward movement of your stride. Imagine running from the hip to the knee, with your lower leg relaxing throughout the stride. You'll notice that you land toward the front of the foot. Athletes who land midfoot and forward typically do not overstride. Also, practice "fast feet"—think about quick tempo (frequency) with manageable stride length. A great way to practice this is running quickly down hills. (More on this later.)

Crossing Over

Crossing over is another malady that plagues triathletes. Crossover occurs when the foot plant crosses over the midline of the body; often, the arm swing crosses over the midline as well. Remember that the shortest distance between two points is a straight line—crossover truly adds to the distance you run. If you cross over a mere two inches with each step, at 1,000 to 1,500 strides per mile the extra distance really adds up!

To fix crossover, think of always keeping your hips moving forward. Relax, and let them move in a straight, flat line parallel to the ground. Swing your arms forward and backward, not left and right—never crossing the chest. Keep your shoulders low and relaxed while forming a 90-degree angle at the elbow. Your lower arm should always be parallel to the ground, with hands relaxed and moving front and back. You can practice arm swing while sitting down, which is a good drill for people with crossover problems. Last, think about your knee-to-foot landing directly below the same hip. You may feel as if you're running "wider," especially if you have chronic crossover, but over time the correct stride will feel more natural, and you'll add less distance to your run.

Excessive Bounce

Bounce adds vertical distance to your run and consumes energy that should be used to move forward. We have all seen runners bounding down the road, almost like kangaroos or long jumpers. Bounce is common in multisport racing, especially after the transition from bike to run. After cycling at 20+ mph during the bike leg, runners perceive their movement as too slow during the initial stages of the run. To compensate, triathletes often bounce and overstride in an effort to feel faster, but this usually results in early fatigue.

You can combat bounce in a couple of ways. First, always imagine the ground as a horizontal force plate rather than a vertical force plate. Drive forward, not upward, with each pushoff. Second, minimize your knee lift; knees should move directly forward and back. You can also keep bounce in check by focusing on stride frequency; a fast tempo can only be supported by a stride that moves forward.

Using a Video Camera

Watching yourself on video is an excellent way to help correct flaws in your running form. While you're running, have a friend tape you from directly in front, from the side, and from behind. Watch the footage in slow motion, and you might be surprised at what you see.

Crossover can easily be detected from a head-on shot. If your hip and foot form an angle at all, or if your arms swing in front of your chest, you are crossing over. If you shoot your video at a track, take the front shot while running over the top or straddling the lane lines. If your foot hits or crosses the line, you are crossing over.

A side shot is the best way to spot an overstride. If your foot is landing beyond your knee, your stride length is too long. You'll notice a classic "heel-to-toe" foot strike. Ideally, your foot should land smooth and more or less flat, directly beneath your knee.

Front and side shots can help you detect bounce. Bounce is easiest to see if there's a building or something in the background. Watch the top of your head: does it bounce up and down? Remember that you want to go forward as you run, so your head should remain somewhat level. Once you minimize bounce, you feel as if you could balance a book on your head while running.

After viewing your initial tape, work on fixing your form while you run for three to four weeks. Then have your friend tape you again while running at race speeds, and see how much improvement you have made. The best runners in the world are always looking for ways to improve their technique to maximize efficiency. You'll notice a big difference in your running ability as you start to control overstride, crossover, and bounce.

Hill Running Technique

There are special techniques to use in running uphill and downhill. Since courses are seldom pancake flat, excellent form on the hills can significantly help running performance.

Uphill Technique

Focus on form and technique running up the hill. Lean slightly into the hill, using your arms, high knees, and rapid turnover. Minimize foot–ground contact time by shifting foot plant to the balls of the feet (see photo *a* on page 158). Keep momentum forward and the level of physical effort relatively constant. Imagine you have a shoulder harness with several balloons attached, lifting you up the hill. Don't make the mistake of putting in too much effort going up the hill—you'll waste too much energy to finish the race!

Downhill Technique

Many great runners, such as Bill Rogers, are average uphill runners but compensate by running super downhills. When going downhill, you must allow gravity to do its work. Learning to allow your arms and legs to move quickly is a must for great downhill running form (see photo *b* on page 158). Also, a natural tendency for some is to lean back against gravity, putting on the brakes. Remember, don't stand in the way of gravity—lean slightly forward, let it grab you and pull you forward, and take advantage of the assistance! You can practice these skills along with many others, after reading the next section on drills.

a   b

Lean into the uphill and let gravity do the work running downhill while keeping your stride quick.

Running Technique Drills

The drills below enhance your running form and help your neuromuscular system adapt to changes in your running technique. In choosing which drills are best for you, ask advice from your coaches or running friends. Try selecting two or three drills to do during your warm-up or after an easy run. You should do them at least once a week.

SINGLE LEG DRILLS

Stand with your body perpendicular to a wall. Place one hand on the wall for balance, assume a proper upright running posture, and plant your inside leg with knee slightly bent. Move your outside leg quickly and repetitiously through several (10 to 20) stroke cycles. Start with your foot highly elevated, at or near the stationary knee. Quickly move through a cycle, with your foot brushing or snapping the ground, landing slightly in front and leaving the ground slightly behind your stationary foot. Use a high recovery behind, with your heal brushing your butt, if possible. Pause momentarily at the top of the stroke, and then repeat. If possible, have a friend view this drill from the side and give you feedback. The entire cycle, or the circle described by the movement of the foot, should be centered below the body. Switch legs and repeat at least twice. This drill enhances balance, strength, and coordination on both sides of the body.

HORIZONTAL BOUNDING

This drill improves strength and flexibility. Run with an exaggerated stride, trying to go as far forward as possible. Think "light feet" and see how few strides you need to cover 50 meters. Do four to six 50-meter bounding runs per session.

VERTICAL BOUNDING (OR HIGH KNEE DRILL)

In this drill you try to get as high as you can with each stride. Drive knees up and forward. This drill improves flexibility and strength, especially in the hip flexors. Do three to five 50-meter repeats.

POWER SKIPPING

This drill emphasizes the leg drive of the leg swinging through. The drill is just like vertical bounding, but you do it while skipping (see photo on page 160). Do three to five 50-meter repeats of this drill.

STRIDE COUNT

We covered stroke count in swimming and cadence in cycling so you understand their importance. Stride count in running is equally important yet receives little attention. Remember that a generally shorter stride with a light foot plant is more efficient than a longer stride. During your more intense running sessions (aerobic power or SP long), count your stride cycles for one minute (count one leg only). Most elite runners complete nearly 90 cycles a minute. If you're not at or near 90, work on shortening your stride a little and increasing your leg turnover or tempo. The process may be gradual, but practicing several one-minute sessions over a few weeks during your warm-up helps the goal of 90 become second nature.

Power skipping helps with form and improves functional strength. It's also a good way to warm up and cool down.

STRIDES

On a flat (and preferably soft) surface, and after a good warm-up, run smooth and fast for 100 to 200 meters (see photo on page 161). This drill should be a "build", and ends when you hit near top speed. Smooth power is the key, as this is not an all-out sprint. Try to imitate your work in the single leg drill: maintain good posture, keep knees high and foot plants fast and light; keep recovery high, also, with heals practically brushing your butt. Concentrate on light feet. Perform four to six repeats, walking back to the starting point between each stride. Then go directly into your main workout. Strides are also beneficial after a long, slow workout, when your muscles feel tight and achy. Strides facilitate recovery and remind you to lengthen your stride, which may have been shortened through fatigue.

Count your stride cycles and be more efficient.

DOWNHILL STRIDES

You can do this drill every time you go downhill. Let gravity do the work as your legs move smoothly and effortlessly down the hill. This drill helps running coordination and is great practice for learning how to run effectively downhill.

Focusing on your running form is your first step to increased efficiency. Always look for ways to move faster, with less effort.

Chapter 13

RUNNING WORKOUTS

Now that your technique is perfected (or at least you're aware of good technique and are working hard to improve), here are some triathlon-specific workout ideas to increase your speed and endurance. If you're like most of us, your training time comes at a premium, so making the most of your workouts is essential. We present the "macroplan" for training in chapter 14, so that won't be covered here. And for very specific training plans tailored to different distance triathlons, see chapter 15. In this chapter, we'll introduce several workouts and running recommendations useful to most triathletes.

Training Zone Summary

As we did for cycling, we'll present a summary of training zones and types of workouts applicable to each. In table 13.1 we show approximate heart rate, actual zone and percentage of maximum heart rate, and also "PE" for "perceived effort." In part V, we'll show you how to put these workouts into a structured triathlon training plan.

Sample Workouts

What follows are sample run workouts for each training zone.

EN Recovery

EN recovery consists of easy runs, usually done the day after a hard or long workout, or after a race. These runs will be about 20 to 40 minutes at EN recovery heart rate (less than 65 percent of your max HR).

EN Overdistance

EN overdistance consists of one- to two-hour efforts at 65 to 72 percent of max heart rate. Build duration of efforts slowly over time. If you're focusing on

Table 13.1

Running Training Zones

Type of training	Zone: %	PE	Type of workouts and tips	Duration
EN recovery	1: <65%	1-2	• Thorough warm-up and cool down, very low effort • Lots of stretching after warm up and completion • Consider soft surfaces—dirt trails or good-quality track • Low speed treadmill	20-40 min
EN overdistance	1: <65% 2: 65-72%	1-4	• Long group runs at your pace; running with others helps with monotony • Try changes of scenery and routes • Hydration is a must, caloric intake advisable • Soft surfaces are wise • Periodic speed bursts of 10 to 30 seconds helps • Lots of stretching afterwards • Water running	50-120 min or more if training ultra distance
AP low	3: 73-80%	5-7	• Moderate "tempo" runs • Moderate "fartlek" (changing tempo, continuous runs) • Run with a friend who is slightly faster, but don't overdo it! • Very moderate hill repeats or simply a hilly course • "Brick" workouts	20-30 min continuous or long intervals
AP high	4: 84-90%	7-9	• Structured track interval workout with thorough warm-up and cool-down • "Training" 5K, 10K, or half-marathon race • Longer, more challenging hill repeats • "Brick" workouts • Group run with the fast guys, but drop to your pace when necessary • Challenging trail run	Medium-distance intervals, 800- to 1,600-meter repeats at 10K or half-marathon race pace 30-60 min

(continued)

Table 13.1 *(continued)*

Type of training	Zone: %	PE	Type of workouts and tips	Duration
SP short	NA	5-6	• Very thorough warm-up and cool-down	10- to 30-sec bursts
			• Track interval workout, short repeats	50- to 200-meter repeats
			• "Bursts" of speed during any workout	
SP Long	5: 91-100%	8-10	• Thorough warm-up and cool-down	30-120 sec
			• Track interval workout	
			• 800 meter to mile track or road race	Up to 400 meter repeats
			• Intense 200- to 400-meter hill repeats	

a sprint or Olympic race distance, overdistance duration should build up to twice the race distance or duration. If you're focusing on a race distance of a half-marathon or longer, overdistance should equal 1 to 1.5 times the race distance or duration. Occasionally, add in four or as many as eight tempo speed bursts of 10 to 30 seconds, spaced 5 to 10 minutes apart (see short speed).

If aches and pains are a problem, try running on softer surfaces to increase shock absorption on your legs. Dirt and grass trails and gravel roads are preferred. Asphalt is the next choice. Concrete is the worst running surface.

AP Low Workouts

The following are some examples of appropriate AP low workouts.

- Fartlek runs, where you change tempos randomly from EN overdistance to in and around AP heart rate. The duration of "on" (up tempo) and "off" (EN tempo) should be about equal. The overall duration of the run should be about 40 to 60 minutes.

- Tempo runs, which are more sustained efforts at AP low heart rate. Warm up easy for 10 to 15 minutes. Build slowly to AP low, hold for 10 minutes, (or up to 40 minutes if training for longer distances), and finish off at EN Recovery for 10 to 15 minutes.

- Any run of 30 to 60 minutes, alternating long intervals of EN overdistance to AP low, back and forth at intervals of 4 to 8 minutes. For example, 12 minutes EN overdistance; 8 minutes AP low; 8 minutes EN overdistance; repeat; finish with 12 minutes EN recovery.

A Word From Wes

Sprucing Up the Looong Run!

Almost every coach and authority on the subject preach that a long run every week or two can help improve your running performance. The long run strengthens tendons and coordinates muscles to prepare the body for more strenuous faster-paced running. More importantly, the long run mentally prepares you for the running segment of a triathlon, which is usually shorter in distance than your long runs. I am much more confident going into the 10K segment of a triathlon knowing that I have run two to three times that distance in training. If I run for two hours in training, there is no reason I can't run for 35 minutes in a race.

Now we know why we should do the long run, but let's figure out how we can enjoy it. To the relief of us all, the general rule is that you should be able to have a conversation with someone while you run; otherwise you're running too hard. The long run should be less than 70 percent of your maximum heart rate. I prefer the unscientific method of "talk rate." If you can talk to someone without gasping between sentences, then you are in your target zone. Talk to yourself: recite the alphabet, National Anthem, Bill of Rights.

The long run varies among athletes from one hour to three hours. The time depends on the distances you race and your running history. To get my butt out the door, I do several things that make the long run enjoyable. The secret behind these methods is to get your mind off what you are doing—running. Don't worry about how many miles you run; just base your run on time. By doing so, you don't strain yourself to reach certain mile marks in a specified time.

- Conversation makes the time pass quickly, so run with a friend or group of friends. If you are breathing too hard to talk, then it's "adios, amigos!" to your running partners. The long run stresses the body in different ways than shorter, more intense runs. You are probably already running hard two times a week, so running hard during your long run will more likely cause injury than enhance performance. The gossip conscious love the long run because the longer you run with someone, the less trivial the conversation will be, and you get to learn more about your running partner.

- Run on trails. Talk about passing time and reducing mental stress. This is the ticket to running bliss. It's worth driving 30 minutes or more to reach a trail site. Enjoy your surroundings. Listen to the birds, streams, and the rattlesnakes. Smell the flowers and pine trees. Notice the cows as they charge you. Before you know it, the long run is over.

- Take a golf ball or tennis ball and create your own game. I like to toss the golf ball in the air and tell myself I have to reach it before two bounces. It often takes a sideways bounce and I have to cut left or right suddenly as well as have bursts of speed to reach the golf ball. This enhances my fast-twitch muscles, and the side-to-side motion strengthens my tendons. You and a friend can also toss a football or Frisbee to get the same results. All these help hand-eye coordination. Warning: Do not do this in the middle of Main Street during rush hour.

- Run with man's best friend. I enjoy my long runs most when I have a dog. Watching a dog observe the world is humorous and enlightening. You can tell how much the dog loves the simple freedom of being outdoors. I vicariously transfer the dog's enjoyment to my run. If you don't have a dog, then take a neighbor's or friend's dog. My "nephew" is Jessie, my parents' dog. He gets so excited when I come over because he knows he's going for a run. I talk to him about life, girls, and other stuff. He doesn't really respond, but I know he's listening.

- Have a destination. I oftentimes break up a long run by running with a purpose. I run to swim practice or to a friend's house. I even run to the video store to return my overdue movie. Running with a purpose gives more credibility to the run, and you also know that you are doing your part in keeping the environment clean.

- Go house hunting. Even though I have no means to buy these houses, I like to dream a little. Many houses that are for sale have free information brochures on the for-sale signs, which also list the asking price. I like to stop at the house and guess the price. It's kind of like "The Price Is Right" with Bob Barker.

- Run on the golf course. Shhh, I know that it is trespassing, but it's hard to resist the feeling of surefootedness on plush, perfectly manicured grass (except for the divots by hackers). I like to start at a hole and run progressively through each hole. It's also fun to run fartlek intervals: run one hole hard, one hole easy. An 18-hole course is usually about 6,000 yards. Anyone for 36 holes? I recommend running the golf course during the winter when there are no golfers up north or in the morning or dusk when there are fewer players. Remember, don't run on the greens, and watch out for the groundskeeper—he can be a beast sometimes.

- Run with music. This is pretty self-explanatory. Radios have become very lightweight and many have straps to secure the radio around your arm. Tune in to some of the morning shows. But beware—you might double over with laughter after hearing some of the dialogue. Again, you get the stares from the civilians who think laughter is passé.

- Run at night. This is great during a full moon. For some reason I always feel faster running in the dark. One of my favorites is running on a typically busy street late at night during a snowfall. Everything is quiet except for the sound of your feet crunching the snow. If you are nervous about safety, run with a friend, and carry mace and a whistle. Another favorite is running the night of the first snowfall of the season. The tranquility is invigorating.

- Finally, run with your spouse, who is always squawking about how you don't spend enough time with him or her and the children. Your mate can ride a bike or in-line skate while you run. You can run with a baby jogger, and your children can ride bikes. Your family can also carry water or munchies. If the rest of the family isn't very athletic, meet them at a park for a picnic or at the swimming pool. Getting the family involved helps them realize what you are doing and the type of dedication that is required. Until a spouse sees you training, it is hard for that person to understand what you are doing.

These ideas should help spice up your long run. Enjoy it, don't dread it. Keep tri-ing and I'll see you on the run.

- Long track intervals of 800, 1,200, or 1,600 meters with equal rest distance at an easy jog. Do up to six repeats at shorter distance, two or three at longer distance. Try to achieve even pacing, even 400-meter splits at roughly race pace or slightly less.

- Two-mile time trial on track once a month at relaxed but steady race pace, record progress.

AP High Workouts

The following are some examples of AP high workouts.

- 15 minutes at EN recovery; 4 × 400 meters at AP high with 400 easy jog between; as season progresses increase to 6 × 400 and 8 × 400 with same rest interval; always cool down with 10 to 15 minutes of easy jogging

- 15 minutes at EN recovery; 4 × 800 meters at AP high with 400 easy jog between; add one 800 per week up to eight. Don't force yourself to do more efforts when "blown"; stop and try again next week. Go for smooth quality. Cool down 10 to 15 minutes.

© Nigel Farrow

Staying relaxed and maintaining form is important in a long run.

- Find a 400- to 600-meter hill of average grade; start again with 15 minutes warm-up at EN recovery; perform repeats at a steady pace; try to keep repeats equal in duration and effort, meaning start a little easy. Keep HR at AP high and back off if going too high. Jog easy to bottom and repeat; don't take too much rest. Add one repeat per week.

SP Short

Adding some short speed sessions to your run training will help you develop power and allow you to put forth bursts of speed in a race. Increased power and speed can be helpful for running up the beach after the swim for a quick transition or surging at the end of the race.

Short speed sessions are best done within an EN overdistance run, at regular intervals of between 5 and 10 minutes. After thoroughly warming up, steadily increase your speed to near maximum over 10 to 30 seconds. Then ease back to EN effort. You can do these "pickups" at regular intervals of between 5 and 10 minutes. Pick a landmark 50 to 200 meters down the road or trail to imagine as the finish line, and build speed to the finish.

SP Long

Longer speed sessions are crucial for a triathlete. This type of training helps you adapt to high levels of lactic acid and oxygen debt. It enables you to vary your speed during a race and put out extra effort (on hills, for example), without depleting your glycogen stores.

Long speed training includes any short interval repeat 400 meters or less. Don't overdo these. Don't do more than four repeats if longer, and not more than eight if shorter. Allow ample time between for recovery.

Here are some sample long speed run workouts.

- 400-meter ladder: 15 minute warm-up; 2×100 meters on, 400 recovery; 2×200 meters on, 400 recovery; 2×400 meters on, 800 recovery; 2×200 meters on, 400 recovery; 2×100 meters on, 400 recovery; finish with 10- to 15-minute easy jog. "On" is building to 90 percent, not all out; recoveries are very easy, full recovery, walk if necessary to get HR under 120.

- Heart rate intervals: After thorough warm-up, do four builds achieving first 82 percent, then 84 percent, then 86 percent, then 90 percent of maximum HR; jog between intervals until HR drops to 120. As fitness progresses, add a few more intervals, starting at lower heart rates and ending as high as 96 percent. Finish with a thorough cool down.

- Hill repeats: Either on a repetitive hilly course or the same hill, carefully time your HR "build" while ascending the hill so that about 90 percent HR is achieved at the top, leaving some power to go over the top, and begin to ease up on the flat or downhill. This will teach you to monitor your progress on hills during a race, so as not to be blown at the top.

General Training Tips

If you're new to running or have just come off an injury, always take it easy for at least six weeks. Train with no intensity whatsoever, and increase distance by not more than 5 percent per week. At any stage in your training, working out with a group can be beneficial. Very long, slow workouts can often be accomplished better if the suffering is shared with someone. Track interval workouts are also much more fun with a partner or even a group. Running clubs exist in all major cities and many smaller cities. Make sure the group's workouts fit your plan; if they don't, don't do them, or possibly do some of them and modify the rest to fit your goals, and then finish on your own. Even better than a running club is a triathlon club. If your city doesn't have one, consider starting one. USA Triathlon sanctions clubs and has information on how to start a club. Log on to **www.usatriathlon.org.**

© Nigel Farrow

Trail running is a great change of pace from pounding the pavement.

Running inevitably causes aches and pains at some point. Here are some pointers for dealing with sore, aching muscles and joints:

- Warm up thoroughly! Unless you're doing a simple recovery run, always warm up easy for 5 to 10 minutes. Most people are warmed up when they just begin to sweat.

- If you are currently sore, warm up and then stretch. After your workout, cool down and then do some light stretching.

- After any workout, particularly an intense or long-distance session, ingest calories within a half hour. Doing so efficiently replaces depleted glycogen stores, producing gains and reducing pains.

- Get a massage—always beneficial for aching muscles.

- Trail running or other soft-surface running is good for sore joints.

- Check the mileage on your shoes; replace them every 400 to 500 miles.

- Try water running.

- Always hydrate—before, during, and after running, and all day long in between. Make hydration a part of your life.

- Get regular medical checkups. Many people continue to train through pain with disastrous results, including stress fractures or tendon, ligament, and cartilage damage that can lead to osteoarthritis.

- Ibuprofen or other pain relievers can help, but don't depend on these or use them on a regular basis.

- When joint pain lasts unusually long, try glucosamine sulfate—many people swear by it.

- Use ice to reduce inflammation.

- Train with weights. Weight training increases strength in muscles, tendons, and ligaments surrounding your joints. Strengthening helps alleviate pain and keeps a full range of motion.

- Get plenty of rest. Running, along with your other training, continually tears down muscle fiber. Sometimes the only way to recover is through complete rest.

Now that we've explored each sport individually, it's time to put them together in a cohesive triathlon training plan. The next section covers planning your season, setting up training schedules, and the mental aspect of training and racing.

Part V
TRAINING

SWIM
BIKE
RUN

Chapter 14

PLANNING YOUR SEASON

Planning a full season of triathlon training and racing takes some thought. You need to look into the future with a clear set of goals, know your limits so you don't blow yourself out early in the season, and train in such a way that you're always able to have a good shot at meeting your goals as races near. As we mentioned before, when it comes to triathlon, failing to plan is indeed planning to fail. If your goal is to get into shape, race occasionally for fun, and enjoy the social benefits of participating in triathlons, you won't need a serious training program. However, if you're into competing and are willing to invest the time, money, and effort in your search for peak performance, then a plan for success and goal attainment is a must.

This chapter breaks down a total plan for peak performance on a seasonal basis. In the next chapter we discuss specific weekly plans for competing at different distances. Our recommendations work best for the athlete who is selecting a few races to be competitive in and also wants to peak for a couple of selected targets over the season.

Define Your Season and Set Your Goals

Your first step down the path to peak performance is to relax, grab a calendar, and plan what you want to accomplish over the next year (or maybe two) . In what race(s) do you want to deliver your best possible effort? What events are you going to use as tune-up? Do you want to plan a prolonged peak for several weeks in which you race several times? These, and others, are questions you'll need to ask yourself before planning a full training season. The answers to these questions begin to form the macroplan of your season.

Not even the best athletes expect lifetime performances over an entire year. Triathletes who focus on shorter events (sprint and Olympic distance triathlons) can plan for a period of four to eight weeks of peak performance in which to set their goal races. Another option is to spread out your big races over the course of the season and plan for periods of training and peaking between events. If you see yourself focusing more on the longer events (long and ultra), fewer competitions should dot your calendar to allow you more time for preparation, longer taper period prior to the race, and substantial recovery time afterward. Longer races take much more out of you, so your ability to race frequently is diminished because of the intensity and wear and tear on your body. Chapter 15 details training for specific types and distances of racing.

Once you decide on the triathlons, duathlons, road races (running or cycling), and swim meets you want to enter during the season, write the events down, including the date. Then, make a competitive schedule, as shown here:

April 15	10K Road Race (run)
April 29	Duathlon (5K/30K/5K)
May 12	State 40K Time Trial (bike)
May 26	Sprint Distance Triathlon (.5K/20K/5K)
June 10	Local Time Trial (bike: 10 miles)
June 24	Olympic Distance Triathlon (1.5K/40K/10K)
July 4	Firecracker 5K (run)
July 21	Sprint Distance Triathlon (.8K/25K/5K)
August 5	Local Time Trial (bike: 10 miles)
August 16	Regional Triathlon Championship (1.5K/40K/10K)
September 4	Sprint Triathlon (.5K/20K/5K)
September 11	Local Time Trial (bike: 10 miles)
September 25	National Sprint Triathlon (.5K/20K/5K)
October 10	Regional Duathlon Championships (5K/30K/10K)
October 24	10K road race (run)
November 5	5K road race (run)

Once you have your schedule on paper, keep it in an area where you'll see it frequently. Also give members of your family and friends a copy, as this will help "cement" your commitment to your goals.

Now grade your races A, B, or C, using this system:

A races: events you want to perform at your absolute best. These races are very important to you.

B races: events that are somewhat important to you, but mainly they are solid tune-ups for the A events.

C races: events in which you're going to compete at the best of your ability but to which you'll devote no special prerace preparation. (Serious athletes call this "training through" these events.)

Only a select few races should be A races, as it's impossible to be at your absolute best for every race in a given season. If you can hold yourself to between two and three A races, you can focus better at all your events and give yourself an excellent opportunity for success. However, it is important to focus on more than one big race so if something goes wrong in that race, like a flat tire or leaky goggles, you won't feel as if your entire season has been wasted. From our sample schedule above, here's how you might grade your races. Note that only three events are graded A.

© iphotonews.com/Brooks

Pace your season so that you're at your best for the big races.

April 15	Grade C
April 29	Grade B
May 12	Grade B
May 26	Grade B
June 10	Grade C
June 24	Grade A
July 4	Grade C
July 21	Grade B
August 5	Grade C
August 16	Grade B
September 4	Grade A
September 11	Grade C
September 25	Grade B
October 10	Grade A
October 24	Grade B
November 5	Grade B

Planning Your Training Season

Once you know what events you're shooting for, it's time to plan your personal map of success. Your map should be detailed, yet flexible, allowing for adjustments along the way for unexpected schedule changes, or to accommodate advances or declines in fitness. The season can be broken down into segments known as macrocycles, which fall into one of five categories: general conditioning, specific preparation, peak, sport-specific, and regeneration phase. Your macrocycles are several weeks of training, strung together, that focus on a certain area of development. After certain times of the year, it's important to vary your training routine to optimize performance. This is the concept of periodization, which means training for a planned peak in performance. Instead of just hoping for a great race, you plan your entire training program at a goal to deliver a great race at a desired time.

General Conditioning Phase

We mentioned the conditioning phase (also called base training) earlier as an integral part of the triathlete lifestyle. General conditioning constitutes the greatest percentage of your calendar year and forms the backbone of your seasonal plan. For example, for a triathlete planning a peak performance in late summer or early fall in the northern hemisphere, general conditioning should occur during the months of January through March. Your foundation (base) is developed during this stage to prepare your body for greater intensity training down the road. Smart athletes understand that if their base is insufficient, intensity training is ill-advised and generally results in injury.

Generally the emphasis during this phase is on training in the EN zone, although you will still do some training in AP and SP zones as well. The general conditioning phase is also the best time to work on your technique or mechanics in the three sports.

Specific Preparation Phase

This is your meat and potatoes time of year, in which your most focused and intense training takes place. Specific prep builds on the fitness you've gained during the conditioning phase and is geared toward making you faster and stronger. In essence, this phase takes you from being a trainer to being a racer. Again, for the above-mentioned triathlete planning on a late-summer to early-fall peak, the specific prep period would be from May through July, taking advantage of the warmer summer months so training is less affected by inclement weather. However, because of such factors as heat and humidity, triathletes must use good sense and judgment regarding the weather, staying well hydrated and training during the cooler times of the day, especially when doing high-intensity running and cycling workouts.

Peak Phase

The fun time of the year. This is the stage at which you reap the rewards of your diligent training, finally racing at the peak events you have been shooting for. Training during this time sharpens your skills and allows for recovery between races. There will be a reduction in overall volume during this phase, and training efforts will be coordinated with your training and racing schedule. Special attention is given to the specifics of your big races, such as being ready for a hilly bike or run course, potential adverse weather conditions, or rough swimming conditions. This phase is also the time when you must be particularly tuned in to your body. If your body needs rest, take the time you need, before you get sick or injured.

Sport-Specific Phase

Since the multisport racing calendar winds down in the early fall, some triathletes use this time to concentrate on one sport exclusively. Perhaps a 10K or marathon, a bike time trial, or Masters swim meet could serve as a goal event for the fall season. During this time, the sport you want to focus on takes priority, as your goal is to improve in this sport. Do the other two sports to add variety and for active recovery from the tougher workouts in the sport you're emphasizing. This phase is your time to strengthen your weak spots and capitalize on the fitness you've gained from a season of multisport preparation.

© Anthony Neste

Planning your season is critical for success.

Regeneration Phase

The regeneration phase consists of recovery or rest weeks, and it is crucial in your overall plan. In fact most elite athletes take a couple weeks to a month completely off training each year. The break is needed physically and mentally. But don't be totally inactive during this phase or you will loose all the conditioning you're worked so hard for. Maintain your fitness with low-key, unstructured workouts. You can continue to swim, bike, and run if you prefer those sports as recreation, but you might also use this time to do some different activities, like hiking, tennis, in-line skating, rowing, stair master, or elliptical trainer. This period is also a good chance to mend relationships that might be stressed with spouse and kids because the rest of the year is shared with training.

Chapter 15

CREATING A TRAINING SCHEDULE

Although form and technique play a roll in swimming, cycling, and running, we cannot escape the fact that the sport is a physiologically based activity. To improve one's physiological capabilities, a plan of consistent development must be executed.

To optimize performance, an athlete needs to blend training volume and intensity into a comprehensive plan. Periodization is the art of properly placing key training periods that will lead to peak performance at your key event(s). The training plans covered in this chapter are based on periodization principles. There will be weeks of gradual increases of volume and/or intensity, followed by a week of lower volume/intensity. To learn more about this principle, please read *The Theory and Methodology of Training* by Tudor Bompa. This text is the bible of periodization concepts.

Daily and Weekly Plans

Before you undertake a training season, determine which days work best for particular types of training. Perhaps the Masters swim team you train with has its tough training sessions on Monday, Wednesday, and Friday mornings, which means you'll need to adjust your run and bike workouts around these times. If you find one sport fatigues you more than another, focus on that training session and keep everything else on that day relatively low key. Many triathletes find they can do tough swim workouts and bike sessions on the same day. Some athletes prefer tough bike days to be by themselves while combining quality swim sessions and run sessions. Most, however, seldom combine quality bike/run days, unless planning brick training. Finally, taking one day off of training per week is wise. This rest goes a long way toward keeping you healthy and refreshed for a long season. Below is an example of a well–thought out week.

Monday	AM Quality swim with Masters team
	PM Easy bike
Tuesday	AM Easy run
	PM Quality bike
Wednesday	AM Quality swim
	PM Quality run
Thursday	AM Easy run
	PM Easy bike
Friday	Day off
Saturday	AM Quality bike/run (brick training)
	PM Easy swim
Sunday	AM Long bike or run (alternate weeks)
	PM Off

Organizing Your Yearly Training Plan

If your goal is to race optimally, take time to consider what you must accomplish during the course of the season. Look at a calendar with an eye toward the month(s) in which you want to peak, and write in key events. In North America, triathletes generally focus on a racing season that spans from June through September. Shorter races are easier to recover from than long races, so you can plan for several peaks over a month or two and still have a good chance to fulfill your goals. As we've mentioned, not every race will be a peak event, but each race should serve as a tune-up leading up to your goal race(s).

If you're a triathlete whose goal is to perform at your best during the summer months and then possibly continue with running road races in the fall, the sample training schedule shown here might resemble yours:

2 to 16 weeks	General conditioning phase
8 to 12 weeks	Specific conditioning phase
8 to 12 weeks	Race phase
4 to 8 weeks	Sport-specific phase
4 to 8 weeks	Regeneration phase

General Conditioning Phase

Those of us in the northern hemisphere are in the middle of winter from January to March, but no matter what the weather is like, this period is an important time to be laying down aerobic foundations. After the holiday season, most athletes are anxious to shed unwanted pounds and get back into shape. As you get back into general conditioning, you'll work most on endurance training. You'll also want to start some aerobic power and speed training during this phase—if you don't, you'll probably find the fast-paced work of the next phase uncomfortable and overly challenging. Start with very light loads of aerobic power (~10 to 15 minutes per AP session) and speed training (~5 minutes per session). Never increase the amount of work more than 5 percent over the previous week, as greater increases lead to overtraining or injury.

Begin by simply making one session per week in each sport an AP low practice. Warm up, then swim, bike, or run at AP low intensities, keeping duration low. AP low sessions during the base phase should not be overly long or arduous. Try warming up for 10 to 20 minutes, starting with light activity and progressing toward moderate effort. Next, complete anywhere from 10 to 30 minutes of AP low work (excluding recovery between efforts,

A Word From Wes

Train the Way You Race

For most of us, training time is limited. Therefore, it is important to train specifically for the triathlon race. Here are a few ideas:

- Swim fast at the beginning of the practice. In traditional swim practices, the first 25 percent of the yardage is used to warm up. On the morning of a triathlon, you may not have any chance to warm up. Try doing one out of every four swim workouts with no warm-up. At group workouts, either get in a faster lane at the beginning or wait until warm-up is over and hop in for the main set.

- Bike train in aero position. People have these aerobars sitting in front of them on rides, yet they never use them. During a triathlon, the lower back gets tight or the hamstrings lock up because triathletes aren't used to riding aero. From four weeks before a triathlon to the race, I try to do at least 50 percent of my riding in aero position.

- Brick workouts. These workouts can be swim to bike or bike to run. The purpose is to get the body accustomed to going from one of the disciplines to another without discomfort. A great method for both types of bricks is to take a bike and place it on a wind-trainer at either a pool or a track. The amount of repetitions is just as important as the length. For instance, I will do a bike–run brick, where I ride 10 minutes on the bike and then run one mile. I will do this continuously four to six times through. I found that the more often I race, the less I need to do in these workouts.

if you're doing interval training). Finish with 5 to 10 minutes of easy activity to cool down.

You'll do less speed training than aerobic power training during this period, but you'll want to include some speed. During one or two endurance sessions per week, throw in a burst of speed about 15 seconds in duration. In the first 5 or 6 seconds build to a pace that feels faster than race pace, and then hold it for the remaining time. For example, build up your tempo until it feels like mile pace only (no need for all-out sprinting!). Once the 15 seconds are over, ease back to endurance pace. Four to 12 such efforts over the course of an endurance workout are sufficient. Training this way also keeps you mentally fresh because the workout is less monotonous.

Ideally, all three components—endurance, aerobic power, and speed—should be done, but intensity and duration need to be kept at reasonable levels and adjusted for the focus of work.

Sample Training Schedules

Tables 15.1 and 15.2 show a typical monthly cycle during the general conditioning phase. Table 15.1 is for athletes training for a sprint or an Olympic distance event and table 15.2 is for athletes training for long or ultra-distance races. Note that training volumes are expressed in units of time rather than mileage. Most successful multisport athletes have realized that gauging training with time is better than using distance and helps put an end to "mindless miles" and allow you to better monitor improvement. Plus, using time rather than distance makes the training tables in this book more applicable to triathletes of different abilities.

Keys to table interpretation:

EN = endurance

AP– = aerobic power (low)

AP+ = aerobic power (high)

SP = speed

Swim practice can of course be with a Masters team; modify the workouts slightly to suit your needs, or move up or down lanes as necessary to increase or decrease intensity. (Masters workouts are divided into lanes by ability.) If you are swim training on your own, go back to chapter 6 and plug in appropriate workouts. Workouts should be low intensity, longer intervals, adequate rest, and medium overall distance/duration.

As you can see in the tables, a progression in training volume occurs over the first three weeks, and then the last week sees a significant reduction in training, even less than in week one. This type of training plan has periodic "unloading" segments to allow recovery from the three preceding weeks. The plan yields excellent results with elite endurance athletes—they all train this way now. Any triathlete must allow his or her body to absorb training, and the only way to do this is through a recovery period.

Table 15.1

Sample Four-Week Schedule During General Conditioning Phase for Sprint and Olympic Distances

WEEK ONE

	Swim	Bike	Run
MON	Focus on AP	40 min EN	
TUE			4 x 4 min AP+ w/2-min easy jog*
WED	Focus on EN	20 min. AP– continuous	
THU			30 min. EN*
FRI	Off	Off	Off
SAT	Focus on EN	2+ hr mountain bike	
SUN			60 min EN 5 x 15 sec SP

WEEK TWO

	Swim	Bike	Run
MON	Focus on AP	50 min EN	
TUE			20 min AP–*
WED	Focus on EN	3 x 8 min AP+ w/2 min easy	
THU			35 min EN
FRI	Off	Off	Off
SAT	Focus on EN	2+ hr mountain bike	
SUN			1:10 EN 6 x 15 sec SP

*Follow run workout with weight-training session.

184

WEEK THREE

	Swim	Bike	Run
MON	Focus on AP	60 min EN	
TUE			4 x 5 min AP+ w/2 min easy jog*
WED	Focus on EN	25 min AP– continuous	
THU			40 min EN*
FRI	Off	Off	Off
SAT	Focus on EN	2+ hr mountain bike	
SUN			1:20 EN 7 x 15 sec SP

WEEK FOUR

	Swim	Bike	Run
MON	Focus on AP	35 min EN	
TUE			15 min AP– continuous*
WED	Focus on EN	3 x 6 min AP+ w/2 min easy	
THU			25 min EN*
FRI	Off	Off	Off
SAT	Focus on EN	2+ hr mountain bike	
SUN			50 min EN 4 x 15 sec SP

*Follow run workout with weight-training session.

Table 15.2

Sample Four-Week Schedule During Conditioning for Long and Ultra-Distance

WEEK ONE

	Swim	Bike	Run
MON	Focus on AP	60 min EN	
TUE			2 x 8 min AP+ w/2 min easy jog*
WED	Focus on EN	30 min AP– continuous	
THU			35 min EN*
FRI	Off	Off	Off
SAT	Focus on EN	2+ hr mountain bike	
SUN			1:20 EN 5 x 15 sec SP

WEEK TWO

	Swim	Bike	Run
MON	Focus on AP	1:10 EN	
TUE			25 min AP– continuous*
WED	Focus on EN	5 x 15 min AP+ w/1-min easy spin	
THU			40 min EN*
FRI	Off	Off	Off
SAT	Focus on EN	2+ hr mountain bike	
SUN			1:30 EN 6 x 15 sec SP

*Follow run workout with weight-training session.

186

WEEK THREE

	Swim	Bike	Run
MON	Focus on AP	1:15 EN	
TUE			4 x 5 min AP+ w/1-min easy jog*
WED	Focus on EN	25 min AP– continuous	
THU			45 min EN*
FRI	Off	Off	Off
SAT	Focus on EN	2+ hr mountain bike	
SUN			1:40 EN 7 x 15 sec SP

WEEK FOUR

	Swim	Bike	Run
MON	Focus on AP	50 min EN	
TUE			20 min AP–*
WED	Focus on EN	2 x 10 min AP+ w/2-min easy spin	
THU			35 min EN*
FRI	Off	Off	Off
SAT	Focus on EN	2+ hr mountain bike	
SUN			60 min EN 4 x 15 sec SP

*Follow run workout with weight-training session.

187

Weight Training

During the general conditioning phase, two workout sessions a week are reserved for weight training, with two or three days of no lifting in between. A triathlete's resistance program should be simple and address two primary goals: total body strength and injury prevention. The best approach is to find a local, certified personal trainer to develop a program geared toward your needs and goals as an endurance athlete. Workouts should take about 30 to 45 minutes to complete and include 8 to 12 exercises. Some triathletes take weight training too seriously and expend more energy than they need to. Explain your needs to a personal trainer and come up with a program that's easy to follow that achieves your two primary objectives.

See table 15.3 for a sample weight-training program for a triathlete.

Table 15.3

Sample Triathlete Weight Program

Exercise	Sets	Reps
Bench press	2	10
Squat	2	12
Upright row	2	10
Hamstrings curl	2	12
Lat pull-down	2	10
Calf raises	2	12
Biceps curl	2	10
Triceps extension	2	10
Bent-over row	2	10
Abdominal crunches	2	50

Specific Conditioning

This training stage progresses your fitness level from aerobic work to faster forms of training. The workouts included in this section focus on improving speed and strength.

Hill Workouts

Hill training significantly increases strength and stamina for both the bike and run. If hill training existed for swimming we'd recommend it as well, but we have not (yet) devised a way to do it. Since most triathlon run and bike courses feature a hill or two (or more), it really helps on race day if you have practiced hills and are comfortable and familiar with techniques and demands for conquering them. Hill work builds sport-specific strength—find an athlete who is strong in the hills, and you have likely found a tough competitor. Hill repeats improve the aerobic power and speed components of training. You should do one cycling hill workout and one running hill workout each week during this training phase.

A good hill for bike training takes two to three minutes to climb at a sustained pace. It's best if the hill is on a lightly traveled road, as you'll be turning around at the top and bottom. Once warmed up, complete several repeats, 4 minimum to 12 maximum. Wear your heart rate monitor and push

© iphotonews.com/Brooks

Hill training gives you a competitive edge on challenging courses.

yourself to see how close you can come to your max. Many cyclists achieve new heart rate maximums during hill training. Once you reach the summit, turn around (watch for traffic!) and spin easy down the hill as a recovery; coasting with your legs motionless can lead to lactic buildup or cramping. Start and end at the same spot, and time each effort. Experiment with different positions (standing and sitting, or combinations of both) and different techniques (handlebar position, butt position, ankle incline, cadence), and ultimately determine which climbing position is best for you. The best position should result in the fastest time with the lowest heart rate. Also, work with different gear combinations in tandem with technique to find the fastest and most efficient way.

Running hill repeats are performed in much the same way as biking hills, fundamentally. A perfect hill for run repeats is between 200 and 400 meters, and fairly steep. Try to find a hill with a soft surface, such as grass or dirt. After warming up, complete 4 to 12 reps; at the top of the hill, turn around and jog easy down to the starting point. Focus on form and technique running up the hill: lean slightly into the hill, use your arms, high knees, and rapid turnover and minimize foot–ground contact time.

Brick Intervals

Brick intervals make for a fun workout that helps you with the dreaded bike-run transition. Take your bike and wind-trainer to the track, setting them up trackside for this all-important session.

Begin with 10 minutes of easy jogging, and then do 10 to 15 minutes of light spinning on the bike. Once warmed up, go directly into the brick intervals. This workout features alternating cycling and running repeats for a set time and distance. The rest interval is the time it takes to change shoes from bike to run and run to bike. Changing shoes is good practice too; much time can be gained in a quick transition—elite triathletes can change shoes in less than 20 seconds. Here are some examples of brick interval sessions:

3 to 6 × 5 minute bike, alternating with an 800-meter run

3 to 5 × 7.5 minute bike, alternating with a 1,200-meter run

2 to 5 × 10 minute bike, alternating with a 1-mile run

The bike efforts are around 85 to 90 percent maximum heart rate, so be sure to wear your monitor for this session. Time your run efforts; goal times for these efforts should be race pace. Once you complete the last brick interval, walk an easy lap, and then spin easy on the bike for 5 to 10 minutes. This workout significantly helps with the bike-to-run transition and makes you faster as well. Brick interval sessions should be done once a week and are always in the AP high category.

Sample Training Schedules

Table 15.4 illustrates a typical month of training in the specific conditioning phase for those specializing in sprint and Olympic distance races. Table 15.5 illustrates a typical month of training in the specific conditioning phase for those training for long or ultra-distance events. Remember to progress your workload over a period of three weeks and lower your volume in the fourth week to allow for necessary recovery. Dropping your volume by 15 to 25 percent under the toughest week really helps with recovery from three weeks of tough training.

Again, swim with your Masters group at appropriate intensities, or plug in AP high swim workouts from Chapter 6. Most Masters swim groups include several (or are sometimes dominated by) triathletes. It is appropriate to present your specific needs to the coach and ask that some workouts be tailored to triathletes at that time. No harm will be done to nontriathlete swimmers.

It is important not to overdo it at this point and become burned out. If you are tired, make sure you perform plenty of active and passive recovery.

Race Phase

This is what all the training is about! This is also where short-distance specialists (sprint and Olympic distance) and long-distance triathletes (long and ultra) really begin to diverge due to different racing needs. In previous phases the difference was mainly volume, with the ultra athlete doing about 1 to 2 times that of the sprint and olympic athletes. During the race phase, the training program must address individual needs of the athletes to maximize performance. It is important for triathletes to remember that during this time training must be geared to racing! Train to race, not train to train. If the athlete feels stale during this time, a small break might be needed. A couple days off followed by 2 to 4 days of short, easy EN training is a simple prescription that can help restore mental and physical health.

Because of the obvious differences in racing needs for the different events, your program must reflect the type of racing you want to place your focus on. Short-distance triathlons place a premium on speed, and longer races call for greater endurance. Training intensity goes up during this time for short-race triathletes. Conversely, training volume increases for those who want to go long!

Race Phase Training for the Short-Distance Triathlete

It's time to get fast! The training during this time builds upon the strength you gained during the specific conditioning phase. Think of this period as

Table 15.4

Sample Four-Week Schedule During Specific Conditioning Phase for Sprint and Olympic Distances

WEEK ONE

	Swim	Bike	Run
MON	Focus on AP+	1:10 EN	
TUE	Optional: easy swim or bike		Hills: 6 x 300 m
WED	Focus on EN	Hills: 8 x 2 min	
THU	Focus on AP–	35 min EN	
FRI	Off	Off	Off
SAT	Optional: easy swim	Brick intervals: 4 x 5 min bike/800m run	
SUN		2 hr EN 8 x 20 sec SP	

WEEK TWO

	Swim	Bike	Run
MON	Focus on AP+	1:15 EN	
TUE	Optional: easy swim or bike		Hills: 8 x 300 m
WED	Focus on EN	Hills: 10 x 2 min	
THU	Focus on AP–		40 min EN
FRI	Off	Off	Off
SAT	Optional: easy swim	Brick intervals: 3 x 7.5 min bike/1,200 m run	
SUN		Optional: easy bike	1:15 EN 6 x 15 sec SP

WEEK THREE

	Swim	Bike	Run
MON	Focus on AP+	1:20 min EN	
TUE	Optional: easy swim or bike		Hills: 10 x 300 m
WED	Focus on EN	Hills: 12 x 2 min	
THU	Focus on AP–		45 min EN
FRI	Off	Off	Off
SAT	Optional: easy swim	Brick intervals: 3 x 10 min bike/1 min run	
SUN		2.5 hr EN 12 x 20 sec SP	

WEEK FOUR

	Swim	Bike	Run
MON	Focus on AP+	45 min EN	
TUE	Optional: easy swim or bike		Hills: 5 x 300 m
WED	Focus on EN	Hills: 6 x 2 min	
THU	Focus on AP–		30 min EN
FRI	Off	Off	Off
SAT	Optional: easy swim	Brick intervals: 3 x 5 min bike/800 m run	
SUN		Optional: easy bike	60 min EN 4 x 15 sec SP

Table 15.5

Sample Four-Week Schedule During Specific Conditioning Phase for Long and Ultra Distances

WEEK ONE

	Swim	Bike	Run
MON	Focus on AP+	1:10 EN	
TUE	Optional: easy swim or bike		Hills: 8 x 300 m
WED	Focus on EN	Hills: 8 x 2 min	
THU	Focus on AP–		40 min EN
FRI	Off	Off	Off
SAT	Optional: easy swim	Brick intervals: 2 x 10 min bike/1 min run	
SUN		3+ hrs EN 8-10 x 20 sec SP	

WEEK TWO

	Swim	Bike	Run
MON	Focus on AP+	1:15 EN	
TUE	Optional: easy swim or bike		Hills: 9 x 300 m
WED	Focus on EN	Hills: 10 x 2 min	
THU	Focus on AP–		45 min EN
FRI	Off	Off	Off
SAT	Optional: easy swim	Brick intervals: 3 x 10 min bike/1 min run	
SUN		Optional: easy bike	2 hr EN 8-10 x 15 sec SP

194

WEEK THREE

	Swim	Bike	Run
MON	Focus on AP+	1:20 min EN	
TUE	Optional: easy swim or bike		Hills: 10 x 300 m
WED	Focus on EN	Hills: 12 x 2 min	
THU	Focus on AP–		50 min EN
FRI	Off	Off	Off
SAT	Optional: easy swim	Brick intervals: 4 x 10 min bike/1 min run	
SUN		4+ hrs EN 12-15 x 20 sec SP	

WEEK FOUR

	Swim	Bike	Run
MON	Focus on AP+	60 min EN	
TUE	Optional: easy swim or bike		Hills: 5 x 300 m
WED	Focus on EN	Hills: 7 x 2 min	
THU	Focus on AP–		35 min EN
FRI	Off	Off	Off
SAT	Optional: easy swim	Brick intervals: 3 x 7.5 min bike/1,200 m run	
SUN		Optional: easy bike	1:45 EN 4-8 x 15 sec SP

© Nigel Farrow

Speed training acclimates you to race-pace.

"sharpening your sword." A new training concept is introduced during this phase to help you get razor sharp: speed training.

Speed training can be done in all three sports and really build economy. Training at paces over what will be encountered during racing helps the body adapt. Once you do a few speedy sessions, AP pace/effort does not seem very difficult.

A triathlete doing this type of work needs to concentrate on grace and ease of movement. Imagine yourself as a great 400-meter runner or 100-meter swimmer when doing speed efforts in running and swimming. On the bike, use the largest gear possible while maintaining 90+ rpm. On the bike, focus on the pace being fast, quick, and light. Almost complete recovery is taken between speed reps.

Here are example speed sessions for each of the three sports:

Swim: 8×50 with fins. Each 50 is all out, and swim an easy 50 between each fast effort.

Bike: 6×1 min with 2 min easy spin between each effort.

Run: 5×300 meter w/500 meter easy jog between.

Table 15.6 gives a typical four-week training block during the race phase for sprint to Olympic distance competitors.

• Straight Bricks: This is more of a traditional bike/run brick in which you train for that particular transition. Complete a longer ride of about 2 hours with 30 to 40 minutes of AP-continuous cycling towards the end of the ride. Then, change quickly into running attire and head back out the door. Jog easy for about 5 minutes, then run 20 to 25 minutes at triathlon race pace. Finish the session with 5 minutes of easy jogging.

Long/Ultra Differences During the Race Phase

The race phase looks very similar to the specific conditioning phase for the triathlete who desires success in these events. However, the major difference is the increased volumes. In order to get your body prepared for the rigors of longer racing, you must get familiar with the time it will take. By alternating a long run and a long bike each week (two each per month), you will be ready for race day! Table 15.7 gives a sample four-week block of training for the long/ultra competitor. You will notice the strong shift to more training volume. This type of training needs to be done for 8 to 12 weeks before you start tapering (the art of tapering will be discussed later in the chapter). This four-week cycle is a good starting point for a triathlete who has a solid base in the general and specific training phases. As each month progresses, increase the volume cyclically by 5 to 10 percent, depending on how you feel. Don't increase volume on your easy week if you are feeling tired.

• Straight bricks for long and ultra competitors: Using your goal race as a guide, complete a bike training session that is approximately the same amount of time that you plan on racing in your goal event. The majority of this workout should be in the EN category, with about 40-60 minutes at AP low intensity, preferably toward the end of the session. After completing the ride, change into running clothes and shoes and head back out the door. Run for 20 to 30 minutes at planned pace for the running portion of your peak race. Then walk easy for 5 to 10 minutes. This session is tough!

Race Week and Tapering

The days leading into a race are probably more for the mind than for the body. It takes the body about two weeks to acclimatize to past training. Thus, what you did two or more weeks ago has more bearing on race-day performance than what you did the prior week. The days leading up to a race are used for sharpening and fine-tuning. You cannot really "win" a race in the days leading up to the competition, but you really can "lose" it if you try to cram in too much work before it.

Table 15.6

Sample Four-Week Schedule During Race Phase for Sprint and Olympic Distances

WEEK ONE

	Swim	Bike	Run
MON	Focus on AP+	60 min EN	
TUE	Optional: easy swim or bike		8 x 200 m SP w/400 m jog between
WED	Focus on EN	9 x 1 min SP w/2 min easy between	
THU	Focus on SP/AP–		30 min EN
FRI	Off	Off	Off
SAT	Optional: easy swim	Straight brick*	
SUN		30 min easy	1:10 EN 8 x 15 sec SP

WEEK TWO

	Swim	Bike	Run
MON	Focus on AP+	60 min EN	
TUE	Optional: easy swim or bike		7 x 300 m SP w/400 m jog between
WED	Focus on EN	10 x 1 min SP w/2 min easy between	
THU	Focus on SP/AP–		35 min EN
FRI	Off	Off	Off
SAT	Optional: easy swim	Brick intervals: 3 x 10 min bike/1 min run	
SUN		2 hr 10 x 20 sec SP	

198

WEEK THREE

	Swim	Bike	Run
MON	Focus on AP+	60 min EN	
TUE	Optional: easy swim or bike		6 x 400 m SP w/400 m jog between
WED	Focus on EN	12 x 1 min SP w/2 min easy between	
THU	Focus on SP/AP−		40 min EN
FRI	Off	Off	Off
SAT	Optional: easy swim	Straight brick*	
SUN		30 min very easy	1:20 EN 10 x 15 sec SP

WEEK FOUR

	Swim	Bike	Run
MON	Focus on AP+	45 min EN	
TUE	Optional: easy swim or bike		6 x 200 m SP w/200 m jog between
WED	Focus on EN	8 x 1 min SP w/2 min easy between	
THU	Focus on SP/AP−		30 min EN
FRI	Off	Off	Off
SAT	Optional: easy swim	Brick intervals: 4 x 5 min bike/800 m run	
SUN		2 hr 8 x 20 sec SP	

199

Table 15.7

Sample Four-Week Schedule During Race Phase for Long and Ultra Distances

WEEK ONE

	Swim	Bike	Run
MON	Focus on AP+	60 min EN	
TUE	Optional: easy swim or bike		3 x 8 min AP+ w/2 min jog between
WED	Focus on EN	8 x 5 min AP+ w/1 min easy between	
THU	Focus on SP/AP–		40 min EN
FRI	Off	Off	Off
SAT	Optional: easy swim	Straight brick*	
SUN		2+ hr EN	40 min EN

WEEK TWO

	Swim	Bike	Run
MON	Focus on AP+	60 min EN	
TUE	Optional: easy swim or bike		3 x 10 min AP– w/2 min jog between
WED	Focus on EN	Hills: 12 x 2 min	
THU	Focus on SP/AP–		45 min EN
FRI	Off	Off	Off
SAT	Optional: easy swim	Brick intervals: 4 x 10 min bike/1 min run	
SUN		30 min very easy	2+ hr EN 10 x 20 sec SP

200

WEEK THREE

	Swim	Bike	Run
MON	Focus on AP+	60 min EN	
TUE	Optional: easy swim or bike		3 x 12 min AP+ w/2 min jog between
WED	Focus on EN	6 x 8 min AP+ w/2 min easy between	
THU	Focus on SP/AP−		50 min. EN
FRI	Off	Off	Off
SAT	Optional: easy swim	Straight brick*	
SUN		3+ hr EN	40 min EN

WEEK FOUR

	Swim	Bike	Run
MON	Focus on AP+	45 min EN	
TUE	Optional: easy swim or bike		4 x 5 min AP− w/2 min jog between
WED	Focus on EN	Hills: 8 x 2 min	
THU	Focus on SP/AP−		35 min EN
FRI	Off	Off	Off
SAT	Optional: easy swim	Brick intervals: 4 x 7.5 min bike/1,200 m run	
SUN		30 min very easy	2+ hr EN 8 x 20 sec SP

If you are planning to deliver peak performance at a race, two weeks prior to the race would be fairly low key. No great increases in volume or intensity. Long and ultra competitors should not complete any long rides or runs the weekend before the big race. The last "normal" long ride or long run weekend should be three weekends before. Two weekends before, reduce your long run or long ride by 50 percent. You will progress to the week before the event more refreshed and rested.

Tapering for Short Races

Table 15.8 shows a typical race week for a competitor who wants to perform optimally at sprint and Olympic distances.

The rationale for this type of week is to have a couple low volume quality days to just feel race pace. It would also be a good idea to bike and run over a similar terrain that will be encountered on race day. If the race is going to be hilly, head for the hills. If the event will take place on a pancake-flat course, go faster in training by staying in the flats. Also, many successful endurance athletes have found taking a day off two days before the event more advantageous. By doing all three sports the day before, you get a chance to loosen up the different disciplines and check your gear before race day.

Table 15.8

Sample One-Week Taper for Sprint and Olympic Distances

	Swim	Bike	Run
MON	Focus on AP	60 min EN	
TUE	Focus on SP—very light		4 x 3 min AP– w/2 min between
WED		3 x 5 min AP– w/2 min between	
THU	Focus on easy swimming		30 min EN
FRI	Off	Off	Off
SAT	400-500 m EN	20-30 min EN	10-20 min EN
SUN	Race day		

Tapering for Long Races

Generally, an athlete should rest slightly more for longer races. This allows you to be well rested on race day and maximize glycogen storage in the working muscles. Table 15.9 is an example of a two-week taper that would be appropriate for a half-Ironman or longer.

Sport-Specific Phase

In North America, September is usually the last month for multisport competition. However, you don't want to stop since you are very fit from triathlon training and simply aren't ready for a break yet. A perfect solution is to key on a sport-specific phase during the fall months.

Pick one of the three sports to train and select a few races to compete in. Many triathletes find the goal of running road-race, personal-best times a great goal for the fall. The weather is often ideal for running, and there are plenty of 5K and 10K road races around. The fall months are also a great time to run a marathon, if that's a goal for you.

If you prefer to key on swimming, there are usually fall Masters swim meets. Autumn kicks off the short-course (25-yard/meter) racing season for swimmers with competitions popping up as early as mid-October. This is a great time to train specifically for a pool mile (1,650 yards or 1,500 meters), try your hand at sprinting, or compete in a nonfreestyle event. Once you compete in a Masters swim meet and try events other than distance freestyle, you will have a whole new appreciation for the sport.

Cycling events in the fall can be more difficult to find, as they traditionally follow the same season as triathlon. However, many cycling clubs have late-year time trials, mountain bike racing, or long tour events in the cooler autumn months. You may need to do some searching to find a bike race, but it can pay huge dividends in the next triathlon season. And, yes, even in the dead of winter, outdoor cycling still goes on, primarily in two categories. For training, there are the infamous long gravel road rides, done on your mountain bike (or a cyclocross bike if you have one). It can be great fun and a great workout to bundle up and ride in the peaceful and quiet winter. And then, there is cyclocross racing—a short event that combines trail riding, grass riding, pavement riding, and low hurdles or other sections where you are forced to dismount and run while carrying your bike. These events are wild and fun and currently constitute the fastest-growing race events in traditional cycling.

Once you choose the sport to prepare for, focus your training on that sport, but don't give up on the other two altogether. The other disciplines can be done in conjunction with your specific preparation but at low EN levels, to promote recovery from the tough sessions of your focus sport.

Table 15.9

Sample Two-Week Taper for Long and Ultra-Distances

WEEK ONE

	Swim	Bike	Run
MON	Focus on AP+	60-90 min EN	
TUE	SP—very light		6 x 3 min AP+ w/2 min easy jog
WED	Optional: easy swim	4 x 5 min AP+ w/2 min easy spin	
THU	Focus on AP–		40 min EN
FRI	1,000 yd/m EN	60 min EN	30 min EN
SAT		2 min EN w/20 min AP– in middle	15 min AP–
SUN	1,000 yd/m EN	60 min EN	45 min EN 5 x 15 sec SP

WEEK TWO

	Swim	Bike	Run
MON	SP—very light	3 x 3 min AP– w/2 min easy spin	
TUE		60 min EN	3 x 2 min AP–
WED	1,000 yd/m EN		25 min EN
THU	1,000 yd/m EN	45 min EN	20 min EN
FRI	Off	Off	Off
SAT	300-500 yd/m EN	30-40 min EN	10-15 min EN
SUN	Race day		

204

Table 15.10 illustrates an example of a weekly training cycle for the triathlete shooting for middle distance (5 to 10K) running races during the fall. Table 15.11 illustrates an example of a weekly training cycle for the triathlete training for a fall marathon.

A similar pattern can be followed for swim or bike preparation. Three to four key workouts in your sport of choice are plenty. It's always nice to close out the year with a great effort, as it helps build confidence and keeps you excited about the next season.

© Rich Cruse

Mountain biking is an excellent sport to try during the triathlon off-season.

Table 15.10

Sample Week for Running Concentration: 5K to 10K

	Swim	Bike	Run
MON	1,000 yd/m EN	30 min EN	
TUE			4 x 5 min AP+
WED	1,000 yd/m EN		6 x 200 m SP w/400 m jog between
THU	Off	Off	Off
FRI		30 min EN	35 min EN
SAT		30 min EN	Run 5K to 10K road race or 20-25 min AP–
SUN			60-90 min EN 6-12 x 15 sec SP

Table 15.11

Sample Week for Running Concentration: Marathon

	Swim	Bike	Run
MON	1,000 yd/m EN	30 min EN	
TUE			20-30 min AP–continuous
WED	1,000 yd/m EN		35-45 min EN
THU	1,000 yd/m EN		3-4 x 8-10 min w/2 min easy jog
FRI	Off	Off	Off
SAT			30-45 min EN
SUN		30-40 min EN	1.5-3 hr EN 6-12 x 15 sec SP

Regeneration Phase

This phase can also be called the recovery stage. After a long year of training and racing, your body needs time to rest and recuperate. No one, not even elite athletes, can handle serious training and competition for indefinite periods. After your fall goal event, take a few weeks break around the holidays. Be sure to stay physically active, exercising at least three times per week for 20 minutes, a little more if you feel like it. And these 20-minute workouts need not be swim, bike, or run. To stay fresh and have fun, try a rowing machine, stair master, elliptical trainer, or whatever it takes to get your heart rate up to the EN level. This phase is also a great time to work on flexibility. Toward the end of the phase, you should feel recovered, re-charged, and excited about starting preparations for the coming season.

Now that we have an understanding of the physical side of training, we must work on what may be the most important factor on race day: mental training. Even the best-trained athlete in the world cannot reach peak performance if he or she isn't mentally prepared. This alone is often the only factor separating the winners from the also-rans.

Chapter 16

MENTAL TRAINING

Preparing the mind for excellent performance helps all athletes. You spend countless hours preparing your body for race day, but if you're like many others, you often leave the mind out of the training equation. We've included this chapter in the training section because we believe that training for the mental side of triathlon is as important as training for the physical side. Most elite athletes will tell you that mental preparation plays a huge role in determining success or failure. No matter how ready your body is for an event, without mental resolve, your performance is going to suffer. When your mind quits your body soon follows. Likewise, when your body is trashed near the end of a race, you can help overcome some of the physical pain with mental training techniques.

Some athletes seem to have a natural aptitude for mental preparedness, able to perform their best in the heat of competition, while others preparing to race experience a monumental struggle of nerves. We've all heard coaches say things like, "she's a great training athlete but a poor competitive athlete." Some athletes regularly underachieve in competition, not because they can't push themselves physically, but because they can't push themselves mentally.

Mental training is essentially sports psychology, a branch of sport science that has been around for many years. The discipline of sports psychology uses many methods to help athletes achieve their optimal mental state. These methods range from simple to complex and have many applications.

Mental training is very individualized. You'll want to experiment until you find mental-training methods that work best for you. Those that handle the stress of competition easily may need little more than a smile on race day to deliver peak performances, while others require elaborate routines that may be complex and time consuming. But everyone benefits from some degree of mental preparation. In this chapter we provide a brief overview of some strategies and techniques you can use to improve your mental training.

Four basic mental tools that really help the triathlete are goal setting, relaxation, visualization, and positive self-talk. You might find one area more important than others and choose to focus your mental training energies within that area. Or you might find a blend of two, three, or all four tools most helpful in preparing for race day. Whatever you choose, keep things as simple as possible, and be consistent in using the mental-training methods that work for you. One of the reasons these methods work is that they become part of a routine that triggers your optimal state of arousal when you most need it. To be able to count on that trigger, you must be consistent in your mental preparation.

Goal Setting

Goal setting is crucial to success not only in sport but in every life endeavor. Setting goals is a process of reevalution. What have you done in the past? Where are you now? What do you hope to accomplish in the future? Goal setting is a way to evaluate past performances and devise measurable milestones for improvement. Once specific goals are set, your path and purpose become clear and you can focus on the steps needed to achieve your goals. If you leave out this crucial step, your training will lack focus and direction.

Goals could encompass a whole career or season, or they may pertain only to your next competition or training session. In fact, you should set both long- and short-term goals. Long-term goals are those you hope to achieve over a longer period of time—say a season or even a couple of years. For example, you might set a goal to finish an Ironman in under 12 hours within the next two years. Short-term goals can be those that you can begin to work on achieving immediately, such as improving your diet, or they can be goals you hope to achieve within a few months, such as cutting your 100-yard swim time by six seconds. Short-term goals allow you to see more immediate improvements, thus enhancing motivation, and can lead to accomplishing your long-term goal.

Typically athletes will set their goals for an upcoming racing season. Try to set no more than three major goals for a season. Setting more than that is unrealistic and complicates matters to the point of diminishing focus. Start by asking yourself the following questions:

- What were my best achievements last year in any and all aspects of triathlon training and racing?
- What seems to be my natural areas of strength in the sport?
- What goals did I not achieve last season?
- What are my weaknesses in triathlon?
- In what areas would I like to improve?

Goals should be specific and they should be measurable. As they say in business, "if you can't measure it, you can't manage it." After going through

© Nigel Farrow

Knowing your goals well before race day will give you focus from the start.

this process and identifying the areas you wish to improve, translate them into simple written goals that are measurable. Successful athletes get goals down on paper, where they can begin to manage specifically how they will achieve them. For example you might set a goal to reduce your 6×400 repeat run interval time from 80 to 76 seconds, or increase your lactic threshold by five beats by June 1. It's not enough to simply set a goal to reduce your 400-interval time or increase lactate threshold; you must make the goals specific and devise some way of measuring your progress.

Other goals may not be as easy to quantify, but you can still devise ways to see how you're progressing. For example, you might set a goal to improve diet by eliminating fast food and junk foods, and ensuring all snacks are either fresh fruit or energy bars by always having them on hand. You could monitor your progress by keeping a food log. Or you might set a goal of correcting an aspect of your swimming, cycling, or running technique by devoting a certain amount of training time to technique drills and monitoring your progress by videotaping your form or getting feedback from a coach.

A second important aspect of goal setting is setting competitive goals, as discussed in chapter 14. Deciding what events you want to shoot for and setting specific performance goals for those events will help structure your training.

Once you've decided which events will be the key events to shoot for, you should set specific goals for those events the same way you did with your training. Often your goal will be to finish the race in a certain time, but there are other performance goals you could set as well, such as placing in the top 10 percent in your age group or beating a certain competitor you always race against.

Relaxation

Everyone has an optimal state of arousal for competition. Some need to be calm and mellow, while others need to be bouncing off the walls. Most athletes fall somewhere in between. Knowing your personal optimal state of arousal is crucial for success. It usually takes a few races to find your best state of mind for peak performance.

One way to identify this optimal state is to keep a log. The log should include what you have done in terms of training and racing, but more importantly it should also include how you *felt*. If you had a good performance write down all the reasons why you performed well. This way you can begin to establish patterns and routines that work to achieve your optimal state of arousal. Grade C events, where the stakes are lower, are great times to experiment with relaxation techniques.

Relaxation is the ability to ease tension in your body while allowing your mind to clearly focus. Although many forms of relaxation are used simply to help people get to sleep (which can be a huge performance enhancement in itself), performance relaxation is a bit different. Usually what we're trying to achieve in prerace relaxation is that optimal state of arousal, especially if you have a tendency to get overly excited or nervous before competition. Both before and during the race, you need to know how to calm your mind if stress is building to an intolerable level.

Perhaps the best way of learning the art of relaxation is to do it several times in the comfort of your own home in a place away from noise and distractions. Start by lying down on something comfortable with nothing touching your body. Take three to five slow, deep breaths, focusing on blowing all your tension out during the exhale. After the deep breaths, focus on each area of your body, moving from your toes to the top of your head. As

© Anthony Neste

Take time after the race to reflect on and learn from the experience.

you progress up your body, feel each area—toes, feet, ankles, calves, knees, thighs, hips, torso, arms, shoulders, neck, face, head—become warm, soft, and heavy. The key is in focusing relaxation on smaller body parts and progressing from one end of the body to the other. Trying to relax your whole body in one action simply won't work. If muscles don't relax at the thought alone, try doing some muscle tightening and releasing. Breathe in and flex the tense area, hold for three seconds, and then breathe out, releasing the contraction. Do this three times to a specific area. Feel the tension melting away from your body. Once you're relaxed from head to toe, feel what it's like to experience total-body relaxation, while your mind is sharp and clear.

Initially, this method takes a while to get through, but with practice you'll be able to achieve total-body relaxation within a couple of minutes. It's easier to feel relaxation happen in a perfect environment and then put what you've learned into practice at the race. This relaxation method is just like any other aspect of successful racing in that it must be practiced. Total relaxation is difficult to achieve the first few times, even in a perfect environment. We recommend trying this technique daily at the same time and place up to 10 days in a row. It's amazing how quickly you can master it with this kind of practice.

Achieving this state prerace or during a race will be even more difficult, but even meager gains in relaxation are beneficial. Offsetting the race jitters has many positives. First, heart rate and adrenaline output are lowered. This saves energy and places you ahead of your competitors before you even start. Many people also experience a host of other symptoms when nervous: stomach upset, excessive sweating, shivering, diarrhea, or vomiting. Some cannot mentally focus enough to carry on a conversation or fill out a race form. But all these symptoms can be controlled or reduced through relaxation techniques.

Another benefit of being relaxed is that it's easier to focus on good form and technique in the swim, bike, and run. How often do you see top professional athletes who don't look completely relaxed and smooth, especially in those sports requiring elevated technique? They seem calm and focused in their athletic environment, despite a very high level of intensity. Successful athletes know that the more relaxed the muscles are, the more quickly and easily they can respond the way the athlete wants them to during competition.

We've discussed achieving relaxation prerace, but how do you initiate it midrace? If you are getting hammered in the swim and start to feel panicky, what can you do? Many athletes have key thoughts that seem to trigger or help them achieve relaxation. Wes Hobson, for example, uses a simple word, uttering "Stop" to himself when his mind tries to shut his body down from race fatigue. This triggers the relaxation and focus needed to overcome a potential mental and physical breakdown and maintains his optimal race state. Kent Dobbins, one of the top 55 to 60 age-groupers in the United States, has his own technique. Kent is the friendliest and most humorous person you'll ever meet but not so on race day and especially not during the race. During the race he is all focus, yet relaxed, often reporting afterwards that he has little memory of the race. He is on autopilot while racing. He won't answer when spoken to or even make eye contact with anyone. Through practice, he's learned how best to achieve his own optimal mental state on race day.

Visualization

The subconscious mind cannot distinguish what is real from what is imagined, which is why the power of visualization can truly help an athlete. Visualization works during and before a race to calm your mind, put you at ease, and get you ready for top performance. The key is the familiarity of stimuli played within your subconscious mind. In effect, you train your subconscious to react in a certain way precisely when you want it to.

There are two useful types of visualization—performance visualization and mental imagery. The former deals with imagining your performance in advance of a race or workout, while the latter deals with using metaphorical imagery to enhance form or to relax and focus on the task at hand.

Performance Visualization

In the week before the race, try visualizing your performance. After going through your relaxation routine, see yourself in your mind's eye as you perform in the upcoming race. Watch yourself execute the entire race from the start to crossing the finish line. Use as many of the five senses as you can in your visualization. See your competitors as they run beside you, smell the salty ocean air, feel the breeze on your bike, hear the sounds of your footsteps, taste your sports drink, and so on. Bring in as many sensations as possible to deepen the visualization experience within your subconscious.

Focus particularly on the important components of the race, including your transitions. The more clearly you see yourself performing small details

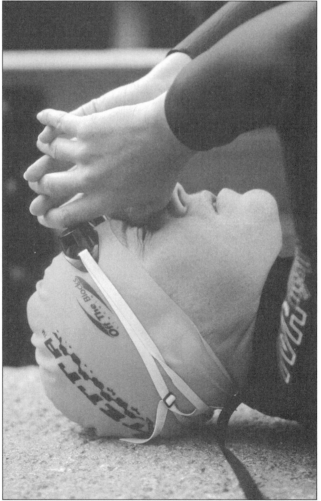

© Nigel Farrow

Stop before the race and visualize yourself performing successfully.

with precision, the better you'll become at doing them; the actions become nearly automatic on race day.

Try to visualize the exact race course. If you live far away from the race course, just generalize and do more visualization the day before the race, after you've had a chance to see the actual route. Also, visualize yourself racing several different times. Visualize the perfect race where you are relaxed and strong and you cross the finish line knowing you did the best you could. Also, visualize things that might go wrong and picture yourself staying calm and fixing or accepting the problem without panicking. Visualize missing the start gun by 30 seconds, goggles that break just before the race starts, a cycling shoe that comes off the pedal in transition before you mount the bike, a flat tire, or a shoe lace that comes untied. The important thing is to visualize the distraction happening and not letting it distract you. So if it does happen in a race, you won't panic. You'll calmly correct it and then continue having a great race.

Mental Imagery

Mental imagery is another form of visualization, and can be used during training and racing. We all have imaginations that run free and conjure up all kinds of imagery throughout the day and night. Elite athletes know how to use imagination as a powerful tool for success, separating positive and strong images from negative and debilitating ones. Whenever you feel you are in a rut with your training, you can use imagery to help you break through the plateau. For example, many athletes use imagery to enhance their swimming technique and break through swimming plateaus. What works for you will be very personal. Some athletes imagine themselves as a gliding dolphin, barracuda, or manta ray. Others may imagine themselves as a certain Olympic swimmer, or picture their body as a racing skull with giant hand paddles. Others may isolate a part of the stroke, doing something as simple as swimming with hand paddles, then removing them and imagining they're still there. Use whatever imagery works best for you and employ it during the race. Drawing upon your personal imagery library in conjunction with race visualization keeps you in your own world, which is where you want to be for top performance. Some call this being "in the zone." As the great basketball star Bill Russell said, "I would rebound the ball before the opponent even took his shot." Bill held all the rebounding records as an active player.

As you get better at visualization, you might be surprised how fast you can "see" yourself complete a race that lasts over two hours. Because of the relationship between visualization and the subconscious mind, your mental practice before the race helps keep prerace tension in the positive realm. You have already seen yourself do the race several times, which keeps the fear of the unknown in check. Once you get to race day, you're much less nervous and mainly excited about fulfilling your dreams.

A Word From Wes

Having a Bad Day? Turn It Around!

Race day! This is why you have spent the past three months of your free time training. You ostracized yourself from the rest of the world to enjoy a precious three hours of sheer enjoyment and personal agony. You dedicated so much time and energy to have the perfect race. Your training plan worked without a glitch. You tapered so well that you are ready to explode.

Boom! The gun sounds. Pow! Stars are bouncing around in your head as an elbow clocks you from your friendly competitor. Your left goggle eyepiece is embedded in your eye socket. Now comes the true meaning of "finding oneself."

What do you do as situations arise that prevent you from having that perfect race? Do you throw in the towel? Or do you take the event as a unique aspect of the sport and make the best of it? I present to you some possibilities to make the best of incidents so that you still cross the line with a smile and an acknowledgment of personal achievement.

To prevent incidents from getting the best of you and ruining your race, mentally prepare for the improbable. Visualization lets you imagine what might occur: getting kicked during the swim, losing your goggles, getting a flat tire, dropping a chain, crashing into other cyclists, running or cycling on bad roads, goofing up on transitions, getting blisters, competing in rain or heat, going off course, running out of water at the aid station, or getting delayed by cows crossing the road. If reality does happen, you have already been there and done that in your mind. With mental imagery, you picture yourself living the incident. Instead of being stressed and panicked, you picture yourself calmly correcting the situation or accepting the situation as part of racing.

Throughout my career, I have had several flat tires at races. Since I have pictured myself calmly fixing a flat in my mind time and time again, I am able to more efficiently fix it when it really occurs. Visualization can be used in every aspect. It's raining. Most people hate to compete in the rain. You have mentally pictured yourself feeling comfortable in the rain, not tense because the pavement is wet. You swim off course. You have pictured this happening in your mind, and you calmly get back on course and continue to race well.

Another way to be prepared if things don't go according to plan on race day is to practice solving a problem before race day. For instance, practice putting your bike chain back on the ring while you ride. On many occasions, I have seen people drop their chains in a race. They become flabbergasted, stop their bike, and yank on the chain, getting the chain stuck even more. Most of the time, an athlete will be able to put the chain back on the ring while the bike is still moving; minimal time is lost this way. Practicing will make the race incident less of a shock to you.

Change your brain waves. Your brain is intelligent and sometimes too smart for its own good. Why does your brain want to race? All racing does is stress the body and make the brain work harder. Many times during the race your brain will tell you to quit or walk. It blurts out negative thoughts and entices you to stop at the local liquor store to buy a beer. When my brain wants to stop, that is exactly what I do. I yell, "Stop!" In doing so, I tell my brain to change its negative thinking and start thinking positive thoughts. Find a key word that you can verbalize, which triggers you to change your thinking.

Visualization, practice, and changing the way you think. These three actions will help you in a time of need. See you at the races.

Positive Self-Talk

In dealing with mental strategies, what you say to yourself during the event has the greatest impact. We all have an internal dialogue that runs constantly. For most this is a distraction or a negative much of the time. Interestingly, in the rather wild book series from the 1960s and 1970s by Carlos Castenada about Southwest Indian sorcery techniques, one of their key "paths to power" was achieved by the focused practice of completely shutting down their internal dialogue for extended periods. This freed up the mind. The technique is difficult, but can be used to achieve relaxation and to initiate a "flushing" of the mind to prepare it for positive thoughts and self-talk.

Also, this technique or others you may devise such as Hobson's technique of the "Stop" trigger, can be extremely useful at those points in a race where your every inclination is to give up. Or, a certain imagery as described in the previous section could be your key to snapping out of a negative, debilitating mind-set. Racing hurts—lactic acid buildup, joints pounding over a marathon, the dreaded "bonk," or onset of dehydration. Some of these situations may require more than positive self-talk, but the first time one reduces pain and suffering by mastery of mind over matter through positive self-talk and other methods, is truly a powerful moment. You may simply amaze yourself. Make sure to make strong mental notes of exactly what got you over the hump. When the race is over, write it down in your log. Practice it, enhance it, and build on it. Soon you will have mastery over your body and sport.

Keep your internal dialogue positive. Start today . . . right now. Start by becoming ultra-conscious of what you say to yourself during training. Is your mind filled with cans and dos, or is it filled with can'ts and don'ts?

Assessing what you say to yourself can be a powerful tool in helping reach your potential.

Generally, if your mind believes it can do something (within reason), the body will follow. Conversely, if your mind believes it cannot do something, your body is inhibited from performing. During a race, embrace the "can do" attitude. It's relatively easy to harness this power, simply by controlling what your body hears from your mind. Practice positive self-talk daily, and it will come easier at race time.

The mental side of competition separates a champion from an also-ran. You should practice mental preparation just as seriously as you practice your physical preparation. Schedule time for it. It might provide you with more gains than any other training.

Part VI
RACING

SWIM
BIKE
RUN

Chapter 17

RACE DAY: SPRINT DISTANCE

Race day has arrived! Whether this race is your big event or a competition you're using to prepare for your goal race, your prerace routine must be one that you have used repeatedly with success. This chapter focuses on race strategies for a sprint triathlon; we'll also give you pre- and postrace ideas to enhance performance.

Race-Day Preparations

Make sure things are ready to go the night before, so you're not scraping around making last-minute changes. Wake up at least two hours before the race start. Start hydrating immediately upon waking up, especially if the weather report calls for a hot day. Have a light breakfast. During sleep, you have essentially fasted since dinner, so a light meal in the morning helps top off your glycogen stores. Some triathletes find one or two cups of coffee helpful in waking up. Since most races start early in the morning, you're likely up and about at 5 A.M., so a couple of cups of java will help get you going. Here's a word of warning, however. Don't start drinking coffee the morning of your big race! If you plan on drinking coffee before the race, make sure you have drunk coffee several times during training so that your body is accustomed to its effects. One of the downsides of coffee is that it is a diuretic for most people, so make sure you drink plenty of water to counterbalance the fluids you'll lose through urination.

Arrive at the race start area no later than an hour and a half before the gun. Once you arrive, check in and set up your transition area. Transitions are vitally important in sprint races, so make sure your gear is strategically placed to save precious time. Know exactly where your bike and gear are located. Many triathletes have finished the swim only to forget the precise location of their bike, which makes for a miserable experience. Make sure your area is easy to recognize; identify a few landmarks that help you get to your transition area quickly, or even mark it with a balloon or other visual marker. After getting your transition area established and organized, get ready to warm up.

The following is a transition checklist:

- Set your bike in the right gear for exiting the transition area, and be sure that your tires are properly inflated and have no cuts.
- An ANSI-approved helmet is required. Be sure it's in position for you to pick up and put on, all in one fluid motion.
- Have your sunglasses or other eye protection ready to go.
- Attach your bike shoes to the pedals.
- Have your running shoes open for ease in putting them on. Use lace locks or elastic laces.
- Have your run number handy, placed either on a singlet or an elastic band.
- If you wear a visor (which we recommend if the course is low on shade), be sure it fits properly and is ready to be put on.
- Your water bottle should have enough fluid to hydrate you after the bike. Leave the top open so you don't have to fumble with it during transition.

Warming Up

How many intense workouts do you perform without thoroughly warming up? If you're smart, the answer is probably none. So, why do we see so many competitors neglect to warm up before a race? Who knows? It makes absolutely no sense, but swept up in the moment, some people just tend to forget the important things. Warming up and getting mentally, physically, and emotionally ready to deliver peak performance is the final piece of preparation left to do before the starting gun is fired. If you're not warmed up before the race, expect to put forth much greater effort than you planned and also significantly increase your chances of injury. This is especially true for a sprint triathlon, in which you must be ready to put the hammer down from the start. A thorough warm-up is absolutely required before the start, and you should warm up more than you do for longer races.

If you arrived at the race area an hour and a half before the start, checked in, and then set up your transition area, you have about an hour before the gun goes off. Use this time wisely, getting in an awesome prerace warm-up, including jogging, stretching, spinning on the bike, and perhaps light swimming.

A Word From Wes

Transitions—The Fourth Sport

Although triathlon consists of three primary sports—swimming, biking, and running—there is a fourth element, transition, which is often overlooked. The time spent between the swim to bike (T1) and the bike to run (T2) is key to beating the clock and the competition. First, it doesn't take a lot of sweat and time to improve your transition. Second, it's a lot easier to catch competitors in transition than on the course. And third, a quicker transition won't crank your heart rate or drain your energy. Here are a few basic tips:

T1 swim to bike. Arrive before the start of the race to organize your transition area. Rack your bike by hanging it by the seat, facing the mounting line. Put your sunglasses in your helmet. Hang your helmet with the front facing toward you and the straps ready to put on as you approach your bike. Do the same with your shoes, but place them on a colorful towel so that you can spot your bike among the others. Tie a balloon to the rack near your bike so that you can spot it quickly. Race numbers can be pinned to your jersey or displayed on an elastic waist belt. Men, tuck the jersey with the race number or race belt into your swimsuit so that you can pull it out while you run from the swim to bike.

Before going to the start, pick out your bike as you walk to T1 from the swim course. Make specific notes of the rack location. Is it the fourth rack over, second row back? Is it near a particular race banner? During the swim leg, visualize what will happen as you exit the water. Think about where your bike is and the order you will do things. Approaching T1, take off your swim goggles and swim cap and untuck your race number while running. Next, put on your shoes, lift your bike off the rack, push it to the mount line, and you are out of T1.

T2 bike to run. This transition is much easier than T1. Simply dismount your bike and run it to the rack. Hang your bike and unbuckle your helmet. Put on your running shoes and—see ya! Consider using elastic shoelaces so that you don't have to tie your shoes. Also consider wearing a lightweight mesh cap to keep the sun out of your eyes. Improving transition time is a simple way to decrease your overall time.

Practice these basic tips as part of your regular training regimen to keep your transitions smooth. Come race day, you will have two chances to gain on your competitors: T1 and T2.

Stage 1: Jog + Stretch + Restroom Break

Leave the transition area for a 5- to 10-minute light jog. Allow your heart rate and body temperature to rise gradually. Go half the time out, and come back to the transition area on the way back. After your jog, stretch lightly and find a restroom once more before you start.

Practice all aspects of transition well before you race.

Stage 2: Spin on the Bike

After stage 1, take your bike out for a 10- to 15-minute spin, or bring your trainer and spin on it, which is a preferred method for many athletes. Go through the gears, ensuring all parts are in working order and that everything is ready to go. Watch for traffic around the race site, for it tends to be a bit crazy with volume and sheer confusion. Try to get away from the potential heavy traffic roads as quickly as possible. Also, keep clear of any debris that may cause a flat tire. Most quality races have a bike mechanic on hand, so check out your bike with plenty of time to allow for adjustments if necessary.

After your bike warm-up, re-rack the bike and make any final arrangements to the transition area for optimal time saving. Make sure your bike is in the right gear for the start. If you have a short climb out of the transition area and your bike is in 53 × 14, you're going to waste time shifting your gears. Select a gear in which your legs can spin freely. Then get your swim stuff and head for the start. If the race calls for a wetsuit, put it on and apply petroleum jelly to possible chafing areas and to your lower legs (which greatly aids in getting the suit off after the swim). Apply the jelly with a rag or towel to keep it off your hands. You don't want to accidentally smear it on the insides of your goggles, and the gel can cut down on the sensitivity of your hands while swimming. Also apply petroleum jelly on your inner thighs and the sides of your bike seat to prevent chafing. We're getting close!

Stage 3: Swim or Not to Swim?

Whether you'll want to swim as part of your warm-up depends on water and weather conditions. It's a good idea to warm up for the swim, as you must be ready to sprint at the start. However, as a rule of thumb, if the water temperature is below 80 degrees Fahrenheit *and* the air temperature is below 60 degrees Fahrenheit, then it's too cold for a swim warm-up. Race personnel can give you a good idea of the water temperature. In all USAT-sanctioned races, temperature must be below 78 degrees (per year 2000 rules) for wetsuits to be allowed, so all sanctioned races will be measuring and reporting anyway.

If the race does not allow wetsuits, but the water is cold and you like a warm-up swim, bring a wetsuit along and use it during the warm-up. You'll need to find a way to stay warm between your warm-up and the race start.

Whether you swim or not, you still need to warm up and get ready for the start of the swim. Two plans are described below.

Swim Warm-Up

Get in the water and swim easy for 5 to 10 minutes, mixing up strokes. Once you have done the initial easy swim, do a couple of race-pace efforts for 10 to 20 strokes. This elevates your heart rate and gets you ready for the start. If the race is an in-water start, time your warm-up so you can stay in the water right up until the gun is fired. If it's a running start, have a friend with a towel and warm-up top nearby as you wait for your starting group to be called to the line; put these on and keep them on right up to the final seconds before start.

No Swim Warm-Up

If you can't get into the water at all during warm-up, don't fret. The effects of a great warm-up can be erased if you venture into cold water or air. Your body-core temperature plummets, and any positive effects of a great warm-up are greatly diminished. You can still do a couple of dryland exercises that help you get ready to swim.

First, do plenty of forward and backward arm circles with both arms. Perhaps go through your typical postswim workout flexibility routine. Jumping-jacks and body rotation help to warm up your arms, legs, and torso. Finally, rub your hands with sand or on rough concrete to help sensitize them and enhance your feel for the water.

The Race

You're now warmed up and ready to race. Before the start, position yourself where you want to be within the heat. Remember that mass-start swims are a mad dash at best, especially in sprint races. If you're a fast starter, get to the shortest point between you and the first course buoy. If you start a bit more conservatively, start at the sides or back. Save yourself a lot of grief by getting in the right area.

Once you have assumed starting position, try to relax, give yourself a few words of encouragement, and get ready to hammer down.

The Swim

The gun firing can create a maddening scene: arms and legs fly everywhere, some athletes start in a dead sprint to get away from the pack, while other swimmers almost immediately go off course. Try to start the race with a calm mind and a race-ready body. The more you can disassociate from the pandemonium of the mass start, the better. Get into your race rhythm as quickly as possible. A sprint triathlon swim should feel like AP high intensity. Keep your strokes long, avoid applying too much force to the water while pulling (attempting to overpower the water), and swing your arms comfortably. Let your stroke carry you. Sight breathe as conditions warrant, and swim in a straight line from turn buoy to turn buoy.

Breathing plays a major role in race-day success. It's very easy to start hyperventilating at the start (especially if the water is cold), and taking in air feels like you're sucking eggs. It is very important that you get your breathing relaxed and under control. If you experience the sucking eggs feeling, slow your breathing and focus on taking full breaths. Concentrate on exhaling completely through your mouth and nose while underwater. When you take a breath, let the air "fall" into your lungs—don't force it or gasp for air. Feel like you're breathing deep, from your belly, not your throat. Keeping your breathing in check significantly helps your stroke stay together and conserves precious energy.

As you near the end of the swim, slightly increase your kick tempo to help bring blood to your lower extremities. But don't overkick and use more energy than needed. Also, visualize your bike location and mentally rehearse the first transition.

Transition #1

Once you complete the swim, make your way to the bike, swiftly but in control. Usually there's some form of running between the water and the transition. If you used a wetsuit, begin to remove the top portion as you jog to the bike. Don't make the mistake of sprinting full-bore from the swim to the bike. Your legs still don't have their usual supply of blood and oxygen,

Slightly increase your kick tempo in preparation for the first transition.

and a hurried sprint to the bike will spike lactic acid production and leave you hurting later in the race. If you gradually increase your running tempo as you progress toward the bike, the run from the water to the bike can help your legs get ready to bike.

Once you arrive at your bike, remove your wetsuit (if used) and get your bike stuff on quickly. In a sprint, a swimsuit is all you need for the body—don't even think about putting on shorts. Don your helmet and sunglasses (to keep debris out of your eyes while flying down the racecourse and to keep your face, and thus your body, relaxed). If you need to wear a race number during the bike, make sure you have that as well. Learn to put on your cycling shoes while they are attached to the pedals. It's a simple trick to learn and makes your transitions much faster. Just pedal with your feet on top of your shoes until you reach a good cruising speed and then put your feet into your shoes while coasting for a short period of time. Secure your shoes with the Velcro strap. Practice this before race day. Make your transition as seamless and streamlined as possible.

The Bike

Some triathletes find biking after the swim challenging, mainly because of the lack of blood flow to the legs. It's important to start the bike portion in a reasonable gear and allow for adjustment. But don't waste too much time, as the bike portion will be over before you know it.

You should already be familiar with the racecourse. Save time by effectively cornering and climbing any hills in the optimal position for you. While in the flats, use the biggest gear you can while maintaining 80 to 100 rpm. Try not to under- or overgear, as both are a severe waste of time and energy.

The pace and tempo of a sprint bike leg should feel at AP high. In your aerobars, assume the most aerodynamic position possible, and stay in that position. Anytime you open up your chest and expose a large frontal area, you'll slow down immensely or cause unnecessary energy expenditure. When you need to shift gears, do it quickly, smoothly, and accurately. Be familiar with the course—anticipate your gear changes or, better yet, completely rehearse them in advance.

Keep your breathing in check on the bike, just as you did during the swim. Exhale completely and fully. Inhalation should be natural and feel as if you're breathing deeply, using your stomach muscles. Focusing on breathing helps maintain concentration and increases your body awareness of the effort you're exerting. If you have a cylcocomputer, keep tabs on your mph or rpm; don't let either get too low.

During a sprint, avoid aid stations on the bike, unless it's impossible. One water bottle will be plenty. Getting a drink or a new bottle slows you down and takes you out of your rhythm. But be sure to drink along the way during the bike; hydrating will pay off later in the run, especially if the weather is warm.

As you near the end of the bike, gear down slightly and stretch your legs briefly. This will help you in the run. Let your heel drop below your pedal to stretch your lower leg, open your knees to stretch your groin, stand up and arch your back to stretch the lumbar region. Just as you did in the swim, visualize a perfect transition from bike to run.

Transition #2

Safety is a big concern now, as you have athletes flying off the bike course into the transition area. Slow down, and pay attention to race officials, who are looking out for your safety. Reckless behavior can lead to disqualification or injury. Any loss in time is negligible if you simply must slow down to play it safe.

Once you reach your transition area, rack your bike and quickly put on your running shoes. Some triathletes struggle with the switch in shoes, but elastic laces and quick-ties help a lot. Also, if you did brick intervals in training, this transition should be a snap. Take off your helmet, and be sure your race number is clearly visible. Now let's get going and finish this!

© Empics

Spencer Smith, a true professional, is always mentally prepared for peak performance.

The Run

The first few steps after the bike can be very awkward, but if you practiced bike–run transitions in training, you should be okay. One tendency sprint triathletes must avoid is taking out too fast on the run. After spending a good deal of time on the bike zipping down the road at 20 to 30 mph, running at 6- to 8-minute-mile pace seems really slow. This is due simply to the kinesthetic "feel" your body adopted while cycling—you became accustomed to what it's like to move fast on the bike. To keep yourself from falling into this trap, pay attention to your stride length and frequency, and again, check your breathing. Keep your stride short and quick. Many triathletes overstride at the start of the run and waste precious energy. Starting too fast will come back to haunt you later. Feel like you're building your tempo the first quarter to half mile.

Settle into a pace that again feels like AP high (a recurring theme during a race of this length). If there are corners to negotiate, be sure to run the shortest distance possible and pick up your pace in and out of them. Keep your effort even up hills, and aggressively attack downhill portions. If people are in front of you, go after them. As you get close to the finish line, start building your speed. Instead of sprinting the last 100 meters in world-record time, use that energy more evenly over the last 400 to 800 meters. Reserve a full, dead-on finishing kick for a potential victory (or for beating your training buddy).

Postrace Recovery

After your race, you'll want to keep moving. Allow time to just walk around and allow your heart rate to lower. Your body temperature will begin to fall quickly, so try to put on warm, dry clothes. Drink some fluid-replacement beverage and have a snack. Some triathlons are famous for their postrace buffets. But before gorging yourself, take time to cool down. If your bike is available, a spin of 10 to 15 minutes significantly helps promote recovery. If your bike is at another location, a short jog of 5 to 10 minutes is also okay. Also, some triathlons have postrace massage available. A massage helps get rid of any potential race soreness. If no masseuse is available, do some light stretching.

It takes one to three days to recover from a sprint race depending on your fitness level. Avoid hard workouts until the postrace soreness is gone. It's usually easier to complete a tough swim practice or bike workout before a tough run. Generally a tough swim workout could be done two to four days after a shorter race, whereas you should wait a minimum of three days before any hard running.

End your day at the races by thanking the race director and as many volunteers as possible. Without their service to and love of the sport, we would not have these tests of our capabilities. Putting on a race is a monumental task, and showing your appreciation helps keep your favorite races around for a long time. If you had a truly wonderful experience, send a note to the race committee to tell them so and to applaud the individuals who were out there helping you.

Chapter 18

RACE DAY: OLYMPIC DISTANCE

Now that triathlon has finally made it into the Olympics, the Olympic distance will increase in popularity worldwide. The international standard is a 1.5K swim (equal to the longest swimming event in the Olympics), 40K on the bike (the standard distance for individual time trials in international cycling), and a 10K run (common track event plus a popular road-racing distance). Tying these three distances together helps a broader audience understand triathlon. A competitive swimmer has probably swum the 1,500, a competitive cyclist has likely completed a 40K time trial, and almost all runners have raced the popular 10K.

This triathlon distance fits well into the Olympic Games format. The race takes a little less time than the marathon, and because of the relative brevity of the event, the racing is intense and exciting, perfect for a worldwide television audience. Triathlon has fought long and hard to be accepted by the Olympic community, and its introduction into the Games benefits all triathletes, amateur and elite.

Although the Olympic standard is 1.5K/40K/10K, the category includes the following ranges of distance: swim—1 to 2K; bike—30 to 50K; and run: 8 to 15K. The category challenges all multisport athletes and serves as "middle ground" among triathletes. The distance is long enough for pacing to be important but short enough for intensity to come into play. Those who focus on sprint events and tend to thrive at the hammer-down approach step up in Olympic distance; competitors who excel at longer events come down to the Olympic distance and consider the event more of a sprint. This makes for exciting competition. Who will succeed, the speedy sprinter or the steady, strong Ironman competitor?

Race-Day Preparations

Prepare for the Olympic distance in much the same way as you do for a sprint event (see chapter 17). Pre-warm-up and actual race warm-up routines are

230

virtually identical to those of a shorter race; you may increase duration slightly, but it's not really necessary. The greater difference is how you execute the event and that's what this chapter will focus on. As mentioned earlier, a race of two to three hours is too long to push at maximum aerobic capacity. Your glycogen stores need to be full, so eat a proper diet up to race day and attend to hydration. A race of this distance pushes your energy stores to the limit, so you can't be depleted in any way.

Because of the time and energy demands of racing an Olympic distance triathlon, it's wise to consume a fluid-replacement beverage, especially on the bike. Have at least one water bottle full of your favorite fluid-replacement drink, and be sure to hydrate often during the bike. Studies have shown that consuming fluid-replacement is superior to plain water during an endurance event. If an athlete is familiar with the mixture, the electrolyte balance enhances the absorption of fluid into the body—just be sure you have used the drink in training.

The Race

Pacing is critical for race-day success at Olympic distance. Savvy competitors push the pace but not so much that they pay for it later. We'll describe how to attack each segment.

The Swim

As with any open-water swim, the start is fast and furious. We hope you have become acquainted with the nuances of a mass-swim start. Prior to race day, completing the World's Best Triathlon Swim Workout (chapter 6) significantly helps prepare your mind and body for a successful swim start.

Once the swim pace starts leveling out, get into a steady rhythm and gain control of your stroke and breathing. If a fellow competitor is slightly ahead of you, get on his or her feet and draft. Be sure to exercise drafting etiquette (see chapter 7), and, if the opportunity presents itself, do your share of the work. And, don't rely totally on the person (or pack) in front of you for navigation. Sight breathe every 4 to 12 stroke cycles no matter what, and swim the shortest possible distance by staying in a straight line.

The overall pace (after the initial quick start) should feel like AP low pace or "comfortably hard." Make sure you don't overuse your legs by kicking too hard, but do elevate your kick tempo the last 50 to 100 meters to increase blood flow in preparation for the bike.

Transition #1

The first transition is a good opportunity to hydrate after swimming for 15+ minutes. Get something to drink as soon as you exit the water. Many races have the first aid station right after the swim. Take advantage. Grab a cup of water and drink as you make your way to the bike.

© Anthony Neste

Conserve your energy while running through shallow water.

Once you get to the bike, speed is of the essence, just as in the sprint distance. Time saved in the transition is "free time." Precious seconds, even minutes, can be lost if your transition is inefficient. Time saved here does not require you to swim, bike, or run any faster. Be organized, smooth, and quick in getting out on the bike course.

The Bike

Many Olympic distance competitors err in taking the bike leg out much too fast. Make sure your legs feel normal during the bike by progressing your gearing and effort the first mile. Stay away from an all-out effort at the start.

This is an important time to gain control of your breathing. Focus on full, deep breaths and relax your upper body as much as possible. You don't want to waste *any* energy. Rapid, shallow breathing and unnecessary upper-body movement saps the strength you'll need later.

The intensity of the bike can be in the AP high range. Focus on spreading your cycling strength over the entire distance. A strong, evenly paced bike leg is generally much faster than an erratic ride of varying speeds. Make sure you take in fluids along the way (especially with a fluid-replacement drink). Toward the end of the bike leg, do a couple of on-bike stretches to get you ready for the run.

A Word From Wes

Racing: What to Eat?

A majority of triathlons are Olympic distance (1.5K swim, 40K bike, and 10K run). I complete this distance in 1:45 to 2:05 depending on the course geography. I have raced more than 200 triathlons in my career, and I have found what energy supplements work best for me. Before the race, I eat enough so that my stomach feels "not empty." This doesn't mean stuffed, but satiated. The amount of calories I eat before the race depends on the time the race starts—my caloric intake for a 7 A.M. race differs from a 2 P.M. race.

Everyone burns a different amount of calories in a triathlon. It depends on a person's fitness level, body type, and the time it takes to finish a race. Usually, 30 minutes before the race I will have half of a Clif Bar. I continue to drink water leading up to the start of the race. On the bike, I have two full water bottles. One contains water and the other contains an electrolyte replenishment drink, such as TeamPro2's ProEndurance. I also have two Clif Shots taped to the top tube of my bike. I prefer the Chocolate Espresso and the Peanut Buzz because they have caffeine in them. I have one shot 20 minutes into the bike ride and one 20 minutes before the bike ride ends.

On the run, I grab two more Clif Shots in the transition area, and I take one at the beginning of the run and then another 20 minutes later. I know that some professional triathletes use only an electrolyte drink in the Olympic distance race. Everyone is different so make sure you experiment in training to maintain a stable energy level. In doing so, you will be less likely to have a surprise bonk at mile four of the run.

Transition #2

Quickly get your running shoes on and make your way to the run course. Have a water bottle near your running gear with the top open, so you can drink right away. Guard against going out too fast by keeping those first few strides short and quick.

The Run

Build slowly and evenly the first mile of the run. This is a good time to reinforce your race effort with positive self-talk. Repeat to yourself phrases like "feeling awesome," "doing great," "flow," and so on. The first half of a 10K run can be the toughest part. You realize that you still have quite a bit of racing to do. Keep your mind filled with happy thoughts and keep the negative ones out.

As on the bike, spread your effort throughout the run course. The overall intensity should feel like AP high but may drop to the AP low range as fatigue sets in. Keep your form as much as possible and avoid any wasted movements, such as overstriding or crossover. Move everything forward toward the end of the run, and finish strong.

Postrace Recovery

Your routine after the race resembles your postrace for the sprint. Walk around a little after finishing and put on warm, dry clothes. Eat and drink a bit and, if possible, head out for an easy spin on the bike. Get a postrace massage or stretch. Treat yourself to a nutritious, high-calorie postrace meal. Your body needs it.

It takes anywhere from two to seven days to fully recover from an Olympic distance race depending on your fitness level. Don't do any hard workouts until all your postrace soreness is gone. Do some easy swimming and spinning on your bike for a few days following the race, as they actually promote recovery. You should wait at least three days before attempting a quality run workout.

Do You Have Olympic Dreams?

With triathlon's inclusion in the Olympic program, you may aspire to compete someday at the elite level or even to represent your country in the sport. The sport has evolved since the early days, and racing at this highest level is much different than it once was. If you do dream of being an elite competitor and becoming one of the best in the world, here is a scenario for the development of a potential Olympian.

Great Olympic distance triathletes need to come from a swimming background. Learn to swim efficiently and effectively early in life. Former swimmers tend to become better sprint and Olympic distance triathletes because they can finish the first segment in contention and expend relatively little energy. Future Olympian triathletes are in the pool right now.

After getting started in the water, a future Olympic triathlete's attention turns from the pool toward the track, with a focus on events such as the 800 meters and mile in running and cycling. The emphasis needs to be on speed versus endurance, as today's best Olympic hopefuls are not only strong at all three sports but are deadly fast runners. It's not uncommon for elite triathletes today to post sub 31:00 (men) or sub 35:00 (women) in the 10K. Running both track and cross-country in college is probably the best way to go for an aspiring triathlete. The prime ages for peak performance in endurance sports are 25 to 35. Thus, post college is the time to start focusing on preparing specifically for the triathlon, with a greater emphasis on cycling.

Cycling in elite triathlon racing today has become mostly draft-legal at the international level. The future great triathlete will need to be comfortable with bike road-race strategies. It will no longer be the time trial effort that initially began the sport. Pace lines, echelons, and team-style racing will dominate the bike leg of triathlon.

Ultimately, the future elite competitors vying for Olympic and international glory will need to

- swim fast enough to stay with the leaders. You might not be able to win the race in the swim, but if you finish too far back, your race is over.

- bike comfortably in a pack and work well with others. It's conceivable that if better swimmers form an alliance and team time-trial together effectively, they can gain time on weaker swimmers who happen to be lightning-quick runners.

- finish with an extremely fast run leg. To truly be in contention for the top spots, an elite triathlete must be able to cover a 10K at blazing-fast times. If you don't have this type of speed, you're probably going to get run down a lot.

Here are some training tips for the aspiring elite triathlete:

- Swim: Always keep your swimming edge. Train with a team, and let the coach know your goals as a triathlete. Five to six sessions a week

© Bongarts Photography/SportsChrome USA

Simon Whitfield winning the gold medal at the 2000 Sydney Olympics.

are a must. If you're a strong swimmer, don't make the mistake of backing off in your best event—keep swimming the cornerstone of your program.

- Bike: Train with a group one to two days a week. Most serious cycling communities have a weekly ride (or two) where cyclists get together and simply hammer each other. This type of training session often turns into impromptu road races. Participating in a weekly ride is a great way to learn how to ride with a group and get a very intense workout as well.

- You also need to complete some bike-training sessions on your own. Hill workouts, AP high/AP low sessions and speedwork all need to be in your program. If you ride with a group once a week, count it as an AP session and fit perhaps one or two other quality sessions in on a weekly basis. Be sure to incorporate easy EN sessions to help you recover.

- It may also be wise to join a cycling team and do bike races at certain points during the year, a practice becoming more common among triathletes. Learning how to time-trial helps all aspects of triathlon racing, but only road-racing and criterium events allow you to further experience the art of riding with a group at high speeds.

- Run: Quality, quality, quality. If you have collegiate running experience, don't get caught up in long, slow runs. Instead, maintain two quality sessions per week, and all other run training can be recovery in nature. Focus on increasing your speed and your ability to run well off the bike. Brick intervals help improve running off the bike. The goal of your preparation should be to see how close you can come to your 10K personal best (track or road) in a triathlon. In the near future, we will see triathletes break 30:00 (men) and 33:00 (women) for 10K.

Chapter 19

RACE DAY: LONG AND ULTRA-DISTANCES

Long and ultra-distance events require special attention for success on race day. Just completing a race of this length is often viewed as a victory in itself, which is an extremely healthy way of looking at these competitions. Racing these events requires huge physical, mental, and emotional demands that are difficult to replicate in training. It is wise to have a modest race goal for your first long or ultra race. Every race is a learning experience, and you will need to run a few longer races to learn the ropes. After a couple, you'll be ready to compete in an event of this magnitude.

Race-day strategies for ultra or long-distance triathlons are similar. Because of the obvious challenge of longer racing, you need a plan to cover the entire day of competition. Start with a positive attitude—after all the time and effort you have put into this day, you deserve a wonderful experience.

Your race-day strategy should be well–thought out and simple to execute. Establish a prerace routine and a competition plan, along with a recovery routine for after the race. Longer racing is quite different from Olympic distance and sprint racing. Choosing the right equipment and clothing is even more important. At the race, you should be prepared for anything that comes up, which might mean bringing a lot of stuff to the race location, especially if weather conditions are hard to predict. During the race, pacing is a huge issue; go a little too fast early, and you'll experience fatigue. Early fatigue is no good in any triathlon and is particularly terrible in a long or ultra race. On the other hand, if you go too slowly, you won't perform up to your expectations. Ideal pacing is the key to a great race.

In this chapter we'll break down the components of race-day planning for an athlete getting ready for an Ironman distance race (2.4-mile swim/112-mile bike/26.2-mile run). Race-day preparations are similar for races up to half the distance of a standard Ironman. These guidelines will help you prepare properly so you can have a great experience.

Before the Race

Later in this chapter we'll tackle specific preparation on race day; first, we need to discuss some advanced preparations that are keys to success in racing longer distances.

Research the Race

Learn all the information you can about your big event. Contact the race director and ask about entry procedures, race management, course terrain, typical weather conditions, lodging options, and pre-event training possi-

© Sport The Library/SportsChrome USA

Pros like Wendy Ingraham learn as much as possible about their races well in advance of race day.

bilities. Many races include a lot of information on the internet as well. The more information you can gather, the easier your decision whether to invest your time and money in this race. You are the consumer in this market—shop around to find the best event that fits your needs.

For some athletes, a question as basic as what energy-replacement drink is used during the race can make or break many competitors. If you train with Gatorade and get to the race and find out they'll be using Exceed, you may have a tough day on the racecourse. Finding answers to the little questions often makes the difference between a good and bad experience.

Once you select an event, make your travel plans early; know what mode of transport you intend to use. If you fly, buy or borrow a hard-shell bike case. Make lodging reservations early, as close to the race site as possible. If you wait too long, many nearby lodging options will be booked, adding unnecessary drive time to your prerace preparations. Also, don't forget that entry fee; many long races fill up well before the entry deadline.

Acclimatize to Race Conditions

Learn the typical weather conditions for the race area during the time of year in which it is held. Too often, a season's worth of training goes down the tubes when an athlete is not ready for the weather or terrain challenges. These races last a very long time, so the run is usually during the heat of the midday. If you normally run in the early morning when the weather is cooler, your body may not be able to handle the stress of severe heat. If the bike course has monster hills and all you have done are flat training rides, be ready for a world of hurt. If the course is hilly, make sure you have trained appropriately and that your bike has the correct gearing.

Survey the Course

A couple of days before the race, take time to survey the racecourse. Drive the bike and run courses in a car. Pay attention to obstacles like rough road, potholes, tight corners, or steep hills. Find the mileage markers, which should be set up in advance. Find out where the aid stations will be so you can plan your hydration and refueling. The more you know about the race course, the better off you'll be during the race.

Establish a Race Hydration/Refueling Plan

In races that last more than three hours, you'll need to determine a systematic way of drinking and eating during the race. Many elite multisport athletes have found success with the simple plan outlined below:

2 hours prior to race	Light breakfast and energy-replacement drink
	Drink water liberally
30 minutes before race	Energy bar (if tolerated) and water

Just before swim	8 to 12 ounces of water
After the swim	Water bottle of energy-replacement drink
Every 10 to 15 minutes eduring the bike	Alternate drinks of water and energy placement
Every 30 minutes during the bike	Eat some solid food (half an energy bar, small banana, two to three fig bars) or gel product
During the run	Alternate drinking water and energy-replacement drink every aid station (usually one mile apart)

Experiment during training with the schedule you plan to follow. Many athletes devise elaborate methods of measuring hydration or caloric loss during a race, making sure they replace exact amounts being depleted. This may be beneficial to the elite athlete; in our opinion simply establishing a plan similar to the one we've suggested above and sticking to it is enough for most athletes. The most frequent problems are caused by insufficient hydration or too-low calorie intake.

A Word From Wes

Airline Travel

Buying Your Tickets

Usually, you will need to purchase tickets at least 21 days before your departure date if you want a cheap fare. For international travel, the cheapest tickets are usually through travel agencies that sell consolidated tickets; with these agencies you can save up to $500. Web sites also offer cheaper fares than airlines, especially if you are flexible on travel dates.

Bike Travel

Airlines have raised the price of bike travel to $75 one way. It is absurd, but airlines have the right to charge what they want to charge. In an attempt to fly their bikes free of charge, people use a myriad of disguises for their bike cases. I've seen bikes covered by tuba cases and scuba gear, which fly free of charge. One triathlete packs his bike in a bike case, but he leaves out a pedal. When the ticket counter person asks if that is a bike, he replies, "No, it's bike parts—it's not rideable." He says about 40 percent of the time he gets on free without having to lie. You can also give the curbside baggage person a $20 tip. If he takes the money and delivers the bike, you have saved up to $55 in bike travel. If you don't want to press your luck, getting a free bike pass is the least stressful way to travel. You can get free bike passes on certain airlines through USA Triathlon or by joining US Amateur.

Seating

When checking in, request an emergency exit row so that you'll have more legroom. You can only reserve an exit row at check-in, and you can reserve an exit row seat on the return flight since they know you are physically able. If exit rows are unavailable, window seats are great on short flights if you don't feel like mingling and if you want to sleep and lean against the window. The aisle seats are good for longer flights where you can stand and stretch your legs often.

Boarding

When the flight attendant calls for boarding, why does everyone hurry up and board? While the herd is waiting in line, use this time to stretch, get water, and use the restroom. Boarding last is less stressful because you don't receive the negative energy and tension from those who are in a hurry to sit. If you do board last, it is a good idea to have a small carry-on because space may be minimal.

Flying Essentials

Full water bottle. The longer the flight, the more dehydrated you'll get. Flight attendants never seem to come around often enough with beverage service.

Earplugs. If you forget them, you'll be seated right next to a screaming baby.

Eye covers. For those who need total quiet and darkness to snooze.

Headphones. Better sound quality than the airline's headphones and you don't have to deal with other people's earwax and hair gel.

Travel partner. Excellent for hand, neck, and back massages in your seat.

Good book and a deck of cards. Helps to pass time.

Exiting

When the plane reaches the gate, everyone jumps up and hurries to grab their overhanging luggage just so they can. . . wait another five minutes! This is an excellent time for triathletes to stay seated, take deep breaths, and visualize the transition to the baggage claim area.

When flying, prepare your mind for possible delays, canceled flights, mechanical problems, or bad weather, and the trip will be more enjoyable.

Race-Day Preparations

Most Ironman races begin at the first light of day. The sheer competition time of these events requires a full day to complete (and some continue well after dark), which means you'll be up early and doing most of your prerace preparation in the dark. You probably won't sleep well the night before, but that's all right, as the most important nights of sleep are the few nights preceding the night before the race. If you sleep lousy, just look around at your competitors and know they probably slept lousy, too. In fact, it's not unusual to have a virtually sleepless night before a race.

Special Equipment Needs

Because long events take so much time to complete, being comfortable and gaining speed advantages are important for race-day success. Here are some extra equipment needs for a long race:

- Sunscreen. Very important for a sunny or hot race. Be sure to use a water-repellent sunscreen that does not cause skin irritation. Use the same brand in training before race day. Choose an SPF 30 or higher since you'll be exposed for a long time.

- Water bottles. Bring along plenty of water bottles to use before, during, and after the race. Make sure you have one to use before the swim and others ideally placed for use during each transition. If you're racing in very warm to hot conditions, try freezing your bottles the night before and letting them thaw gradually during the day—or purchase insulated water bottles.

- Petroleum jelly. Apply to all parts of your body that chafe in the three sports. Also have a small container available before the run so you can reapply if needed.

- Sunglasses. A must for any race to protect your eyes and keep your facial muscles relaxed.

- Visor. If it's sunny and hot, wear a visor during the run. Keeping the sun off your face helps beat fatigue.

- Appropriate clothing for all events (which we'll discuss later).

- Heart rate monitor. It's a must on the bike and helps on the run by making sure you're at the right intensity and accurately calibrating your pace.

Preparing Equipment

Organize your race-day equipment well before race day. Many Ironman competitions require you to check in your bike and race gear the day before the race (which helps cut down on confusion for race organizers). If you're confronted with checking in your equipment early, here are some tips:

- Make sure you have everything. Once you get to race check-in, you should not have to go back to the hotel to get the bike helmet that you forgot. Make a checklist and go through it a couple of times before leaving for check-in.

- Organize your equipment precisely. Set up your first transition exactly how you want it. If you have to bag your clothing for the different transitions, make sure you have everything you need. Place a plastic cover over all your equipment to keep away night moisture. Also, make sure the plastic cover is weighted down to prevent the wind from uncovering your equipment. Soggy, damp shoes and clothes will slow your transition before the bike or run.

- Deflate your tires and cover your bike. Excessive heat can build up from sitting in the sun causing tires to explode. Also, this forces you to inflate to proper pressure the morning of the race, always a good idea. Covering your bike prevents night moisture from building up on sensitive bike parts, such as the chain, derailleur, and brakes.

- Make sure all race numbers are properly placed. Most Ironman races require lots of numbering of your equipment. Double check that you number everything properly.

Taking advantage of checking in the day before is so beneficial—it helps free up time race morning so you can concentrate on a great race.

Selecting Clothing

Clothing selection for the three sports has a huge impact on race day. For the swim it's pretty basic: wear a wetsuit if it's legal (remember a wetsuit is always faster, even for an accomplished swimmer), and your actual swimsuit should be very comfortable and easy to take off. Make sure you have antifog goggles and a race cap. If the water is cold, wear double caps or a thermal cap.

Since you'll spend most of your time on the bike, bike clothing is important. Many elite competitors race in swimsuits or have their cycling shorts on under their wetsuit, and this might work for you, too. However, the most important consideration is comfort for the 112 miles. Changing into full cycling garb is the ticket for most. Cycling shorts with a well-padded crotch and a very aerodynamic top works well. Wearing a swimsuit under your cycling shorts may be an option, but it needs to be comfortable. A tight suit can put a world of hurt on you late in the bike. Whatever you wear, just make sure it has been tried on a long training ride as well—don't ever try something new and untested on race day. A fanny pack can be helpful if your cycling top does not have pockets; a pack is a good place to store snacks.

© iphotonews.com/Brooks

Changing in to full cycling gear is a good idea for Ironman-distance events.

Socks and gloves are important and go a long way toward protecting your hands and feet.

For the run, traditional running shorts or a swimsuit will work fine. A running singlet helps hold your race number in place. Unless you are an elite athlete or have lots of experience racing in flats, we recommend wearing broken-in running shoes with ample support and cushioning. Comfort is vastly more important than light weight for running 26.2 miles. A marathon is also no place for brand-new shoes. Also, be sure to put on that visor before heading out.

Race Morning

Wake up at least two hours before the race starts. Eat a light breakfast and start hydrating. If coffee works for you, have two cups maximum. Also, relieve yourself before heading to the race staging area.

Once you're at the first transition area, get your bike ready. Air up the tires and make sure everything is in working order. Remove the plastic covering from all your gear and go over that as well. If you need to check in with race personnel, do this early. If you need your body marked with your race number, bring a black, waterproof marker and have a friend or family member do it for you. This saves a few minutes standing in line. Once everything is prepared, you're ready to warm up.

Warming Up

Because of the distance and duration of long events, your warm-up is very different from what you do before shorter races. In the long races, you can use the first portion of each event as your warm-up. More on this later.

If you have the opportunity to spin before the race, do it. A simple 5- to 10-minute easy bike before the race is enough to loosen up the legs in a manner that is more gentle and easy than running. But if you checked in your bike the night before, chances are race personnel will not let you remove it before the race. In this case, you have three options:

1. Bring two bikes to the race. Many athletes (most notably Dave Scott, seven-time Ironman Hawaii Champion) bring a second bike with them to the race. Because they know it's impossible to remove their race-day chariot, a second one is used expressly to warm up the morning of the race.

2. Bring a portable wind-trainer with you to the transition area. Many companies make portable wind-trainers that can be used anywhere and travel very easily. This makes warming up at the transition area a snap.

3. Go without a bike warm-up. Run a short jog in lieu of a bike warm-up. However, it's probably a better idea to spin before a long race because it's easier on the legs.

If the water temperature is warm enough for you, a short swim is appropriate. Remember to be smart when deciding if this is for you; if taking a dip will lower your core temperature too much, simply swing your arms and stretch lightly. A light stretch before the race should be the last part of your warm-up.

As mentioned above, consider using the first part of each event to warm up. Let the pro and elite competitors sprint for position. Try to choose the path of least resistance for the swim. Stay away from crowds. Settle into a pace and draft in the swim. The bike and run portions should also start gently.

The time just ahead of the gun can be the most anxious moment for a triathlete. Think happy thoughts and talk positively to yourself. You have

Look forward to the opportunity to use the tools you've acquired in training.

done the work, and this is simply a celebration to show off your talents. Avoid turning a long race into a fear fest. If you've done the preparation, your equipment is in good working order, and you have a solid race strategy, you'll be fine.

The Race

You'll need a pacing and eating game plan for during the race. Earlier we described an eating plan for a longer race. You should have put this plan, or your own alternative, into practice during training leading up to the event so you'll be ready with food and drink during the event.

A pacing plan is also important for each discipline. You should complete all three at an effort that feels on the low side of AP low intensity. Now we'll outline strategies for the five parts of your race.

The Swim

As mentioned earlier, start in an area with the least congestion. If you were unable to warm up for the swim, start the race with the idea of gradually increasing the pace to the level you want to achieve. Unless you're an elite competitor or are trying to get away from a large group of unruly swimmers, don't start out at a sprint. Keep your effort even, keep a check on your breathing, and use your legs only for balance. A light, two-beat (two kicks per arm cycle) kick is plenty. You will have practiced your kick pattern in training, so it should feel natural. Avoid overusing your legs during the swim. Sight breathe as little as possible to save energy from going up and down; direct your energy into moving forward.

Transition #1

If you raced in salt water, quickly shower with freshwater to rinse off the salt residue. If this is your first experience with a race of this length, take time to change into cycling clothing. Practice this transition well before race day. You'll make up any time lost changing later by being more comfortable on the road. Also, put on your heart rate monitor chest unit. If possible, drink a full bottle of fluid-replacement beverage during this transition.

The Bike

Start by monitoring your heart rate. Remember you want to stay in the AP low range. Most triathletes find it easy to stay in this area and feel that it's perhaps too slow. Don't make the mistake of tuning out the signals your body gives you, as it will call for paybacks later. If you trained at 150 to 155 beats per minute for AP low training, stay in that range, even if it means sacrificing a couple of places early. You'll likely catch those rabbits later.

Get into your eating and drinking pattern quickly to avoid forgetting to eat and drink at the right times. It is extremely important to have a set plan for hydration and caloric intake and stick to that plan during the bike. The consequences of not doing so will catch up with you prior to finishing the bike and leave you in trouble during the run. Make sure your clock is visible, or set a countdown timer that reminds you when to eat and drink. You should consume 4 to 6 ounces of water every 15 to 30 minutes, and up to 200 calories per hour of racing (adjust up or down for temperature and intensity of exercise). Remember, you just swam for an hour or so and consumed no water or calories, so you should start consuming quickly. A good, simple plan is to set a countdown timer for 15 minutes. At every interval take a couple swigs of water (this will be two to four ounces). It is better if intake is frequent and small instead of infrequent and large. Every half hour take in calories. Calorie intake can be via a sports drink (which doubles as hydration) or a gel packet, energy bar, or if you can handle it, some fruit. Gel packets are convenient and easy to digest. They are generally just over 100 calories each and some gels contain caffeine if you like that. But beware!

Eating three or four gels during a medium-distance race is one thing, but ingesting 8 to 12 during an Ironman may cause an upset stomach. Most find that mixing in a sports drink and some solid food works best. All these energy sources have labels stating caloric level. Another important aspect is sodium intake, and these labels give you that information as well. If conditions are hot, two to three grams of sodium can be lost per hour; make sure your intake of calories includes sodium at this rate. Ideally, you will have practiced grabbing food and drink from aid-station helpers in past races. Slow down when you go for a bottle or food and focus on what you are doing.

Change your position on the bike frequently. If you're on a flat course, periodically stand up and ride out of the saddle briefly. This helps shift some of the burden from the same muscle units and redirect blood flow to other areas. If you're on a challenging course that varies in terrain, climb in the most efficient position and choose appropriate gearing. Never try to overgear a climb; keep spinning. Focus on your breathing and make sure you are exhaling calmly and fully.

Toward the end of the bike, take time to stretch your worn muscles by standing and dropping your heels, which helps to stretch your lower legs. Arch your back to stretch your spine, and open your knees to the side to help stretch your groin.

Transition #2

Once you're off the bike, you might experience rubbery legs—cycling for 5+ hours can do that to you. Having completed brick sessions in training really helps at this point. During transition, get mentally into the run by thinking positive thoughts. Make sure to apply petroleum jelly to any areas on your body susceptible to chafing. Change into running clothing and take a water bottle with you for the first quarter- to halfmile of the run. This bottle should contain plain, cold water. Drink liberally, and pour some over your head to cool off.

The Run

Start the run with very short strides and gradually increase the length during the first mile or two. Your first priority is to get your "running legs" underneath you. As you feel better, you'll be able to get into a normal rhythm. Focus on running the shortest distance possible by running the tangents. Keep corners and angles as short as possible. Run in a straight line, and avoid stride crossover, bounce, and overstriding, all of which waste precious energy.

On uphill portions of the course, keep your effort as you did on the flats. Don't aggressively pace the uphill sections by running with greater intensity. Imagine you have a shoulder harness attached to balloons overhead. As you make your way up the hill, envision those balloons helping you up. Once you reach the crest and descend, keep your strides short and quick. If your legs are feeling good, it's okay to pick up your pace while descending, as doing so requires no extra physiological effort. Just keep your foot strike light.

Take your time to get into the rhythm of running when first getting off the bike.

If the run gets tough for you, concentrate on progressing from one aid station to the next. Most Ironman marathon courses have aid stations every mile. By focusing on each station, you in essence break the course down into smaller, more manageable sections. Maybe walk the aid stations and drink an entire beverage, or use a sponge to cool off. Drink cool liquids when possible, as they are more rapidly absorbed by the stomach.

A secret of some top performers in longer races is planning for a caffeine/sugar pick-me-up in the later stages of the marathon. What can work perfect is de-fizzed cola. Drinking flat cola was popular among marathoners in the 1970s and works well for some competitors. Some races provide this beverage, but bring some along just in case. It doesn't matter what kind of cola, but it shouldn't be diet (as artificial sweetener can cause stomach upset) and it must be flat. If you want to try this drink during the race, be sure to use it in training before race day.

You should have ingested sufficient water and calories during the bike, where it is more efficient to do so. You should stay with your intake plan during the run. If you have decided on hydration every 15 minutes, this may translate to drinking at every other water stop if they are at one-mile intervals, and every fourth for calories (whatever sports drink they have, if it's agreeable to you, or your own source of calories if you're carrying it).

In a marathon, lactic acid pain or joint pain can sometimes build up to almost unbearable levels. Walking breaks are one solution, but stopping at an aid station and stretching is another. It's amazing how much better you can feel with one minute of stretching; this may be much more efficient in the long run than walking. Additionally, if there is a decent (not too rough or uneven) softer surface along the side of the road, consider running there for a while, but don't twist an ankle!

As you make your way to the finish, try to enjoy the moment. You're about to finish one of the ultimate feats of human endurance. You shouldn't count on it, but in the last half mile it's not uncommon to get a boost of adrenaline to carry you across the line.

Postrace Recovery

Sometimes athletes neglect the importance of recovery after a big event. It takes at least one to two weeks (after a long race) or up to a month (after an ultra race) before you're fully recovered from the effort.

An active cool-down is not as important right after a long race as it is for a shorter event. Keep moving after crossing the finish line. Walk around and check yourself for signs of dehydration. Signs of dehydration can include loss of coordination, bright yellow urine (urine should be pale yellow), sunken eyes with dark circles, dizziness, and nausea. If you experience these things you should allow a medical support staff doctor to evaluate you. Continue to monitor yourself for 24 hours following the race.

Do some very light stretching and get a postrace massage, but only after you've walked around enough to cool down properly. Eat as much as you want to, and drink more than you think you need. Enjoy a big dinner later to celebrate. Avoid heavy stretching for up to two days after the race, as your muscles have experienced some cellular damage and need time to recover.

The day following the big race, go out and spin easily for 20 to 30 minutes on the bike and maybe swim 500 to 1,000 yards very easily. Stay away from running until all postrace soreness is gone. Two or three weeks of easy bikes and swims helps you recover quickly and prevent injury from coming back too fast, too soon. Also, try to schedule a couple of professional massages during this time—they feel great and help promote recovery.

INDEX

Note: The italicized *f* and *t* following page numbers refer to figures and tables, respectively. Bold page references refer to photographs.

ABOUT THE AUTHORS

Wes Hobson   **Clark Campbell**   **Mike Vickers**

Wes Hobson is one of the top triathletes in the United States and has been for the past decade, ranking in the U.S. top five at the Olympic distance since 1990. A member of the U.S. national team from 1997 to 1999, he was the bronze medalist at the 2000 ITU North American championships. He has won more than 30 triathlons in his professional career, including the 1999 Escape From Alcatraz triathlon. A graduate of DePauw University with a degree in economics, Hobson and his wife Jennifer reside in Boulder, Colorado.

    Clark Campbell is the head men's and women's swimming coach at the University of Evansville in Indiana. He spent seven years as a professional triathlete. He was the 1986 national long Course Champion and the runner-up in the United States Triathlon Series national championship in 1990. He has been a collegiate swimming coach since 1992, including stops as an assistant coach at Kansas and Minnesota before coaching at Evansville. Campbell holds a B.S. in exercise science from the University of Kansas and an M.S. in physical education/athletic coaching from West Virginia University. He and his wife, Cassie, reside in Newburgh, Indiana.

    A competitive age-group triathlete and race director, **Mike Vickers** owns Lawrence Triathlon, Inc., a sports management company that runs the LMH Triathlon in Lawrence, Kansas, and the USAT national championship in St. Joseph, Missouri. He and his wife, Caylen, live in Lawrence, Kansas.